Saying No to Hate

University of Nebraska Press
Lincoln

SAYING NO TO HATE

Overcoming Antisemitism in America

Norman H. Finkelstein

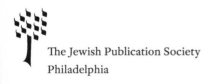

The Jewish Publication Society
Philadelphia

© 2024 by Norman H. Finkelstein

All rights reserved. Published by the University of
Nebraska Press as a Jewish Publication Society book.

Library of Congress Cataloging-in-Publication Data
Names: Finkelstein, Norman H., author.
Title: Saying no to hate: overcoming antisemitism
in America / Norman H. Finkelstein.
Description: Philadelphia: Jewish Publication Society; Lincoln,
Nebraska: University of Nebraska Press, 2024. |
Includes bibliographical references and index.
Identifiers: LCCN 2023048992
ISBN 9780827615236 (paperback)
ISBN 9780827619203 (epub)
ISBN 9780827619210 (pdf)
Subjects: LCSH: Antisemitism—United States—History—21st
century. | Jews—United States—Social conditions—21st century. |
United States—Ethnic relations—History—21st century. | Anti-
Jewish propaganda—United States—History—21st century. |
BISAC: SOCIAL SCIENCE / Jewish Studies | HISTORY / Jewish
Classification: LCC DS146.U6 F56 2024 |
DDC 305.892/4073—dc23/eng/20231221
LC record available at https://lccn.loc.gov/2023048992

Set in Adobe Text Pro.

For Tova, Joseph, and Kit
the next generation

Contents

Illustrations

Acknowledgments

It takes a village . . . a book does not spring full-grown on its own. I am indebted to Rabbi Barry Schwartz, now director and editor-in-chief emeritus of The Jewish Publication Society (JPS), for inviting me to write this book. His suggestions and observations guided me throughout the process. Joy Weinberg, the JPS managing editor, was my shepherd, painstakingly reviewing, nudging, and steering me every step of the way. She is the consummate professional, and I very much appreciate her skill, patience, and unerring advice.

I offer thanks and appreciation to the librarians and archivists who assisted me along the way, including AJC Archives director Charlotte Bonelli and Hebrew College Library director Harvey Sukenic. And I thank the University of Nebraska Press for copublishing this volume.

I thank the American Jewish Committee for permission to excerpt their article that appears as appendix 1, "How to Fight Antisemitism with Advocacy and Pride." Michael Masters of the Secure Community Network (SCN) has also been particularly helpful; the safety information he provides in appendix 2, "How to Prepare for an Active Shooter Attack," will be most useful for readers. Thanks as well to Craig Fifer of the SCN for providing additional information.

My family has been especially supportive. Throughout my writing life, my wife, Rosalind, has been patient and understanding and a first reviewer of my early drafts. And I thank my children: Jeffrey, for sharing insights into the Jewish communal world; Robert, an attorney, for guiding me through historical legal issues covered in the book; and Risa, for her constant encouragement.

Introduction WHY THIS BOOK?

In the more than two-thousand-year history of the Jewish diaspora, no country has offered Jews more freedom, legal protection, and opportunity than the United States of America. Yet, American Jews have always been aware of a residue of anti-Jewish hate lurking in the background, ready to emerge at any time.

Today, in a time of social media and instant news, Jews experience different levels of hate, sometimes resulting in actual violence. Yet, many are not aware of the history of antisemitism that affected preceding generations or the steps taken by Jews to counteract that hate. For readers to understand and confront the antisemitism of today, they need to know the history of the past. That's what *Saying No to Hate* is about.

No single book could possibly document every incident of antisemitism in the United States. That certainly is not this book's intent. Instead, *Saying No to Hate* delves into specific anti-Jewish events that captured general public interest and galvanized the Jewish community to action. The book makes these events accessible to high school, college, and adult learners. No previous knowledge of Jewish history is required.

About the Book

Saying No to Hate is organized chronologically, allowing readers to best understand the world that surrounded American Jews at a given point in time.

It begins with the European roots of anti-Judaism, which preceded the 1654 arrival of the first North American Jews and continues through the centuries. Subsequently, the seventeenth century saw the fledgling Jewish population in the colonies, led by Asser Levy, fight back against the hate that targeted them in their new land. By the time of the American Revolution in the eighteenth century, the Jewish population had reached over two thousand. While Jews fought and died in battle, they often dealt with anti-Jewish discrimination. The positive response by George Washington to American Jews brought them comfort, as did the protection of the new United States Constitution.

The nineteenth century saw a steadily increasing Jewish population. There were legislative and legal battles, represented by the passage of Maryland's Jew Bill. For the first time, Jews used their growing numbers and confidence to respond as a community to anti-Jewish incidents abroad, particularly the Damascus and Mortara affairs. At the same time, they began to build national organizations, such as the Board of Delegates of American Israelites, hoping to represent the expanding American Jewish community.

Later that century saw Jews on both sides of the Civil War standing up for their rights. They fought General Ulysses S. Grant's infamous General Order no.11, which for the first—and only—time expelled Jews from their homes on American soil. They fought for and received the right to have Jewish chaplains in the military. Yet Judah Benjamin's leadership role in the Confederacy stirred an undercurrent of anti-Jewish feelings. After the war, when Jews were barred from many social clubs, hotels, and resorts, they not only fought back legally but created their own institutions.

The twentieth century witnessed a dramatic growth in the Jewish population as immigrants fled Russian pogroms. The "Great Wave" forever changed the complexion of the American Jewry. The early part of the century witnessed a rise in antisemitic fervor, first with the lynching of Leo Frank and then with the incendiary writings and actions of industrialist Henry Ford. The Jewish community responded to both challenges. Organizations such as the American Jewish Committee, the American Jewish Congress, and the Anti-Defamation League, founded early in the century, rose to prominence to defend the rights of American Jews as the Holocaust raged in Europe.

Even after World War II, however, antisemitism continued. Discrimination in employment and housing affected Jews, who turned to legislation and the courts to bring change. In the midcentury, Jews became involved in the civil rights movement, playing an important role in the legal and political fight for equality for all Americans. Blacks and Jews worked together to advance justice in America but later diverged on some issues; today, they are beginning to find common purpose again in twenty-first-century America.

The birth of the State of Israel in 1948 exhilarated the Jewish world even as the young nation faced the enmity of surrounding Arab countries. After the 1967 Six-Day War, some progressive elements in Western countries and developing nations proceeded to portray Israel as a vicious aggressor against people of color. The UN's November 1975 resolution declaring Zionism a form of racism and racial discrimination led to an organized movement to boycott and delegitimize the Jewish state. Anti-Zionist feelings extended into the twenty-first century, with Jewish university students especially singled out. The Jewish community responded with educational and legislative initiatives.

Today, American Jews continue to experience unparalleled success in all aspects of American life. The American Jewish community has become confident as well as successful just as social media has allowed hatred to go virtual, increasing the level and ferocity of antisemitism. Jewish institutions now monitor the growing number of social media outlets that empower antisemites and the hate groups that feed off them. Violent attacks on the Pittsburgh and Poway synagogues, among others, have led the American Jewish community to reassess and take steps to reduce its vulnerabilities. *Editors' Update*: The significant increase in antisemitism in America after Hamas's October 7, 2023, massacre in Israel and Israel's war against Hamas induced further reassessment and self-protective operations.[1] As the undercurrent of antisemitism lingers and the threat of attacks continues, Jews are embracing vigilance.

This book's appendices provide readers with practical techniques to combat antisemitism and ways to potentially protect themselves from attacks. In showing how American Jews have used legal, political, and educational strategies to address antisemitism and examining the steps being taken to safeguard Jews and their institutions, *Saying No to Hate* is ultimately a testimony to Jewish resilience and courage.

A Personal Note

As a child growing up in Chelsea, Massachusetts, just across the river from Boston, I could imagine that the whole world was Jewish. Walking down Broadway in Chelsea I heard people speaking Yiddish. Kosher butchers and bakers abounded. Chelsea's 1.8 square miles encompassed over fifteen synagogues. Many of my public-school classmates were Jewish, many from first-generation homes. Even non-Jews understood Yiddish words and phrases.

Yet even there, I experienced subtle (sometimes not so subtle) reminders that Jews were still a minority in America. Each morning we pledged allegiance to the United States, recited the Lord's Prayer, and heard a Bible passage—sometimes from the New Testament—read to us. At Christmastime, even when we had Jewish teachers, we all sang Christmas carols and decorated the classroom tree. I remember sitting on Santa's knee (the gym teacher) and being asked what I wanted for Christmas.

It all washed over me. I knew I was Jewish. My father, a *Shomer Shabbat* (Sabbath observant) Jew, had to secretly make his way to his workplace on Sundays so as not to lose a day's pay for not working on Shabbat. At the time "Blue Laws" in the state prohibited work on Sundays, and he made sure not to attract attention from passing police officers. In winter he worked in the cold, since chimney smoke would give him away. Fixing some loose bricks outside our house one

Sunday, he was accosted by a neighbor who told him to stop what he was doing since it was the "Lord's Day."

When Rabbi Barry Schwartz, then director of the JPS, asked me to write this book, I quickly said yes. It was not just the memory of my childhood that made me accept the challenge but my experience as a writer of Jewish history and especially as a teacher of high school and adult education Jewish history classes. My high school students in the Prozdor department of Boston's Hebrew College were bright and proud of their Judaism and attachment to Israel. Some have experienced personal incidents of antisemitism—swastikas on bathroom walls or antisemitic taunts—while at the same time witnessing unprecedented security measures implemented at their houses of worship and institutions. Like many of my adult students, they recognized that antisemitism exists but knew little of its history in America. I hope that through *Saying No to Hate*, they—and you—will be better prepared to recognize, understand, confront, and combat the injustice and hatred lurking around us.

What has stood out to me in researching and writing about high-profile antisemitic events in America is that in each instance the Jewish community was not shy about responding to hate and discrimination as best as they believed they could, even when their population was small in numbers. Their public reactions could take place because of the rights guaranteed them by the U.S. Constitution and Bill of Rights. It was clear from the beginning: America was not Europe. Especially in the early years, standing up for their "inalienable rights" could not have happened anywhere else on earth.

Centuries after the first Jews arrived in America, the October 27, 2018, shooting at the Tree of Life synagogue building in Pittsburgh, in which eleven congregants were killed—the worst violent attack on Jews in American history—was personal for me, as I watched my son, Jeffrey Finkelstein, the president and CEO of the Jewish Federation of Greater Pittsburgh, and other local leaders comfort their community while rallying Jews and non-Jews to, in their words, "Say no to hate." What most impressed me was the massive display of support for the Jews of Pittsburgh by the country at large. This gives me hope that despite the despicable acts of the few responsible for hatred, the majority of Americans support their Jewish neighbors.

With their support, and American Jewry's continuing commitment to protecting the rights of Jews and other minorities in America—grounded in the knowledge of how previous generations of Jews stood up to past injustices—we are better prepared to sustain the well-being of Jewish life in America, today and in the future.

Saying No to Hate

1

Origins of Hate

At the Passover seder each year, Jews repeat the words in the Hagga-dah, *she bchol dor v'dor* . . . "in each generation, enemies have arisen to destroy us." Hatred of Jews, former Anti-Defamation League director Abraham Foxman once remarked, is "an ancient virus without an anti-dote or vaccine."[1] And yet, after two thousand years of anti-Judaism (hatred of Jews because of their religion) and antisemitism (hatred of Jews based on race or ethnicity)—the former of which first emerged with the beginnings of Christianity—the Jewish people survive.

Way back then, Jesus was Jewish, as were his earliest followers. When the Romans destroyed the Second Temple, Judean Jews, including early followers of Jesus, were cast into exile, many finding themselves in other parts of the Roman Empire. At first, both Jews and Christians sought converts in their new homes, but ultimately Christianity's casting aside of food restrictions and circumcision made it the more appealing choice for those seeking a monotheistic religion. In 313 CE Emperor Constantine made Christianity the official religion of the Roman Empire. Jews became one of the most visible groups in Europe that was not Christian.

To separate from its Jewish beginnings, the early church claimed that God had rejected the Jews and that Christians had superseded (taken the place of) Jews as God's chosen people. Moreover, some early Christians taught that the Jews were responsible for deicide, the murder of God (or God's Messiah) through the trial and the death of Jesus. These same writers claimed that the destruction of the Second Temple and Judea and the Jews' dispersion from their homeland were in fact punishment for his death.

Root of Historical Anti-Judaism

The New Testament, written after the death of Jesus, remains the root of historical anti-Judaism and a major factor in modern antisemitism. Embedded in its messages of love and compassion is a clear contempt for Jews and Judaism. At the trial of Jesus, Jews are portrayed as admitting guilt for his death by saying, "His blood be upon us and on our children" (Matt. 27:26). 1 Thessalonians 2:15 refers to Jews "who killed the Lord Jesus and the prophets, and drove us out and displeased God and oppose all men." Jesus is quoted as telling the Jews, "You are of your father the devil, and your will is to do your father's desires" (John 8:44). Demonization followed, with depictions of Jews as disciples of the devil with horns on their heads and their house of worship maligned as the "synagogue of Satan" (Rev. 2:9). "The Jews are the most worthless of men," the early church leader St. John Chrysostom (349–407 CE) declared in his oration *Against the Jews*. "They are lecherous, rapacious, greedy. . . . They worship the Devil. Their religion is a sickness. . . . The Jews sacrifice their children to Satan. They are worse than wild beast. The Synagogue is a brothel, a den of scoundrels, the temple of demons devoted to idolatrous cults."[2]

Christianity, the church announced, had superseded Judaism. To distance itself even further from Judaic roots, the church moved the Sabbath from a Saturday observance to Sunday and transformed Passover into Easter. Constantine explained the complete break: "It was, in the first place, declared improper to follow the custom of the Jews in the celebration of this holy festival, because, their hands having been stained with crime, the minds of those wretched men are necessarily blinded. By rejecting their custom, we establish and hand down to succeeding ages one which is more reasonable, and which has been observed ever since the day of our Lord's sufferings. Let us then, have nothing in common with the Jews, who are our adversaries."[3]

Early church councils (ecclesiastical assemblies to decide major matters of faith) cast Jews as outsiders and introduced restrictions on Jewish life to encourage and often force them to convert to Christianity. Church laws decreed that Jews could not employ Christians and that Christians could not live in Jewish homes or consult Jewish doctors. In 1215 the Fourth Lateran Council instituted dress requirements to further set Jews apart from Christians: Jews had to wear different clothing than Christians, could not go out in public on major Christian holidays, and could not hold any public office. In 1227 the Synod of Narbonne enacted one of the first badge laws, requiring Jews over the age of thirteen to wear a yellow patch on their garments. Other European communities followed the practice. In some places, Jews were forced to wear strange-looking hats. In 1266 the Council of Breslau forbade Christians from living in the same house as Jews. Jews became increasingly marginalized from the larger communities in which they lived.

Christian leaders also claimed that the Talmud (a compilation of Jewish writings on a wide variety of subjects ranging from law and customs to history and folklore) contained insulting references to Christianity. As an example, the church pointed to how Sanhedrin 43a portrayed the death of Jesus. "On the eve of Passover Yeshu was hanged. For forty days before the execution took pace, a herald went forth and cried, 'He is going forth to be stoned because he has practiced sorcery and enticed Israel to apostasy.'" From the Talmudic rabbis' point of view, two hundred years after Jesus's death, they were attempting to place the event within the accepted legal practices at the time for bringing a suspect to trial. The Sages were attempting to refute the New Testament narrative that Jesus faced trial and execution immediately after his arrest. Christians did not take kindly to the argument.

Talmud Disputations, Censorship, and Burnings

Beginning in the thirteenth century, several highly publicized disputations took place in Europe. Convened by church leaders with support from local rulers, respected rabbis were invited (or sometimes ordered) to defend the words of the Talmud by debating learned

Christians, who were sometimes converted Jews. These were public events often conducted with pomp and ceremony. The not-so-subtle intention was to ban the Talmud and deprive Jews from a major religious source, thus denigrating rabbinic Judaism and hoping that this would lead Jews to convert. Defenders of the Talmud were always in a no-win situation.

In 1239 a converted Jew, Nicholas Donin, persuaded Pope Gregory IX to conduct an investigation of the Talmud, and the next year a disputation between Donin and four rabbis proceeded in Paris in the presence of bishops and Blanche, the French queen mother. Despite the rabbis' efforts, twenty-four cartloads of handwritten Talmuds and other Jewish writings were burned.

Such burnings took place even without disputations in Vienna, Rome, and other European cities. Meanwhile, disputations continued. A well-known one took place in 1413 in Tortosa, Spain, again instigated by a converted Jew. Convened by Pope Benedict XIII, the yearlong disputation on how the Talmud viewed whether the Messiah had already come pitted the church against a number of rabbis and, unsurprisingly, concluded with the pope banning Talmud study.

In other localities, the church, aided by converted Jews, censored parts of the Talmud by removing the few passages deemed blasphemous. After the invention of moveable type, new printed editions of the Talmud sometimes required the permission of the church printed on the title page. Such censorship, which permitted Jews access to the Talmud albeit with minor excisions, continued well into the nineteenth century.

The Crusades

In 1095 Pope Urban II called for a crusade to liberate Jerusalem from the Muslims. A year later, bands of Christians marched their way through Europe to the Holy City to fight the Muslim infidels. It did not take the mobs long to realize that their fight against infidels did not have to wait until the end of their prolonged journey. Along their route through the Rhineland in today's Germany, they encountered established Jewish communities. Rape, murder, and plundering of Jews quickly followed. Jewish populations in Mainz, Speyer, Worms, and Cologne were decimated and synagogues burned. More than ten thousand Jews are believed to have died. Many committed suicide *al Kiddush Ha Shem*—in sanctification of God's name—rather than submit to forced conversion. Albert of Aix described what happened when the mob entered the city of Mainz:

> Breaking the bolts and doors, they killed the Jews, about seven hundred in number, who in vain resisted the force and attack of some many thousands They killed the women, also, and with their swords pierced tender children of whatever age and sex. The Jews, seeing that their Christian enemies were attacking them and their children, and that they were sparing no age, likewise fell upon one another, brother, children, wives, and sisters, and thus they perished at each other's hands.[4]

Upon reaching Jerusalem, the crusaders killed most of the Muslim and Jewish residents of the city.

A series of other crusades followed. During the Second Crusade (1147–49), comparatively fewer Jews—perhaps 250 to 300—died as the crusaders passed through their lands. The Third Crusade (1189–92) had its greatest impact on Jews in England, where anti-Jewish feelings were rising. A new form of anti-Jewish hate had begun in Norwich in 1144 when the dead body of a twelve-year-old Christian boy, William, was discovered with knife wounds and suspicion fell on the local Jewish community. It was just before Passover, and false claims circulated that Jews required the blood of a Christian in their rituals, particularly to bake matzot—unleavened bread—for the festival. William became a church martyr, and while the local sheriff protected the Jews of Norwich from retaliation, other Jews in subsequent years were not as fortunate.

In 1189 prominent English Jews who arrived to honor the coronation of King Richard I were instead flogged and thrown out of the event. A circulating rumor that the king had ordered the English to attack Jews resulted in dozens killed and their houses burned. The king denounced the killings, yet when he left to participate in the Third Crusade in 1190, attacks on Jews resumed. The worst violence occurred in York, where the religious fervor of the Crusades led residents to attack their Jewish neighbors. Jews sought refuge in a tower at the local castle, and 150 died when the mob burned it down. Some Jews killed themselves rather than be forced to convert.

Blood Libels, Host Desecration, and the Bubonic Plague

More blood libels emerged in England, with the best known occurring in 1255, when nine-year-old Hugh of Lincoln was found dead in a well and eighteen Jews were executed in retaliation. The story was retold in songs, ballads, and verse, including in Geoffrey Chaucer's *Canterbury Tales*. The blood libel motif spread throughout the European continent, where it continued to percolate over the centuries.

In Trent, Italy, in 1475, two-year-old Simon went missing during Passover. When the Christian boy's body turned up, it was assumed that Jews had killed him to use his blood in the baking of matzot. Seventeen Jews of the town were burned at the stake. When miracles were attributed to the dead child, a cult developed around him, and he was declared a martyr of the church, thus perpetuating the antisemitic charge that Jews required Christian blood in their rituals. In 1965, a time when the Roman Catholic Church sought rapprochement with Jews, Pope Paul XI removed Simon's martyr designation.

It is unsurprising given the above that Jews were blamed for many catastrophes in Europe as the centuries progressed. The Bubonic plague of the fourteenth century, known as the Black Death, decimated the population of Europe. Jews suffered doubly, facing both the pandemic and the aspersion that they themselves were responsible for it, by purportedly having poisoned the wells. Thousands of Jews were murdered in cities across the continent.

In the early nineteenth century, the brothers Jacob and Wilhelm Grimm began to collect and preserve popular German folktales such as *Snow White*, *Sleeping Beauty*, and *Cinderella* before the stories disappeared. Among the stories the brothers discovered were antisemitic blood libel fairy tales such as *The Jews' Stone* and *The Girl Who Was Killed by Jews*—fables passed down through the centuries that promulgated the belief that Jews killed Christian children to use their blood in religious rituals. As *The Jews' Stone* reads:

> In the year 1462 in the village of Rinn in Tyrol a number of Jews convinced a poor farmer to surrender his small child to them in return for a large sum of money. They took the child out into the woods, where, on a large stone, they martyred it to death in the most unspeakable manner. From that time the stone has been called the Jews' Stone. Afterward they hung the mutilated body on a birch tree not far from a bridge.
>
> The child's mother was working in a field when the murder took place. She suddenly thought of her child, and without knowing why, she was overcome with fear. Meanwhile, three drops of fresh blood fell onto her hand, one after the other. Filled with terror she rushed home and asked for her child. Her husband brought her inside and confessed what he had done. He was about to show her the money that would free them from poverty, but it had turned into leaves. Then the father became mad and died from sorrow, but the mother went out and sought her child. She found it hanging from the tree and, with hot tears, took it down and carried it to the church at Rinn. It is lying there to this day, and the people look on it as a holy child. They also brought the Jews' Stone there.
>
> According to legend a shepherd cut down the birch tree, from which the child had hung, but when he attempted to carry it home he broke his leg and died from the injury.[5]

Along with tales of blood libels, another accusation stigmatized European Jews: host desecration. In the Catholic Church, bread and wine are used during Consecration of the Mass to represent the body and blood of Jesus Christ. The bread, in the form of an unleavened wafer, is called the host, after the Latin word for sacrifice. Once consecrated, the wafer symbolically becomes holy and is handled with greatest respect since, for believers, it becomes the Body of Christ. During the Middle Ages Jews were accused of stealing the consecrated wafers and stabbing or otherwise defiling them. Charges of host desecration led to more Jewish deaths throughout Europe.

Expulsion and Inquisition

In 1290 King Edward I expelled the Jews of England. Aside from religious hatred, there were economic reasons as well for this action. Under church law, Christians were forbidden to charge interest to Christian borrowers. Moneylending was left to Jews as one of the few professions they could hold. This state of affairs led to continuing anti-Jewish charges equating all Jews with money, greed, and wealth. With crusader debt mounting, expelling the Jews automatically erased any debts owed by Christians.

This expulsion was followed by others in Europe over the next centuries. Jews were expelled from Linz, Cologne, Bavaria, Frankfurt, and other cities. As a result, European Jews moved eastward to Poland, Ukraine, and Lithuania.

Perhaps the most consequential of the expulsions took place in Spain in 1492, the same year that Columbus set sail for the New World. Centuries earlier, Jews living in Spain had endured periodic calls to convert to Christianity and expulsions. The Muslims invaded Spain in 711 CE and ushered in a new era of relative tolerance. The next five hundred years would lovingly and later longingly be known as a "Spanish Golden Age," a literary period associated with the flourishing of the arts. While Jews did not enjoy the same status as Muslims in Spain, they were active participants in the country's political, social, and business life. Jewish learning existed side by side with secular learning; Jewish philosophy and poetry reached new heights, often informed by the literary milieu of Spanish Muslim culture.

As Catholics began a successful reconquest of Spain and Christian life renewed itself, the Jews of Spain once again came to be targeted, on the basis of jealousy and bigotry. While Jews thrived for a time in Christian Toledo and Aragon, blood libels resurfaced, as did old charges that Jews poisoned wells to kill Christians. Violence against Jews, usually incited by religious fanatics, became commonplace. In 1355 nearly twelve hundred Jews were killed in Toledo, their homes savagely attacked. In 1371 King Henry II decreed that Jews had to wear distinctive badges on their clothing. In certain areas, Jews were restricted to special residential quarters called *juderías* where they were allowed to engage in limited occupations. In some cities, Jews were prevented from appearing in public on the Christian holy day of Good Friday. In June 1391 a violent attack in Seville led to the killing of four thousand Jews. Thousands more converted to Christianity to save their lives. The violence spread through Spain, with synagogues sacked or transformed into churches. Mobs entered Jewish quarters to offer a cruel choice: convert or die. Afraid for their lives, many Jews quickly accepted baptism. Some embraced their new religion while others secretly continued connections to Judaism. It didn't take long for Christians who had rejoiced over the conversion of Jews to realize that the New Christians, known as *conversos*, were now legally competing with them for jobs and in business. Now, significantly, hatred of Jews for religious reasons (anti-Judaism) was replaced by hatred of Jews for racial reasons (what later became known as antisemitism). Those who were converts or even had Jewish ancestors were suspect. *Limpieza de sangre*, purity of blood, now determined how Jews were viewed in Spain. Even conversion could no longer protect Jews from ingrained suspicions. Now that Judaism was a racial rather than a religious category, there was nothing you could do to remove it—once a Jew always a Jew.

Concern about the true devotion of conversos to Christianity led religious courts established by the church—the Inquisition—to investigate those thought to be not totally loyal to the church. The Inquisition only had power over Catholics, which legally included converted Jews, who were now officially Catholic. As such, despite the prevalent anti-Jewish feelings among the populace, the Inquisition could only deal with baptized Catholics like conversos and not unconverted Jews.

With particular zeal, the Inquisition set out to unmask and punish the new Christians who showed even the slightest sign of supporting or observing Jewish law, customs, or traditions. Accused conversos were often tortured for their confessions; those found guilty had their property confiscated, were sent to jail or, in the most severe cases, were burned at the stake.

In the years before the 1492 expulsion, Jews who had not converted faced increasing humiliation as church leaders continued to demonize them. Disputations about the Talmud in Barcelona and Tortosa only inflamed anti-Jewish sentiments. The hard life took its toll. Many Spaniards believed any evil rumor about Jews, including the blood libel. People throughout the country demanded the removal of the "Jewish menace" from Spain. They feared that the presence of unconverted Jews kept conversos connected to Judaism.

King Ferdinand and Queen Isabella agreed. An estimated two hundred thousand Jews were expelled from Spain alone, and more from Portugal. Their descendants would create the Sephardic diaspora, a vast network of families throughout the Ottoman Empire, especially Turkey, Greece, Italy, and the Netherlands (Amsterdam). The Dutch colonies in Brazil and Curacao would include some of the first settlements of Jews in the New World (as would the Spanish outpost of Mexico). A contingent of Sephardic Jews seeking to return to Amsterdam from Recife, Brazil, were waylaid and became the first Jews in North America.

Restrictions and Revolts

In 1517 a monk by the name of Martin Luther dramatically altered the path of Christianity by founding Protestantism as an alternative to the Roman Catholic Church. At first, Luther decried the church's treatment of Jews in the hope that the Jews would convert to his updated version of Christianity, but when they refused, Luther's anger against them grew. In 1543 he wrote *On the Jews and Their Lies*, which expressed the centuries-old beliefs that Jews were an accursed people deserving of hate:

We are at fault in not slaying them. Rather we allow them to live freely in our midst despite their murdering, cursing, blaspheming, lying, and defaming; we protect and shield their synagogues, houses, life, and property. In this way we make them lazy and secure and encourage them to fleece us boldly of our money and goods, as well as to mock and deride us, with a view to finally overcoming us, killing us all for such a great sin, and robbing us of all our property (as they daily pray and hope). Now tell me whether they do not have every reason to be the enemies of us accursed Goyim, to curse us and to strive for our final, complete, and eternal ruin![6]

Throughout Western Europe Jews were no longer allowed, as Luther said, to live freely. Instead, they were severely limited in their occupations and places of residence. In Venice, Jews were restricted to an area near an old foundry, the Ghetto, a name later applied throughout Europe to the segregated, closed-in parts of cities where Jews were permitted to live. In 1555 the Jews of Rome were relocated to a confined area near the banks of the Tiber River, where they lived in squalid, crowded, and unhealthy conditions until late in the nineteenth century. Walled in and required to wear identifying garb, Jews became ever more separated from their Christian neighbors. Unable to pursue professions or own land, many became peddlers or hawkers of used clothing. Everywhere they went, they faced taunts of "dirty Jew." Moreover, negative depictions in literature and the theater further denigrated Jews in Christian eyes. For example, William Shakespeare's Jewish moneylender in *The Merchant of Venice*, Shylock, became a stand-in for the mythical greedy and villainous Jews. Later, in the nineteenth century, Charles Dickens would similarly vilify Jews with the character of Fagin in *Oliver Twist*.

As European Jews moved eastward, the accusations, hatred, and myths followed them. By the late 1500s, an estimated 80 percent of Jews worldwide lived in the Kingdom of Poland (which then included Lithuania and Ukraine). Originally invited by Polish rulers to function as agents of absentee landlords, the Jews in Poland developed a rich social, cultural, and religious life largely separate from their Christian neighbors. Their lives fell apart in 1648 when Ukrainian Cossacks led by Bogdan Chmielnicki began a multiyear violent revolt against their Polish masters. During the revolt, the Cossacks turned on the Jews as prime targets, for political, economic, and religious reasons. Three hundred Jewish communities were destroyed and one hundred thousand Jews were massacred. Until the rise of Hitler centuries later superseded the levels of depravity faced in the seventeenth century, Jews invoked curses using Chmielnicki's name.

Wherever they lived in Europe, Jews were a people apart. It was not until the Age of Enlightenment in the eighteenth century that they began to be legally freed from their restrictive lives in Western Europe. In 1791 France become the first country in Europe to declare Jews equal citizens. But even their new legal rights and assimilation could not erase the centuries of demonization.

"Respectable" Antisemitism

Antisemitism adopted a new, scientific look at the end of the nineteenth century. Ironically, in the modern age of reason and science, antisemitism was made to appear respectable. Pseudoscientific studies "proved" the inferiority of Jews. Throughout Europe, new books challenged any rights the Jews had won thus far. Antisemitic political parties won seats in legislative bodies, where hatred for the Jews was legitimized as part of the democratic process. In Vienna, as Theodor Herzl was creating modern political Zionism, the notorious antisemitic politician Karl Lueger led the city's chief political force for years. At the tail end of the nineteenth century, France and the world were convulsed by the case of a French army officer, Alfred Dreyfus, falsely accused of treason simply because he was a Jew.

By the close of the century, as many Jews throughout Western Europe assimilated into modern society, most of the world's Jews were confined in the Pale of Settlement in the Russian Empire. With the annexation of Poland in the late eighteenth century, Russia inherited a large Jewish population, which it isolated in the Pale, keeping Jews mainly out of larger Russia. There, in what today constitutes large areas of Western Russia, Poland, Lithuania, Rumania, and Ukraine, Jews lived a largely insular experience, mostly in Yiddish-speaking shtetls (small villages), and developed their own rich Jewish culture. Yet they also experienced discrimination and frequent pogroms (violent physical attacks that killed and maimed many). The massive pogroms of 1881 after the assassination of Czar Alexander II, which many Russians blamed on liberals and Jews, prompted millions of Jews to vote with their feet and emigrate when they had the chance. They would leave Russian lands behind for the *Goldene Medina* (Yiddish for "Golden Land" of America) and beyond.

For the millions who stayed, no matter where Jews lived in Europe, they continued to experience the tropes of Jew-hatred from the previous centuries. In 1879 the German propagandist Wilhelm Marr coined a term for it—"antisemitism"—building upon a belief dating from the Middle Ages that Jews are not defined by their religion alone but by their genealogy (race). Soon enough, the situation would take a terrible turn.

Nazism

Once the Nazis rose to power in 1930s Germany, they marginalized Jews as the "other" in German society. The Jews, they proclaimed, "are our misfortune."

The Nazis utilized newspapers, radio, and film to demonize Jews as vermin infecting larger society. They caricatured Jews as sinister power brokers and sexual deviants with exaggerated physical characteristics. They also reinvented the purity of blood trope. A Jew was a Jew whether religious or atheist, whether converted to Christianity or not. If someone's ancestor was Jewish, that person was suspect. Laws segregating Jews from the larger society further marginalized them, as the Nazis reinstated the centuries-old practice of forcing Jews to wear markers that identified them as Jewish.

The Holocaust that followed was the culmination of two thousand years of anti-Jewish hatred in Europe. Using twentieth-century technology, the Nazis transformed medieval antipathy and violence on a scale earlier haters would have found astonishing. Swords and then guns gave way to gas chambers. By the end of World War II, two out of every three Jews in Europe were dead: an astounding six million souls. Almost all of the Jewish communities in the Nazis' path were destroyed. So much of the vibrant, centuries-old European Jewish civilization was gone.

Contributing to the annihilation was the ancient charge of deicide: Jews had killed Jesus. While the Nazis did the killing, in many cases ages-old hatred predisposed church leaders to ignore the killing of Jews or sometimes to aid the Nazis. Only in 1965 would Pope Paul VI issue a document, titled *Nostra Aetate*, rejecting Jewish responsibility for the death of Jesus, denouncing antisemitism, and establishing formal dialogue between the Catholic Church and Jews. In Europe, the new attitude toward the Jews had a marginal effect—there were so few Jews left in Eastern Europe, and the communities remaining in France, England, and elsewhere were still beset by prejudice. In America the situation of the Jews had always been better, and Vatican II, as the new church doctrine was called, had a positive effect. But as we will see, antisemitism persisted even in America.

2

In the Beginning

The antisemitism of Europe that had made its way across the Atlantic with the early colonists greeted the first Jewish arrivals to North America. In early September 1654, after a voyage from Cuba, the French ship *Sainte Catherine* docked in New Amsterdam (today's New York City) and discharged a bedraggled group of twenty-three Jewish men, women, and children. In the little colony, their identity as Jews was immediately revealed. In response, Reverend Johan Megapolensis, the leader of the American colony's Dutch Reformed Church, the only religious denomination permitted to hold public services in the colony, complained that there would be "a still greater confusion if the obstinate and immovable Jews were to settle here."[1]

New Amsterdam governor Peter Stuyvesant was also not pleased with the newcomers. He immediately wrote to his superiors at the Dutch West India Company in Amsterdam, chartered by the Dutch Parliament to organize and oversee all Dutch ventures in the Western Hemisphere. The Jews were "repugnant" and a "deceitful race," he wrote, requesting permission to "require them in a friendly way to depart."[2]

The Jews, however, were not willing to oblige. They had been through hell to get to New Amsterdam, and they were not about to leave. They had come from Recife, an important seaport in Brazil. Most of them were descended from *conversos*. Starting in the early fifteenth century, conversos had come to the New World hoping to find refuge far away from the Inquisition. When the Dutch captured the colony in 1630, those secret Jews who had not already reclaimed their Jewish identity in Amsterdam openly and proudly did so in Recife. Holland was a welcoming place for Jews, and now that the Dutch were in control, the Jews of Recife could maintain their reclaimed identity. They established synagogues, created a Jewish communal organization, and imported a rabbi from Holland. They even raised money for poor Jews in Palestine. Yet, by the 1640s, military skirmishes were increasing between the Dutch and the Portuguese troops attempting to reclaim Recife, and in 1654 the Portuguese retook control of the area. For the Jews, Recife now became a dangerous place. Once out of the closet, it was impossible for them to return to their secret lives. Haunting memories of the Inquisition reemerged.

Fortunately, the Portuguese commander, General Francisco Barretto, gave the conversos three months to leave Brazil. Most found ships to take them to nearby friendly Caribbean colonies or to Amsterdam. Yet one of the ships, bound for Holland and possibly commandeered by pirates, landed in Jamaica, a Spanish territory. Afraid of the Inquisition there, the twenty-three Jews on board quickly boarded another ship bound for Cape Saint Anthony in Cuba. There, they found the French ship *Sainte Catherine*, which brought them to New Amsterdam. That destination made sense: it was a Dutch colony, and the Jews of Recife had been loyal Dutch citizens.

At the same time that Governor Stuyvesant sent his request to remove the Jews, the Jews wrote their own letter to coreligionists in Amsterdam asking for help. The well-to-do Amsterdam Jews then composed a petition to the Dutch West India Company directors, pointing to the sacrifices made by the Jews of Recife as well as to the loyalty shown the Dutch by Jewish inhabitants wherever they lived. The petition also reminded the directors that the company had invited industrious people to settle in the Dutch colonies of the New World:

> It is well known to your Honors that the Jewish nation in Brazil have at all times been faithful and have striven to guard and maintain that place, risking for that purpose their possessions and their blood. Yonder land is extensive and spacious. The more of

loyal people that go to live there, the better it is in regard to the population of the country.

Perhaps the clincher argument was this sentence in the petition:

Your Honors should also please consider that many of the Jewish nation are principal shareholders in the Company.[3]

The Dutch were a merchant nation whose concern for trade and profit overrode religious zeal. Thus they denied Governor Stuyvesant's objections and granted the Jews official recognition:

These people may travel and trade to and in New Netherland and live and remain there, provided the poor among them shall not become a burden to the company or to the community, but be supported by their own nation.[4]

The directors' attitude was clear. Soon, other Jews began arriving to the colony, directly from Holland.

Asser Levy's Protest

A stubborn Stuyvesant, whose view of tolerance only extended to members of the Dutch Reformed Church, would continue to place obstacles before the Jewish residents.

He did not count on an equally stubborn Jewish arrival, Asser Levy, to fight back.

The little colony of New Amsterdam numbered fewer than one thousand souls. To protect the settlers from surrounding Native Americans, in July 1655 the governor issued a call to form a militia of all able-bodied men. The question now arose whether or not to include Jewish men. The governor made the decision: "Owing to the disgust and unwillingness of the trainbands [militiamen] to be fellow soldiers and to be on guard with the same at the guard house . . . Jews cannot be permitted to serve as soldiers but should be exempt."[5] Instead, for the privilege of not serving, Jews alone were required to pay a monthly tax of sixty-five stuivers.

Asser Levy refused to pay the tax. In November 1655 he formally petitioned Stuyvesant, requesting that he and another Jew, Jacob Barsimson, be allowed to stand guard duty like other citizens of New Amsterdam or be excused from paying the unfair tax. Stuyvesant denied the request with the advice that if they didn't like living there, they "might go elsewhere if they liked."[6] Nonetheless, after apparently turning to the directors of the Dutch West India Company in Amsterdam to help resolve this matter, Levy and Barsimson began to stand guard alongside the other men of New Amsterdam.

In September 1655, as Native Americans continued threatening the little colony, the decision was made to build a wall around it. That required money, so Stuyvesant and the colony leadership requested "voluntary contributions" from all the residents. The Jews were required to pay one-twelfth of the total despite constituting only one-thirtieth of the total population.

The Jews again protested to the directors of the Dutch West India Company. In a letter dated March 14, 1656, they described their previous petitions to them and made clear their current demands to be treated equally with other residents being taxed. One hundred years before the Declaration of Independence, they called for no taxation without representation.

Trade was important to the economy of New Amsterdam. Yet Stuyvesant also prohibited the Jews from trading up the Hudson River at Fort Orange (today's Albany). "To give liberty to the Jews will be very detrimental," he told the directors. "Giving them liberty, we cannot refuse the Lutherans and Papists."[7] (The governor was an equal opportunity hater.)

Once again, Asser Levy took the Jews' case to Amsterdam. Again, the directors' response to Stuyvesant was clear. The Jews had every right to trade and "enjoy the same liberty that is granted them in this country."[8]

The directors were by now more than a little annoyed with their governor. "We have seen and learned with displeasure" of your denial of trading rights to Jews, they wrote to him on June 14, 1656. "We wish that this had not happened but that your Honors had obeyed our orders which you must hereafter execute punctually and with more respect."[9]

Stuyvesant's anger grew. Frustrated, he wrote to the directors, "What they [the Jews] may be able to obtain from your Honors, time will tell."[10] Still, he could not give up. Stuyvesant had his council pass a new ordinance limiting trade to those who held "burgher [full citizenship] rights." Only one of the Jews in New Amsterdam could claim that right.

Yet, Asser Levy could not be stopped. He appeared before the New Amsterdam court requesting to be admitted as a burgher and showing proof that he had previously held that right when he'd lived in Amsterdam. The court initially denied his admittance, but perhaps by now realizing that all his efforts to curtail the rights of Jews had failed and that it was not in his best interests to ratchet up tensions with Amsterdam, Stuyvesant grudgingly ordered that all the Jewish men of the colony, including Levy, be recognized as burghers with full rights.

Asser Levy was not afraid to stand up for the rights due him and his fellow Jews. He set an example that would long be remembered by the fledgling Jewish community both then and later (in fact a park, a school, and a recreation center are all named after him in New York City). By the time Levy died around 1680, the growing Jewish community was taking root on American soil.

Jews in Colonial Boston

In 1664 the British wrested control of New Amsterdam from the Dutch and renamed it New York. By 1732 much of the American East Coast was divided into thirteen British colonies.

While the New Amsterdam Jews were first to create a real Jewish community on North American soil, individual Jews had arrived earlier in the colonies, with unequal results. For example, in 1649, when businessperson Solomon Franco arrived in Boston, the Puritan leaders ordered him to leave, after having voted to "allow the said Solomon Franco, Ye Jew, six shillings per week out of the treasury for ten weeks for his subsistence til he could get his passage into Holland."[11] (What happened to Franco remains unknown.)

Another Jewish arrival in Boston fared a bit better than Franco, but at a price. Harvard College needed a qualified teacher of the Hebrew language, then a course requirement, so in 1722 the Hebrew teacher Judah Monis received good and bad news. Harvard would hire him as an instructor in Hebrew but possibly with the recommendation or requirement that he convert to Christianity.

The Puritans loved the Hebrew Bible and gave their children biblical names but they didn't care much for other religious groups, including Christian sects like the Quakers, never mind living Jews (unless they converted). The influential minister Cotton Mather expressed his goal in a prayer: "This day, from the dust, where I lay prostate before the Lord, I lifted up my cries: For the conversion of the Jewish Nation . . . to baptize a Jew."[12] The popular hope of the time was that Jews "see the error of their ways and accept the divinity of Jesus."[13]

Monis did proceed to convert, in a public baptism, yet his colleagues continued to refer to him not as a fellow Christian but as a converted Jew. Although now a Christian, he may have continued to observe the Jewish Sabbath on Saturdays throughout the rest of his life. In 1735 he published the first Hebrew grammar book in America. He would remain at Harvard until 1759, when he retired.

Most other universities of the time were connected to specific Christian denominations. Brown University, founded in 1764 near Newport, Rhode Island, required that all faculty members be Protestant and, more specifically, that its president be a Baptist. Jewish students, however, were welcomed. In 1770, after receiving a sizable contribution from Jewish merchants based in the South, Brown voted that "the children of Jews may be admitted into this Institution, and entirely enjoy the freedom of their own religion without any restraint or imposition whatever."[14]

Despite this relative liberalism, most schools required all of their students to attend Christian prayer services regardless of their own religious practices. Shortly before his death in 1826, Thomas Jefferson lamented that Jewish students might miss out on a college education because of these schools' requirement that students attend Christian prayers. "I have thought it a cruel addition to the wrongs which that injured sect have suffered," he wrote, "that their youth should be excluded from the instructions in science afforded to all others in our public seminaries, by imposing upon them a course of theological reading which their consciences do not permit them to pursue."[15]

After fleeing Newport ahead of the British occupation in 1776, Moses Michael Hays arrived in Boston. A wealthy merchant, Hays helped found a major bank and insurance companies. He and his family, the only Jews in Boston at the time, were socially and financially connected to the town's leading families. He was elected Grand Master of Masons in Massachusetts. His Grand Lodge deputy was his friend Paul Revere. That still did not stop another "friend" from referring to Hays as the head of "one family of the despised children of Israel."[16]

Naturalization and Intermarriage

In the early 1700s Luis Moses Gomez arrived in New York by way of Spain, France, and England. An international merchant and trader, as a Jew he was considered an alien resident in the colonies, unable to conduct business and own property without taking a Christian oath. To get around this restriction, he appealed directly to Queen Anne, who granted him an Act of Denization giving him and his family the rights of British citizens living in the colonies "with all the privileges of one of the most favored subjects."[17]

Even in the American colonies, naturalization did not automatically grant Jews the right to vote or hold political office. Jews in the colonies were "tolerated." They could be permanent residents and were free to trade and practice their religion but did not have many rights of citizenship.

Still, letters sent home to Europe reporting glowingly about life in America induced more Jews to cross the Atlantic. By the outbreak of the American Revolution, less than twenty-five hundred Jews were scattered among the thirteen colonies, with the largest groups living in major seaports on the East Coast. Jews' everyday interactions with their Christian neighbors were largely peaceful and polite. Jews were well integrated into business and social life; their lives were much better than those of Jews elsewhere. With so many peoples of diverse backgrounds arriving in the underpopulated colonies, it was best to keep private thoughts private.

And so, despite the existence of unflattering views on Jews among the various other colonists, those first generations of Jews in America saw a number of intermarriages. Through the American Revolution there were about nine hundred Jewish marriages. Historian Malcolm Stern estimated that 15 percent of these were between Christians and Jews.[18] Apparently for those colonial families, love overcame any negative feelings they may have harbored about Jews—a theme that we will see repeat itself throughout American history.

In the colonial period Jews were able to find success and establish important relationships within the confines of a predominantly white, Protestant society even though the looming threat of antisemitism served as a poignant reminder that their acceptance was not absolute or unconditional. This too became a recurring pattern in later periods.

The Colony of Georgia

The last of the British colonies to be established was Georgia, founded by James Oglethorpe in 1732. A year later a boatload of forty-two Jews arrived unannounced in Savannah. Without instruction from the colony's trustees back in London, Oglethorpe had no choice but to let them in. When news of their arrival did reach London, the trustees expressed their displeasure and hoped "not to make a Jew's colony of Georgia."[19] But it was too late to reverse what had happened.

Among the arrivals were Perla and Benjamin Sheftall. Their son Mordecai born in 1735, became a successful merchant and landowner. As the country headed for revolution, he actively participated in the patriot cause. Joining the Sons of Liberty, he was in a group that stormed the Royal Arsenal and took off with gunpowder later shipped to Boston and used against the British in the Battle of Bunker Hill. In 1777 Mordecai Sheftall was appointed commissary general to the Continental Army in Georgia with the rank of colonel, making him the patriot army's highest ranking Jewish soldier. The British named him a "very great rebel."[20]

With the Continental Congress in Philadelphia often short of cash to pay for supplies, Sheftall, devoted to the revolution, used his own funds to ensure that troops were adequately fed, clothed, and armed. He was never fully repaid.

In November 1788, knowing that the British were about to invade Savannah, Sheftall and other Jewish heads of families sent women and children to safety in Charleston, South Carolina. Reading a Charleston newspaper, Sheftall was surprised to discover the "firsthand" account of "an American" who falsely alleged that men "of the Tribe of Israel who, after taking every advantage in trade the times admitted of in the State of Georgia, as soon as it was attacked by an enemy, fled here for asylum with their ill-got wealth, dastardly turning their back upon the country, when in danger, which gave them bread and protection."[21] In an angry response published soon thereafter, a "Real American"— perhaps Mordecai Sheftall himself—informed readers that the Jewish men of Savannah actually remained behind, preparing to fight the invading British.

On December 29, 1778, British troops came ashore at Savannah. Facing them was an armed but greatly outnumbered citizen army, including Mordecai Sheftall and his (uniquely named) son, Sheftall Sheftall. As bullets and cannon balls burst all around, the patriots were cornered. The Sheftalls surrendered and soon found themselves on the British prison ship *Nancy* in Savannah harbor. Knowing they were both Jewish, their captors went out of their way to make them suffer. A fellow prisoner, the Reverend Moses Allen, remembered, "Pork for dinner. The Jews Mr. Sheftall and son refused to eat their pieces and their knives and forks were ordered to be greased with it."[22]

Despite his suffering at British hands and losing his wealth to aid the patriot cause, Sheftall never regretted his fate. Writing to his son after the war, he enthused, "An entire new scene will open itself and we have the world to begin again."[23]

The Revolutionary War

As with other Americans, the revolution divided Jewish families. Out of a total American population of around two million, there were no more than twenty-five hundred Jews. While some maintained loyalty to the British Crown, most favored the patriot cause. They were hopeful that the words in the Declaration of Independence, "All men are created equal," would foretell a more inclusive equality. Nonetheless, there were some patriots who accused Jews of disloyalty to the revolution; conversely, some loyalists thought Jews were disloyal to the king.

Today, Haym Solomon remains the best-known Jewish hero of the Revolutionary War. A successful financial broker who sold stocks and bonds as investments and lent money, Solomon negotiated war loans from France and Holland to fund the Continental Army and as such had business relations with many Revolutionary leaders, including Thomas Jefferson and James Madison. When money was lacking, he dug into his own pockets to loan the American government more than $300,000. He died nearly penniless, having contributed so selflessly to the patriot cause. Madison later wrote, "The kindness of our little friend on Front Street [Solomon], near the Coffee House, is a fund which will preserve me from extremities, but I never resort to it without great mortification, as he obstinately rejects all recompense."[24]

While Haym Solomon was a great patriot, he did not bear arms during the revolution. More than one hundred Jewish men did fight in the Continental Army, and many of them held high ranks. Francis Salvador of South Carolina, who was shot and scalped during a battle in 1776, became the first Jew to die in the war.

The U.S. Constitution and Its First Amendment

With the war over, the new country set out to recreate itself. For Jewish Americans the adoption of the United States Constitution in 1788 provided an official guarantee of equality. In particular, they welcomed Article 6: "The Senators and Representatives before mentioned, and the Members of the several State Legislatures, and all executive and judicial Officers, both of the United States and of the several States, shall be bound by Oath or Affirmation, to support this Constitution; but no religious Test shall ever be required as a Qualification to any Office or public Trust under the United States."[25]

A year later, the First Amendment to the Constitution provided further assurance: "Congress shall make no law respecting an establishment of religion, or prohibiting the free exercise thereof; or abridging the freedom of speech, or of the press; or the right of the people peaceably to assemble, and to petition the Government for a redress of grievances."[26] For Jews, the First Amendment was remarkable; its guarantees of religious freedom were unknown to them in Europe, where governments were intertwined with religion. In America, Jews were on an equal legal footing with everyone else.

Individual states, however, continued to erect roadblocks to the equal treatment of Jewish Americans. In other words, while a Jew could, if elected, now become a member of the House of Representatives or the United States Senate, and, theoretically, could also become president of the United States, holding office in most of the new states was still a problem, since the state constitutions required the taking of a Christian oath. In Delaware, for example, the required oath was "I, do profess faith in God the Father, and in Jesus Christ, His only Son, and in the Holy Ghost, one God, blessed for evermore; and I do acknowledge the holy scriptures of the Old and New Testament to be given by divine inspiration."[27]

Removing those restrictions would be an uphill battle. In Pennsylvania, one letter to a newspaper opposing change stated, "Jews or Turks may become in time our greatest landholders . . . so as to render it not only uncomfortable but unsafe for Christians."[28] Still, by 1830, prompted by Jewish protests, most states would remove this constitutional barrier, with New Hampshire finally bringing up the rear in 1877.

George Washington's Letter

When George Washington assumed the presidency of the United States in 1789, the Jews of America still harbored a bit of nervousness. Over their long history, a change of government had invariably raised the question, "Will this change be good for the Jews?" American Jews now wondered, "Would they be harassed and hated as they had been for so many centuries in Europe?"[29]

The Jewish leaders of the major Jewish population cities, Newport, New York, Philadelphia, Richmond, Charleston, and Savannah, desired to write a joint letter of congratulations to George Washington upon this election to the presidency. They wanted to express the Jewish population's loyalty to the new government and, perhaps indirectly, to sound out the first president's feelings about Jews.

Given the lack of modern communications and internal disputes, a delay ensued as the geographically distanced leaders debated the letter's wording. Meanwhile, time passed. The president was about to embark on a tour of Rhode Island to express his thanks for the state's ratification of the Constitution. One of his first stops was Newport, in August 1790, where he would meet the populace.

Moses Seixas, leader of the Hebrew Congregation of Newport—now known as the Touro Synagogue—could wait no longer. He composed his own letter on behalf of the Newport congregation, which he is said to have read aloud to the president personally.

> August 17, 1790
>
> Sir,
>
> Permit the children of the stock of Abraham to approach you with the most cordial affection and esteem for your person and merits—and to join with our fellow citizens in welcoming you to NewPort.
>
> With pleasure we reflect on those days—those days of difficulty, and danger, when the God of Israel, who delivered David from the peril of the sword,—shielded Your head in the day

of battle:—and we rejoice to think, that the same Spirit, who rested in the Bosom of the greatly beloved Daniel enabling him to preside over the Provinces of the Babylonish Empire, rests and ever will rest, upon you, enabling you to discharge the arduous duties of Chief Magistrate in these States.

Deprived as we heretofore have been of the invaluable rights of free Citizens, we now with a deep sense of gratitude to the Almighty disposer of all events behold a Government, erected by the Majesty of the People—a Government, which to bigotry gives no sanction, to persecution no assistance—but generously affording to all Liberty of conscience, and immunities of Citizenship:—deeming every one, of whatever Nation, tongue, or language equal parts of the great governmental Machine:— This so ample and extensive Federal Union whose basis is Philanthropy, Mutual confidence and Public Virtue, we cannot but acknowledge to be the work of the Great God, who ruleth in the Armies of Heaven, and among the Inhabitants of the Earth, doing whatever seemeth him good.

For all these Blessings of civil and religious liberty which we enjoy under an equal benign administration, we desire to send up our thanks to the Ancient of Days, the great preserver of Men—beseeching him, that the Angel who conducted our forefathers through the wilderness into the promised Land, may graciously conduct you through all the difficulties and dangers of this mortal life:—And, when, like Joshua full of days and full of honour, you are gathered to your Fathers, may you be admitted into the Heavenly Paradise to partake of the water of life, and the tree of immortality.

Done and Signed by order of the Hebrew Congregation
in NewPort, Rhode Island
Moses Seixas, Warden

Later that month, President George Washington penned his reply to the Jewish congregation in Newport—a response that would become the iconic affirmation of acceptance to successive generations of American Jews. Washington understood by Seixas's choice of language—"generously affording to all Liberty of conscience, and immunities of Citizenship"—that the Newport Jewish community sought his personal guarantee that Jews would be included in the word "all." He sent the congregation's words back to them: "All possess alike liberty of conscience and immunities of citizenship."[30] He also incorporated into his response Seixas's phrase "To bigotry no sanction," proclaiming, "For happily the Government of the United States, which gives to bigotry no sanction, to persecution no assistance, requires only that they who live under its protection, should demean themselves as good citizens."

August 21, 1790

Gentlemen—

While I receive, with much satisfaction, your Address replete with expressions of affection and esteem; I rejoice in the opportunity of assuring you, that I shall always retain a grateful remembrance of the cordial welcome I experienced in my visit to Newport, from all classes of Citizens.

The reflection on the days of difficulty and danger which are past is rendered the more sweet, from a consciousness that they are succeeded by days of uncommon prosperity and security. If we have wisdom to make the best use of the advantages with which we are now favored, we cannot fail, under the just administration of a good Government, to become a great and happy people.

The Citizens of the United States of America have a right to applaud themselves for having given to mankind examples of an enlarged and liberal policy: a policy worthy of imitation. All possess alike liberty of conscience and immunities of citizenship. It is now no more that toleration is spoken of, as if it was by the indulgence of one class of people, that another enjoyed the exercise of their inherent natural rights. For happily the Government of the United States, which gives to bigotry no sanction, to persecution no assistance requires only that they who live under its protection should demean themselves as good citizens, in giving it on all occasions their effectual support.

It would be inconsistent with the frankness of my character not to avow that I am pleased with your favorable opinion of my Administration, and fervent wishes for my felicity. May the children of the Stock of Abraham, who dwell in this land, continue to merit and enjoy the good will of the other Inhabitants; while every one shall sit in safety under his own vine and figtree, and there shall be none to make him afraid. May the father of all mercies scatter light and not darkness in our paths, and make us all in our several vocations useful here, and in his own due time and way everlastingly happy.

G. Washington

Historian Harry V. Jaffa wrote that Washington's letter meant that Jews would be "full citizens for the first time, not merely in American history, but since the end of their own polity in the ancient world, more than two thousand years before. From no one else could such a statement about Jews have carried the authority it did carry, when it came from Washington. No one could repudiate these words, once they had come from Washington, without making himself contemptible."[31]

For American Jews, George Washington's letter remains only second to the United States Constitution as a guarantor of their equal rights. The Touro Synagogue in Newport honors the letter with an annual public reading both of it and the Seixas letter.

Each year, at the reading, a notable American also delivers an address. In 2013 it was given by United States Supreme Court Justice Elena Kagan. Referring to the letter, she said, "I don't think this was just a polite, perfunctory exchange of official correspondence. In those early years of the republic, everything George Washington said or wrote or did was addressed to an audience as wide as the nation. He

Fig. 1. Consecrated in 1763, the Touro Synagogue is the home of Congregation Jeshuat Israel and the oldest synagogue building in America. The Newport, Rhode Island, community received George Washington here in 1790. Historic American Buildings Survey (Library of Congress).

was self-consciously constructing the country by his words and his deeds about what it meant to be an American and what it meant to live in accordance with the country's founding principles."[32]

Continuing with personal remarks, the justice said, "I am a Jew and I am an American and not once have I thought of those two parts of my identity as in any tension with each other. Not once have I thought of myself as any less a Jew because I am an American or any less of an American because I am a Jew. When you think about it, that's an amazing thing. Most Jews in most places in most times couldn't have said that, never felt so free of conflict."[33]

A year later, Dr. Christina Paxson, president of Brown University, spoke at the Touro event. "Even more extraordinary," she said, "the letter makes plain that this was not a special gift given to Jews alone. Instead, Washington expressed the idea of liberty of conscience as a universal principle that would be applied to all citizens."[34] In 2014 Paxson's role at Brown University also symbolized how far America had come in its acceptance of Jews: Paxson, who is Jewish, presided over a university which at its founding required the person holding that office to be a Baptist, as we learned earlier in this chapter.

The early Jewish arrivals were not dissuaded by the discrimination they faced in their new land. America was still different from other countries Jews had experienced and those colonial era Jews were resilient. Here, legal and political avenues offered protections they could and did pursue. Standing firm and facing their detractors, they created the foundation of the most unique Jewish community in the world.

Free to practice their religion and to engage in business and the professions, Jews began to assume their places in American life. As the eighteenth century ended, American Jews felt confident in their future. The United States Constitution guaranteed their legal rights while President Washington's letter provided personal assurance that these would be observed.

Still, despite these two vitally important documents to American Jews, the specter of antisemitism continued to loom.

3

Settling In

George Washington was quite clear. In the United States, Jews were to be not just tolerated residents but citizens with full equal rights.

Yet those rights were not always automatically assumed. They had to be fought for and defended.

The experiences of the three of the most visible Jews in early nineteenth-century America, Mordecai Manuel Noah, Uriah P. Levy, and Rebecca Gratz, speak to the difficult position many other Jews faced: fully participating in American life while standing up against antisemitism.

Mordecai Manuel Noah

Mordecai Manuel Noah was born in Philadelphia, likely on July 19, 1785, into a family of American patriots. His father, Manuel Noah, served with distinction in the Continental Army and his mother, Zipporah, was the daughter of Jonas Phillips, also an army veteran. He was raised by the Phillips family, and his grandfather instilled in him a love of country. He apprenticed to a wood carver while attending school and reading voraciously at the public library. His love of literature led him to the theater and to the world of writing.

In 1811 young Noah, seeking greater opportunities, moved from Philadelphia to Charleston, South Carolina, where he studied law and continued writing. His first play, *The Fortress of Sorrento*, was published as early as 1808. Sometime after his arrival in Charleston, he became a writer and editor of the *Charleston City Gazette*. At the same time he actively participated in political life as an outspoken supporter of the Democratic-Republican Party (later to become the

Fig. 2. American playwright, diplomat, and politician Mordecai Manuel Noah. John Wood Dodge, *Mordecai Manuel Noah*, 1834, watercolor on ivory, sight 3⅛ x 2⅝ in. (7.9 x 6.7 cm) rectangle, irregular, Smithsonian American Art Museum, Bequest of Ettie W. Noah Wilson, through John L. Laskey, 1957.11.4.

modern Democratic Party) and of President James Madison (1809–17). Through the newspaper and public speeches, he expressed his support for war against Britain.

The British were attacking American ships and forcing captured American sailors to serve in the British Navy. Noah's outspoken political views were not always popular and led to three separate challenges to duels. Yet President Madison recognized his loyalty to the Democratic-Republican Party and his support of the looming War of 1812. In 1811 Madison offered Noah the position of American consul in Riga, then part of the Russian Empire (today the capital of Latvia). Although delighted at the offer, Noah was aware of the chaotic situation that would greet him there. Russia was in economic turmoil, and a war with Napoleon's France was looming. He declined.

Two years later, President Madison offered Noah another diplomatic appointment, which he now accepted: American consul to Tunis, on North Africa's Barbary Coast. This, too, was a fraught position. For centuries, shipping in the area faced the danger of attack from Barbary pirates operating under the protection of local leaders. The young American government was concerned about pirate attacks on U.S. ships, in which sailors were often enslaved or held for ransom. Recently, pirates had captured eleven white American sailors on board the *Edwin*, out of Salem, Massachusetts. Noah was specifically instructed to obtain their release, with the authorization "to go as far as three thousand dollars a man, but a less sum may probably effect the object."[1] He was also reminded that it was official U.S. policy not to pay ransoms so as not to encourage future acts of piracy. Noah was to make it appear that whatever ransom money he offered actually came from the families and/or friends of the enslaved sailors.

But the pirates and their local protectors had been in the ransom business for centuries and were skilled negotiators. To free the Americans, Noah had no choice but to agree to a much larger payment than the American government expected. Satisfied that he had accomplished his mission of freeing the captured sailors, Noah continued with his diplomatic work. Yet when news of the enlarged payment reached Washington, it created a political firestorm. It turns out that Noah had engaged, perhaps accidentally, a dishonest broker who paid above the limit for the sailors, charged an extra fee, and had fallen out of favor with Madison.

To his total dismay, Noah received the following letter from Secretary of State James Monroe:

Department of State, April 25, 1815

Sir,

At the time of your appointment, as Consul at Tunis, it was not known that the RELIGION which you profess would form any obstacle to the exercise of your Consular functions. Recent information, however, on which entire reliance may be placed, proves that it would produce a very unfavorable effect. In CONSEQUENCE OF WHICH, the President has deemed it expedient to revoke your commission. On the receipt of this letter, therefore, you will consider yourself no longer in the public service. There are some circumstances, too, connected with your accounts, which require a more particular explanation, which, with that already given, are not approved by the President.

I am, very respectfully, Sir,
Your obedient servant
James Monroe[2]

Noah reflected on the letter's contents. "I was at a loss," he later wrote in his book, *Travels*, "to account for its strange and unprecedented tenor; my religion an object of hostility? I thought I was a citizen of the United States, protected by the constitution in my religious as well as my civil rights."[3] The government representatives who had sent him to Tunis knew very well that he was Jewish. And his religion could not have been an obstacle to dealing with the Barbary rulers, since those rulers were unaware of his religion, knowing only that he was the official representative of the United States. "Why am I to be persecuted for my religion?" he lamented.[4]

Upon Noah's reluctant return to the United States, he self-published a pamphlet defending his actions, while urging the government to exonerate him, which it finally did in 1817. It did not take him long to resume his versatile life as a journalist, playwright, and political activist. He settled in New York City where his uncle, Naphtali Phillips, owner of the *National Advocate*, offered him the position as the paper's chief editor. This began Noah's lengthy career editing other New York newspapers. Politically, he became active in the affairs of Tammany Hall, with the *National Advocate* as a supportive newspaper. Founded in 1789 as a political discussion group, Tammany became New York City's political power base with its connections to the Democratic Party, working people, and immigrants. Its corruptive power controlled the outcome of elections and the appointment to political offices. Despite its reputation, Noah wrote supportive editorials in the newspaper and became Tammany's principal spokesperson.

He took an active interest in the city's Shearith Israel Congregation and in 1818 delivered the keynote address at the dedication of the synagogue's new building on Mill Street. Despite his own experiences, he held patriotic views about America and the place of Jews within it. "Until the Jews can recover their ancient rights and dominions, and take their rank among the governments of the earth," he said, "this is their chosen country; here they can rest with the persecuted from every clime, secure in person and property, protected from tyranny and oppression, and participating of equal rights and immunities."[5]

Never shy about publicizing himself, Noah sent copies of the speech to former presidents John Adams, Thomas Jefferson, and James Madison. Madison, as if ignoring his previous treatment of Noah, responded, "I observe with pleasure the view you give of the spirit in which your sect partakes of the common blessings, afforded by our Government and laws."[6]

Noah's political life took a turn in 1822 when Tammany leaders appointed him high sheriff of New York, responsible for the city's jails and overseeing, when necessary, the hanging of convicted criminals. Not every New Yorker was pleased. When he stood for election for a second term one citizen said, "Pity that Christians are to be hung by a Jew." Noah responded, "Pretty Christians, to require hanging at all."[7] The position was made an elected one during his first year, and he was defeated for a second term in part because of religious prejudice. "Mr. Noah is a Jew and adheres to the religion of his fathers," the *United States Telegraph* reported. "This operated powerfully against him at the former election."[8]

Despite the antisemitism Noah faced, he still believed in the American promise of equality and opportunity. His thoughts turned back to the speech he had given at Shearith Israel about the condition of Jews in Europe who did not enjoy the freedoms of America. He decided what was needed: a temporary place of shelter where downtrodden Jews from around the world could seek refuge. Noah even selected the place: seventeen-acre Grand Island in the Niagara River, just offshore Buffalo, New York, and gave it a name, Ararat, after the place where Noah's ark was said to have landed.

Throughout the nineteenth century Christian missionaries had been endeavoring to convert Jews in the United States. In the 1820s some Christian missionaries tried to create a colony in upstate New York to welcome European Jews who had converted overseas. Their attempt never materialized but perhaps led Mordecai Manuel Noah to act. On September 15, 1825, Noah produced, scripted, and starred in a lavish theatrical event to announce the creation of a Jewish colony in America for European Jews.

Military units, leaders of Masonic lodges, elected officials, clergy, and the curious gathered in Buffalo, New York, for the riveting ceremonies. At dawn, a cannon salute was fired in front of the court house. At 10 a.m., uniformed troops led a parade to St. Paul's Episcopal Church, where the foundation stone of the refuge was unveiled. Inscribed on the monument were these words chosen by Noah:

Hear, O Israel the Lord our God is One (in Hebrew)

ARARAT

A CITY OF REFUGE FOR THE JEWS

Founded by Mordecai M. Noah in the Month Tizri 5586
September 1825 in the 50th year of American
Independence

Noah, dressed in crimson robes trimmed with ermine borrowed from a local theater and a large gold medal adorning his neck, then began a grand speech:

I, MORDECAI MANUEL NOAH, Citizen of the United States of America, late Consul of the said States for the city and kingdom Of Tunis, High Sheriff of N. York, Counsellor at Law, and by the GRACE of GOD Governor AND Judge OF Israel, Have issued MY Proclamation.[9]

He then read a list of laws and regulations for the government of the new refuge. The ceremony ended with music and a twenty-four-gun salute outside the church, after which the participants headed to the Eagle Tavern for refreshments.

Newspapers around the world reported on the grand spectacle, but in the end, it amounted to nothing. Noah's plan for a Jewish colony in the United States never materialized. At the time, America was open to Jewish immigrants without restrictions on where they could live. The Jews who arrived from Europe saw no need for a ghetto to remind them of the life they were leaving behind. Nothing was built on Grand Island, and the only memento remaining today is the foundation stone itself on view at the Buffalo Historical Society.

In the space of four years leading up to the failed launching of Ararat, Noah wrote three popular plays, *She Would Be a Soldier* (1819), *Siege of Tripoli* (1820), and *Marion, or the Hero of St. George* (1822). In 1824 he was elected Grand Sachem (the leader) of Tammany Hall. His staunch support of Andrew Jackson in the 1829 presidential election was rewarded with his selection as surveyor of the Port of New York, but the requisite Senate confirmation of his appointment failed on May 10, 1830, in a close vote of twenty-three to twenty-five. Days later, taking advantage of the sickness of one senator and the absence of another, a second vote was held, with Vice President John C. Calhoun casting the deciding vote. Despite one newspaper referring to him as "this outcast of Israel," Noah was confirmed.[10]

Perhaps the best-known Jewish American of his time, Noah was maligned by a *New York Herald* article as "the self-proclaimed king of the Jews at Grand Island, and the associate of everything that is terrible and destructive to Christian civilization and Christian morals." He died on May 22, 1851, in New York City.

Isaac Leeser

The Pennsylvania Society for Evangelizing the Jews formed in 1843 "to promote Christianity among the Jews, by employing missionaries among the Jewish population in this state and promoting their conversion."[11] It followed other such organizations, like the American Society for Evangelizing the Jews (1816) and the American Society for Meliorating the Condition of the Jews (1820). By the 1860s, the missionary society evangelists had established free schools for Jewish children in immigrant areas to convert them to Christianity.

Jews knew that the United States Constitution allowed missionaries to do their work. To defeat the missionaries, they realized they needed to take more affirmative steps, especially by improving both Jewish education and the English-language education immigrant Jews needed. As Isaac Leeser, hazzan at Philadelphia's Mikveh Israel congregation, wrote, "Let us take care of ourselves: we are as competent to do as they can be."[12]

Leeser, the most influential Jewish leader of his time, instituted sermonizing in English during services. The decision, influenced by many Jewish women who had advocated for it, was a consequential step in educating worshippers in synagogue. Concerned that the growing and scattered American Jewish population was largely disconnected, Leeser also founded the first widely circulated Jewish periodical in the United States, *The Occident and American Jewish Advocate*. He aimed to provide American Jews with a knowledge bank to maintain the vitality of their religious practices, as well as a way to connect with the Jewish community even if they lived in a place with no other Jews.

Leeser also supported synagogues' establishment of Jewish day schools as well as Jewish Sunday schools out of concern that the public schools of the day were often unofficial extensions of evangelical Protestantism. "We are not illiberal," he wrote in the December 1843 issue of the *Occident*, "but cannot shut our eyes to the dangerous tendency of placing Jewish children under the inclusive care of gentile teachers."[13] Even hospitals were places of public evangelization, and Jewish hospitals, like Mt. Sinai in New York, were founded in part as a response to this.

Leeser's remarkable efforts to bolster the Jewish community and combat aggressive Christian evangelizing were manifold and also included two more landmark accomplishments. Leeser published a new translation of the Hebrew Bible into English, beginning with the Torah (1843) and later the Prophets and Writings (1853). He also established the first American Jewish Publication Society (1845). Though short-lived, it was a forerunner of The Jewish Publication Society (1888), the publisher of this book.

Fig. 3. Rebecca Gratz of Philadelphia is credited with founding the first Jewish Sunday School in America. Tibbut Archive / Alamy Stock Photo.

Rebecca Gratz

By the 1830s, as more Jewish children began attending public schools, congregational day schools established by synagogues grew out of favor. In this context, Leeser supported Rebecca Gratz's idea of Sunday schools.

Gratz was born into a prominent Pennsylvania Jewish family in 1781. Her father, Michael, was a successful merchant and a signer of the 1765 Non-Importation Resolutions to protest unfair British taxation. In contrast to many women of her time, Rebecca Gratz was self-educated. She attended women's academies and read freely from her father's extensive library.

Impressed by the existing Sunday school model of Protestant churches, which offered free religious education to Christian children, Gratz created and wrote the curriculum for the first Jewish Sunday school for children in Philadelphia in 1838. Her Sunday school became a model for Jewish communities around the country and eventually evolved into today's supplementary Jewish religious schools. In honor of her family's contributions to Jewish American life and their financial contribution to creating a Jewish college, Gratz College was founded in 1895 as the first pluralistic college of Jewish studies in the United States.

Uriah Phillips Levy

Like his older cousin Mordecai Manuel Noah, Uriah Phillips Levy endured antisemitism while pursuing public service. He chose an even more adventurous path.

Born on April 22, 1792, Levy left home at age ten to go to sea as a cabin boy. Within ten years he became master of his own trading ship, the *George Washington*. When the War of 1812 began, he received a commission from the United States Navy as a sailing master aboard a ship stationed in New York harbor, the USS *Alert*, responsible for navigating, keeping the ship's log, rigging sails, supervising cargo, and maintaining the vessel.

In 1813 he was assigned to the USS *Argus*, a warship heading through the British blockade to Europe. And so his naval career progressed for decades, as he moved from ship to ship while steadily rising through the ranks.

On board his assigned ships, Levy was welcomed by some, yet encountered continued insults and provocations. As a young lieutenant on the *Franklin*, he "was immediately made to feel the effect of social ostracism by his fellow officers, who tried to compel the Jew to resign."[14] Proud of who he was and known to be strong-minded and sometimes even disagreeable, Levy often responded by physically attacking his tormentors, leading to a career total of six court martial trials. His superiors understood the torments Levy faced, and the charges were often dismissed or resulted in token punishments. Throughout, Levy's spirit and patriotism did not flag.

While at a dance in Philadelphia, he was purposely jostled by another naval officer, Lieutenant Peter Potter, who shouted, "You damned Jew."[15] Levy struck him, Potter challenged Levy to a duel, and Levy reluctantly agreed. At the assigned time, both men paced off, turned, and fired at each other. The first time, both missed. Levy wanted to end the duel, but Potter insisted on continuing. With the fourth shot, Levy killed Potter and was arrested, since dueling was illegal. A court released Levy based on the knowledge that Potter had persisted in continuing the duel.

For sailors who broke rules or otherwise disobeyed an officer, flogging was the usual penalty. The secretary of the navy officially ended the practice in 1831, but his order was largely ignored aboard ships of the fleet. Levy abhorred this cruel punishment and created his own methods of castigation. In command of the USS *Vandalia* in 1838, he refused to order the flogging of a drunken sailor. Instead, he sent the man to bed and the next day had him wear a wooden bottle around his neck.[16]

In 1839, still in command of the *Vandalia*, Levy earned a final court martial on the charge of "scandalous and cruel conduct, unbecoming an officer and a gentleman."[17] Instead of the expected flogging of a sailor, Levy had ordered the man "to be seized to a gun, his trowsers [*sic*] to be let down, and a [small] quantity of tar and feathers to be applied to his naked skin."[18] A newspaper account of the trial reported that Mordecai M. Noah was there to offer legal advice to his cousin. In April 1842 Levy was found guilty and dismissed from the Navy, but President John Tyler quickly overturned the dismissal since Levy was acting under naval regulations to avoid flogging by substituting a lesser punishment. The symbolic tar and feathering Levy had ordered was certainly less painful to the sailor than flogging. Due in part to Levy's own example and his lobbying to end flogging, Congress totally abolished the practice aboard U.S. Navy vessels in 1850.

In 1855, under the guise of removing unpopular officers from active duty, a naval committee flagged Levy for dismissal, perhaps because of his faith. Although ordinary sailors approved of Levy's role in ending flogging, antisemitic officers opposed Levy. An outraged Levy fought for reinstatement. At a formal Navy hearing in 1857, he spoke forcefully about his faith:

> My parents were Israelite and I was nurtured in the faith of my ancestors. In deciding to adhere to it, I have but exercised a right, guaranteed to one by the constitution of my native State, and of the United States,—a right given to all
>
> Men by their Maker—a right more precious to each of us than life itself. . . .
>
> Remembering always that the great mass of my fellow citizens were Christians; profoundly grateful, to the Christian founders of our Republic, for their justice and liberality to my long persecuted race; I have earnestly endeavored, in all places and circumstances to act up to the wise and tolerant spirit of our political institutions. . . . I have to complain—more in sorrow than in anger do I say it—that in my official experience I have met with little to encourage, though with much to frustrate, these conciliatory efforts.[19]

A few months later, Uriah P. Levy was reinstated with full rank and given command of the USS *Macedonian* with orders to cruise the Mediterranean. In 1860, on that voyage, Levy was promoted to commander of the entire Mediterranean Squadron with the rank of commodore, the highest rank in the United States Navy.

After gathering earth from the Holy Land as ship ballast, Levy returned home. Knowing that religious Jews used small amounts of that earth in burials, he gave some to his New York congregation, Shearith Israel.

After fifty years of naval service, Levy died on March 22, 1862, and was buried with full naval honors.

Today, Uriah Phillips Levy is primarily remembered as the savior of Monticello, the home Thomas Jefferson designed and occupied. Levy had great admiration for Jefferson and his ideals of religious freedom. In 1834 Levy bought Monticello from Jefferson's descendants. The home had fallen into great disrepair; Levy rebuilt and remodeled it. It remained the Levy family home until 1923, when it was sold to a foundation that maintains the architecturally significant building as a national historic site. Visitors on the grounds today can pay their respects at the tomb of Uriah Phillips Levy's mother, Rachel, and ponder the link between two remarkable Americans.

Solomon Etting and the Jew Bill

When Levy spoke about his love of country and his faith, he referred to the guarantees of both the Pennsylvania and United States constitutions. For Solomon Etting of Baltimore, Maryland, however, the state constitution of Maryland was an obstacle. It required anyone holding an elected or appointed state office to take an oath declaring one's belief in the Christian religion.

In 1797 Etting began submitting petitions to the legislature for a change in the state constitution. In 1802 he petitioned again, explaining that "the Jews are deprived of holding any office of profit and trust under the constitution and laws of this state."[20] To a certain extent this was grandstanding; Jews, including Etting and his brother, had received appointments and served in public office even while they were technically prohibited from doing so under state law. Still, Jewish political leaders pushed for the Jew Bill, as it was called, as the status quo put people like the Etting brothers at the mercy of the state legislature. Without constitutional protection, their informal acceptance could be revoked at a moment's notice.

The *Jew Bill* was written in a universal way that included other non-white, Christian groups like "Turks" (aka Muslims) and free African Americans. It failed to garner enough political support and was defeated in 1802. An opposing legislator stated he "did not think it proper or expedient to grant the rights and privileges which we enjoy, to a sect of people who do not associate with us, and who do not even eat at our tables."[21] The bill was defeated once more two years later and was not considered again in the state legislature until 1818, when a legislator named Thomas Kennedy reintroduced it. "There are few Jews in the United States," Kennedy said. "In Maryland there are very few. But if there was only one—to that one, we ought to do justice."[22]

It took Kennedy eight years to get the Jew Bill passed—and by then it was a different version, having been narrowed to specifically reference only Jews. During that time, Kennedy's persistence caused his own loss of reelection twice, but he continued to fight in favor of the bill's passage. When opponents mentioned the false claim that the Jews killed Jesus, Kennedy responded. "We all feel the force of political prejudice, but religious prejudice is even stronger, since it has been passed from father to son for eighteen hundred years."[23] In 1823 he ran on a Jew Bill ticket of supportive legislative candidates, which lost heavily.

At a meeting that year of opponents to the bill, a resolution emerged: "As Christians, we hold this to be our country; and while we are willing to extend toleration, hospitality, personal freedom, and the enjoyment of prosperity, to all men, we wish none to be in office who cannot or will not declare their belief in the christian [sic] Religion."[24] An opposing newspaper article from Washington County stated, "The ticket opposed to religious freedom has prevailed two to one, that is, the new testament Jews have beat the old testament Jews."[25] In 1826 Kennedy, reelected, finally succeeded and the Maryland Assembly passed the Jew Bill. Legally Jews were not just tolerated but equal citizens, able to seek any political office in Maryland. That year, Solomon Etting became the first Jew elected to the Baltimore city council.

The Damascus Affair

By the 1840s the Jewish population in the United States reached fifteen thousand. It was a large enough number for American Jews to begin thinking about a unifying organizational structure for themselves. Until then, Jewish leadership had solely resided in far-flung individual synagogues, each with a limited geographic presence. With growing concern about antisemitism at home and abroad, American Jews needed to respond unilaterally. Incidents far from U.S. shores, in Syria, Italy, and Switzerland, created a desire for a central organization to represent the growing and diverse American Jewish community with one voice.

In Damascus, Syria, on February 5, 1840, Father Thomas, a Catholic priest of the Capuchin order, disappeared. For decades he had worked in the city offering medical care and vaccinations to residents regardless of their religion. When last seen, he was in the city's Jewish Quarter. Priests of his order turned to civil authorities to accuse Jews of killing Father Thomas. They had no evidence but resorted to the ancient blood libel accusation (see chapter 1) that Jews had killed the priest in order to use his blood in baking matzah for Passover, to be held that April.

A Jewish barber by the name of Solomon Negrin was arrested and subjected to extreme torture to obtain a confession. When he could stand the pain no longer, he named seven wealthy Jews who were immediately imprisoned and tortured. Two died, one converted to Islam, and the others were "flogged with rods; they were kept plunged for hours together in cold water . . . their ears were torn off, their faces flayed, and their chins, beard, and noses burnt with red hot irons."[26] Several rabbis were also arrested and tortured. When none of the tortured prisoners admitted knowledge of the father's disappearance, the local governor rounded up dozens of other innocent Jews and took more than sixty young Jewish children as hostages, hoping their parents would come forward to confess.

Syria was then under the control of Mehemet Ali, pasha and viceroy of Egypt. France was closely allied with the viceroy and supportive of Egypt's control over Syria. Its consul in Damascus, Count Ratti-Menton, actively supported the accusations against the Jews. Christians and Muslims committed violence against Jews throughout Syria.

News about the mistreatment of the Damascus Jews slowly reached other countries. Concerned about negative world reaction, Mehemet Ali issued a proclamation ordering a stop to the riots: "Such aggressions displease us; they are contrary to our wishes. I command you therefore to prevent their occurrence."[27] Throughout Western Europe, reaction to the Damascus events expanded, with rallies and calls for action to free the imprisoned Jews. Philanthropist Sir Moses Montefiore, president of the Board of Deputies of British Jews, and Adolphe

Cremieux, president of its counterpart in France, the Israelite Consistory of Paris, sailed to Alexandria, Egypt, on a diplomatic mission in July to protest directly to the pasha. In effect, their organizations were officially recognized by their governments as representing the Jews of their countries.

Meanwhile, news of the Damascus Affair reached the United States and was widely reported in American newspapers. From the 1820s to the 1840s the Jewish population in the States had grown, with most of the Jews hailing from German-speaking countries. Many newcomers had begun their careers as peddlers, and several would eventually open some of the country's best-known stores: Filenes in Boston, Kaufmanns in Pittsburgh, Bloomingdales in New York. Others would make their mark in mining, like the Guggenheims, or in banking, like the Lehmans.

The Damascus Affair aroused American Jews to act as well, but unlike in France and Britain, no central Jewish organization then existed in the United States. Belatedly, Jewish communities independently organized mass meetings in New York, Charleston, Philadelphia, and Richmond. At the August 19, 1840, meeting in New York City, Jewish representatives passed a resolution asking President Martin Van Buren to direct the American consul in Egypt to intervene on the Damascus Jews' behalf. Meeting chair J. B. Kursheedt urged Van Buren by letter to "use every possible effort to induce the Pasha of Egypt to manifest more liberal treatment towards his Jewish subjects."[28]

A quick response to Kursheedt came on August 25 from John Forsyth, the secretary of state. By direction of the president, Forsyth wrote, "I have the honor to inform you, that the heart rending scenes which took place at Damascus had previously been brought to the notice of the President. . . . Our Charge d'Affaires at Constantinople was instructed to interpose his good offices in behalf of the oppressed and persecuted race of the Jews in the Ottoman dominions."[29]

Indeed, several weeks earlier, in response to messages he had received from the Lord Mayor of London, the secretary of state sent a message to John Gliddon, the United States Consul at Alexandria, on

President van Buren's behalf: "In common with all civilized nations, the people of the United States, have learned with horror the atrocious crimes imputed to the Jews and Damascus, and the cruelties of which they have been the victims. . . . he [the President] has accordingly directed me to instruct you to employ, should the occasion arise, all those good offices and efforts . . . to the end that justice and humanity may be extended to these persecuted people, whose cry of distress has reached our shores."[30]

As in New York, a series of resolutions were passed in Philadelphia and sent to the White House. At the Philadelphia meeting on August 27, 1840, Isaac Leeser observed that this affair marked the first time since 1654 that American Jews had united to stand up for themselves as a community. "Another happy effect has already resulted from the same cause," he said. "It has awakened anew the spirit of brotherly love among us, and we have had an opportunity of experiencing that oceans may intervene between our dispersed remnant, that mountains may divide us, but that yet the Israelite is ever alive to the welfare of his distant brother."[31]

Meanwhile, Montefiore and Cremieux arrived in Alexandria and began negotiations with the pasha. Perhaps the power of world condemnation and the specific intervention of important British and French Jews led the pasha, on August 28, 1840, to order that "all the Jews who have been imprisoned be released, and those who have abandoned their dwelling be permitted to return with perfect safety. Each of them may resume his trade or occupation as usual."[32]

The U.S.-Switzerland Treaty

A decade after the Damascus Affair, what should have been an ordinary trade treaty between two countries emerged as a serious threat to American Jews. On February 13, 1851, President Millard Fillmore submitted a proposed treaty with Switzerland to the United States Senate for routine confirmation. The first article of the proposed treaty opened with "the Christian citizens of the United States of America, and the citizens of Switzerland."[33] It seems that Ambrose Dudley

Mann, the American Consul to Switzerland who drafted the treaty, had acknowledged laws in certain Swiss cantons (provinces) that prevented Jews from entering the area and engaging in commerce. On November 17, 1851, a new law in the Canton of Basel was more explicit. "No Jew," it ordered, "without exception, is permitted to settle, to carry on commerce, trade, or any handicraft."[34] According to the letter of the law, Jewish merchants, including American Jews, were prohibited from even setting foot in Switzerland.

Public reaction in the United States was swift and clear. President Fillmore and his secretary of state, Daniel Webster, objected to the treaty, as did various newspaper editorials which pointed out the obvious discrimination against American Jews. Senator Henry Clay wrote, "I disapprove entirely the restriction limiting certain provisions of the treaty, under the operations of which respectable portion of our fellow-citizens would be excluded from their benefits."[35]

Jews across the United States immediately called for Senate rejection of the treaty. Among those leading the fight were Isaac Leeser and Captain Jonas Phillips Levy, the younger brother of Uriah P. Levy. The two worked closely with Senator Lewis Cass of Michigan, who was deeply sympathetic to their cause. Senator Cass ultimately presented to his fellow senators a petition circulated and signed by leading Jews in various cities.

The United States Senate, largely influenced by the reaction of American Jews, rejected the treaty and sent it back to Switzerland for renegotiation. In 1855 a revised treaty was submitted to the Senate. The new first article now began, "The citizens of the United States of America and the citizens of Switzerland, shall be admitted and treated upon a footing of reciprocal equality in the two countries, where such admission and treatment shall not conflict with the constitutional or legal provisions, as well Federal as State and Cantonal of the contracting parties."[36] Except for removing the word "Christian" from the 1850 version, the new treaty practically remained the same. But the term "reciprocal equality" meant that Jews still were subject to Swiss law banning them from the country.

Outrage continued. Jews in several communities held mass meetings and issued resolutions condemning the new treaty version. The Jews of Charleston, South Carolina, wrote to President James Buchanan that "reciprocal equality" effectively deprived the "American citizens of the Jewish Faith from the rights and privileges to be derived therefrom since Federal as well as Cantonal laws of Switzerland do not grant the same political and civil rights to Israelites."[37] Nonetheless, and with little publicity, the U.S. Senate passed the revised treaty in November 1855.

In September 1857 a protest meeting of local Washington DC Jews issued a resolution accusing the Senate of "ratifying a treaty which would have been worthy of the dark middle ages."[38] Tensions were further inflamed when news arrived that an American Jewish merchant, A. H. Gootman, had been ordered out of Switzerland a year earlier. A resolution passed at an Indianapolis gathering declared that "the Israelites of Indiana, in particular, consider it as the greatest tyranny against one citizen of the United States, not to be allowed in foreign countries the rights guaranteed to any other citizen, when such distinction is founded only upon an intolerant religious prejudice."[39]

Newspapers around the country publicized the injustice while petitions and letters opposing the treaty reached the White House and Senate. An announcement in the *Israelite* urged action. "Agitate! Call meetings! Engage the press in your favor!!!! Israelites, freemen and citizens! Let not the disgrace of the treaty . . . remain upon the history of our country."[40]

A small convention of Jewish leaders in Baltimore appointed a committee to call on President Buchanan, who agreed to take up their cause. The American consul in Switzerland appealed to the Swiss government, and eventually Mr. Gootman was allowed to remain in the country—not because of any change in the restrictive laws, but as a diplomatic favor to the American government. The restrictive clauses were finally removed from the treaty in 1866. It would take until 1874 for the Swiss government to adopt a new constitution that finally guaranteed Jews full civil rights and equality.

The Kidnapping of Edgardo Mortara

The next international incident drawing the attention of American Jews occurred in Bologna, Italy, a city in the Papal States ruled by the Catholic Church with the pope as their spiritual and secular leader. By the middle of the nineteenth century some two hundred Jews were living there, including the Mortara family. On the night of June 23, 1858, Marianna Mortara was awakened by loud knocking at her door. Papal police announced they had come to take a family member into custody. Dealing with this on her own (her husband Salomone was elsewhere with one of their children, Riccardo), she was frightened and then astonished when she learned the police had come for her six-year-old son, Edgardo. The little boy, crying for his mother, was legally abducted and taken to Rome to be raised as a Catholic under the protection of Pope Pius IX.

Slowly, the reason why Edgardo was snatched became clear. The Mortaras had formerly employed an illiterate Christian servant girl by the name of Anna Morisi. Several years earlier, when Edgardo was two years old, he became seriously ill. With best intentions, Anna, fearing for the child's health, consulted with a local druggist, who may have advised baptizing the child. This she did, sprinkling water over the boy and reciting a prayer. In the eyes of the church, this was all it took to instantly make little Jewish Edgardo a legal Catholic. In 1858 Anna's deed was revealed to a priest, who notified the local Inquisition office, which ordered that the boy be seized. According to church teachings, a Jewish family could not raise a baptized Catholic. To compound the issue, the Mortaras were also accused of breaking another church rule, usually overlooked, forbidding Jews from employing a Christian in their home.

The kidnapping of Edgardo Mortara quickly became an international scandal. While the Mortaras tried in vain to have their son returned, news of the kidnapping spread around the world. In Europe, heads of state joined Jews in protesting to the pope. Sir Moses Montefiore, who had interceded for the Jews of Damascus nearly two decades earlier, traveled to Rome, but Pope Pius IX refused to see him.

When the news reached the United States, American Jews were shocked and again went into action. Mass meetings were organized throughout the country. In Boston, St. Louis, Philadelphia, Chicago, San Francisco, Charleston, and New York, large assemblies gathered to denounce the outrage. These meetings attracted not only Jews but others who considered what happened to Edgardo an assault on liberty and humanity. A resolution adopted in San Francisco stated, "The Israelites and other citizens of San Francisco, in mass meeting assembled, denounce this act of the Papal authorities at Bologna, as being sacrificial of the dearest rights of humanity—social, political and religious liberty."[41] In New York, more than two thousand gathered in the largest meeting of Jews in that city since the Damascus Affair of 1840. Meetings such as these were widely reported in newspapers throughout the country.

While these meetings evoked great public empathy, they had no impact on the authorities in Rome. Knowing this, the Philadelphia meeting attendees drafted a message to President James Buchanan requesting that the president take action against the Papal States for the abduction and demand Edgardo's return to his parents. Secretary of State Lewis Cass responded, "It is the settled policy of the United States to abstain from all interference in the internal concerns of the country."[42] Some historians add that Buchanan had another motive not to interfere: doing so might draw attention to American slavery.

Young Edgardo continued to grow up within the Catholic Church and eventually became a priest under the pope's patronage. Some historians believe his abduction was a major factor in the church's losing control of the Papal States. In 1870 the Papal States became part of the new Kingdom of Italy. Perhaps with some regret in his voice, Pope Pius IX later told Edgardo, "I have bought thee, my son for the Church at a very high price."[43]

Board of Delegates of American Israelites

Until this point, American Jews' responses to antisemitism at home and abroad had been ad hoc, reactive to circumstances. After the

Damascus, Swiss, and Mortara affairs, some American Jewish community leaders determined that, had they had been more organized, they could have had a greater influence on the American government to intervene in these events. What the growing American Jewish community needed was a single national organization to speak for the Jews.

In 1859 Rabbi Samuel M. Isaacs of New York City's Shaaray Tefila synagogue called for a meeting of representatives from all congregations in the United States to discuss the matter. Twenty-four congregations responded and formed the lay-led Board of Delegates of American Israelites, modeled after the Board of Deputies of British Jews.

Now, for the first time, there was a single official umbrella organization purporting to represent the American Jewish community. In reality, the community was fractured and the Board of Delegates of American Israelites represented fewer than one-fifth of American synagogues. Nonetheless, its goal—"to keep a watchful eye on all occurrences at home and abroad, and see that the civil and religious rights of Israelites are not encroached on, and call attention of the proper authorities to the fact, should any such violation occur"—marked an important development in serving as a watchdog for American Jews.[44]

Their work would be cut out for them, as the Civil War was about to divide the country.

4

A Country Divided

Cesar Kaskel did not understand why he'd been summoned to the provost marshal's office in Paducah, Kentucky, early on a Sunday morning.

One of hundred and fifty thousand Jews amid the two million German immigrants arriving in the United States between 1820 and 1860, Kaskel had opened a men's clothing store in Paducah just four years earlier. He didn't have to wait long at military headquarters before being presented with this official notice:

Office of the Provost Marshal

Paducah, Ky, December 28, 1862

C.J. Kaskel-Sir: In pursuance of General Order No. 11, issued from Gen Grant's headquarters, you are hereby ordered to leave the city of Paducah, Ky, within twenty-four hours after receiving this order.

By order
L. J. Waddell
Captain And Provost Marshal[1]

Kaskel was shocked. Here he was, a respected merchant, a supporter of the North's cause in the ongoing Civil War, even a vice president of the Paducah Union League Club—with twenty-four hours to leave his home and business! When he asked the officer for an explanation, Kaskel was told that that the order did not apply to him alone but to all the Jews—men, women, and children—in Paducah. With that, the officer gave him a copy of Major General Ulysses S. Grant's General Orders no. 11:

General Orders No. 11

HDQRS. 13TH A.C. DEPT. OF THE TENN.

Holly Springs, December 17, 1862.

The Jews, as a class violating every regulation of trade established by the Treasury Department and also department orders, are hereby expelled from the department within twenty-four hours from the receipt of this order.

Post commanders will see that all of this class of people be furnished passes and required to leave, and any one returning after such notification will be arrested and held in confinement until an opportunity occurs of sending them out as prisoners, unless furnished with permit from headquarters.

No passes will be given these people to visit headquarters for the purpose of making personal application for trade permits.

By order of Maj. Gen. U.S. Grant:
JNO. A. Rawlins
Assistant Adjutant-General[2]

General Grant's Order no. 11

Why had General Grant issued this blanket order concerning the Jews?

Grant had succumbed to the anti-Jewish imagery that was often associated with developments hindering the war effort. In all likelihood he was attempting to limit the smuggling and economic speculation threatening his military success. Many of the speculators were looking to purchase cotton, which was in short supply at the time. Jewish communal leader Isaac Leeser explained, "It has been the fashion to call all who were engaged in smuggling or blockade running, as it was termed, Jews."[3] In truth, an angry Grant would later discover his own father was dealing illegally in cotton trading.

The order did not make sense. "If the order was directed against Jewish cotton dealers only," Leeser later wrote, "why not also against Yankee cotton dealers? Why were old residents, women, and children, exiled, who never dealt in cotton? Why were all the Jews in creation stigmatized and disgraced as a lawless band?"[4]

Meanwhile, Kaskel could not comprehend why this was happening. At that very moment thousands of Jewish soldiers were fighting and dying for the Union. He could not keep quiet. He had to do something, and quickly.

Together with several Jewish shop owners from Paducah, Kaskel sent an emergency telegram to President Abraham Lincoln, appealing for him to intervene:

Paducah, KY, Dec. 29, 1862

Hon. Abraham Lincoln, President of the United States.

General Order No. 11 issued by General Grant at Oxford, Miss., December the 17th, commands all post commanders to expel all Jews without distinction within twenty-four hours from his entire Department. The undersigned, good and loyal citizens of the United States and residents of this town, for many years engaged in legitimate business as merchants, feel greatly insulted and outraged by this inhuman order; the carrying out of which would be the grossest violation of the Constitution and our rights as good citizen under it, and would place us, besides a large number of other Jewish families of this town, as outlaws before the world. We respectfully ask your immediate attention to this enormous outrage on all law and humanity and pray for your effectual and immediate interposition. We would especially refer you to the post commander and post adjutant as to our loyalty, and to all respectable citizens of this community as to our standing as citizens and merchants. We respectfully ask for immediate instructions to be sent to the Commander of this Post.

D. Wolff & Bros

C. F. Kaskel

J. W. Kaskel[5]

Hours later, Kaskel and other Jewish residents of Paducah boarded the mail packet *Charley Bowen* for a trip up the Ohio River to Cairo, Illinois, out of the territory controlled by General Grant's army.

News of the expulsion had already reached newspapers. On January 3, 1863, the very page of the *New York Times* that reported President Lincoln's Emancipation Proclamation also mentioned the events in Paducah. Readers were astonished that just as the United States was freeing African American slaves, Jewish Americans were being expelled from their homes. The *Louisville Daily Journal* (Kentucky) commented, "This is a terrible wrong, which if reported to us from Turkey, Russia, Austria, or Morocco, would excite the indignation of every liberal man in the free land. Of what offence have the Jews as a class been guilty? . . . Are there smugglers or traitors among them? If so, let the guilty ones suffer, but not the innocent. . . . What in the name of heaven has the offender's religion to do with his offence?"[6]

Still, not everyone was supportive of Jews' rights in America. When in 1844 Jewish residents of Charleston, South Carolina, protested the governor's issuance of a Thanksgiving proclamation inviting citizens to offer "devotions to god the Creator, and his son Jesus Christ," the governor replied that America was a Christian country and accused Jews of "inheriting the same scorn for Jesus Christ which instigated their ancestors to crucify him."[7] An 1863 article in Washington DC's *Daily Morning Chronicle* stated, "The Jews have, since the very unhandsome trick played by Jacob on his brother, been notorious for their fondness for illegitimate, or, at least, unusual modes of making money . . . the Jews are the boldest speculators in the world."[8]

Throughout the Civil War, in both North and South, Jewish merchants were accused of being war profiteers. Images in political cartoons featured Jews with stereotyped hooked noses. People used the word "Jew" to mean cheating or acting deceitfully. A reporter wrote, "The Jews in New Orleans and all the South ought to be exterminated. . . . They run the blockade and are always to be found at the bottom of every new villainy."[9] In the North, another reporter commented, "The Israelites have come down upon the city like locusts. . . . Every boat brings in a load of the hooked-nose fraternity."[10]

While on board the steamer, Kaskel penned a personal account of what had happened. When the boat docked in Cairo, he handed the write-up to an Associated Press reporter, who quickly forwarded it to newspapers around the country:

> I, a peaceable, law-abiding citizen, pursuing my legitimate business at Paducah, Ky., where I have been a resident for nearly four years, have been driven from my home, my business and all that is dear to me, at the short notice of twenty-four hours; not for any crime committed, but because I was born of Jewish parents. Nearly thirty other gentlemen, mostly married, all respectable men, and old residents of Paducah, two of whom have served their country in the three months' service, and all loyal to the government, have suffered the same fate.
>
> On my way to Washington in order to get the most outrageous order of General Grant countermanded. I ask you gentlemen, to lend the powerful aid of the press to the suffering cause of outraged humanity; to blot out as quick as possible this stain on our nations honor, and to show the world that the American people, as a nation, brand the author of that infamous order as unworthy of their respect and confidence.[11]

The publicity did not change the reality. Kaskel knew he had to go to Washington DC without delay to see the president.

After a long and uncomfortable train trip, a bedraggled Cesar Kaskel reached Washington on Saturday, January 3 (traveling on the Sabbath, as the urgent mission required). His first stop was the office of Congressman John Addison Gurley, a friend of President Lincoln. It was already dark when Gurley accompanied Kaskel to the White House. When the president was told of their arrival, he sent word that he was "always glad to see his friends."[12]

Kaskel, still wearing his dusty travel clothes, was ushered into President Lincoln's office. After introductions, Kaskel told Lincoln about the unjust order and the expulsions. The president listened attentively but could not believe what he was hearing until Kaskel presented him with the copy of Grant's Order no. 11 handed to him by the officer in Paducah.

It was obvious that the president knew nothing about it. An often quoted but perhaps not entirely accurate account of their exchange begins with Lincoln saying,

> "And so the children of Israel were driven from the happy land of Canaan?"
>
> Kaskel: "Yes, and that is why we have come unto Father Abraham's bosom, asking protection."
>
> Lincoln: "And this protection they shall have at once."[13]

The president then sat at his desk and wrote a message to Henry Halleck, general-in-chief of all Union armies, which he gave to Kaskel to deliver personally to Halleck at his office in Washington.

Kaskel reached Halleck shortly thereafter. Upon reading the presidential message, the general told Kaskel, "You may leave for home at once if you wish and before you reach there Grant's order will have been revoked."[14]

Much relieved, Kaskel traveled back to his expelled neighbors in Cairo and together they returned to Paducah. An officer who apparently had not yet heard of President Lincoln's action asked by what right they had returned. Kaskel proudly responded, "By order of the President of the United States."[15]

Cesar Kaskel was not alone in fighting back against General Grant's order. The Board of Delegates of American Israelites and officers of B'nai B'rith (the Jewish fraternal organization founded in 1843) sent messages to the White House from across the country. Delegations of Jews from Cincinnati and Louisville were already on their way to the White House when they found out the order had been countermanded; they decided to continue in order to thank Lincoln for his intervention on American Jews' behalf. During their meeting with the president, Lincoln reputedly said, "To condemn a class is, to say the least, to wrong the good with the bad. I do not like to hear a class or nationality condemned on account of a few sinners."[16]

Meanwhile, Congress commended the president for rescinding General Grant's order, but in both the House of Representatives and in the Senate no resolution censuring the general was passed. Grant was too important to the success of the war.

Fortunately, meanwhile, Grant's order had not reached most of the territory under its jurisdiction. By a twist of fate, Confederate raiders had cut the telegraph wires at Grant's headquarters in Holly Springs, Mississippi, before the order could be widely sent. A few small towns like Paducah were the only places where the order was received and carried out by local troops.

The Thomasville Expulsion

In August 1862 a similar expulsion order occurred within Confederate States of America territory in the town of Thomasville, Georgia. On August 30 a group of white gentiles led by a wealthy slave trader accused Jews of passing counterfeit currency, engaging in speculation, and not being loyal to the Confederate cause and passed a resolution ordering all Jews to leave Thomasville in ten days else be expelled by force. Only five Jewish families lived in the area, but many more itinerant Jewish peddlers sold their wares door-to-door locally. Newspaper accounts of the expulsion order resulted in a quickly organized Jewish response. The long-established and important Jewish community of Savannah, Georgia, two hundred miles from Thomasville, organized an emotional protest meeting which led to the unanimously adopted resolution: "This wholesale slander, persecution and denunciation of a people, many of whom are pouring out their blood on the battle fields of their country . . . can find no parallel except in the barbarities of the inquisition."[17]

The reaction of German Jews serving in the Confederate Army had a more direct impact on the implementation of the order. Jewish soldiers of Georgia's Thirty-Second Regiment gathered, spoke of their sacrifices on the Confederacy's behalf, and passed a resolution holding the residents of Thomasville in "contempt and deeming the motive of the same based only upon selfishness and envy."[18] They further advised all Jews to retaliate against those who supported the expulsion.

Cooler heads eventually prevailed. The Thomasville Jews were not expelled and the issue was quickly forgotten. Jews saw once more that they could speak about prejudice without isolating themselves socially and politically. In other words, Jews had become socially prominent enough that they could speak out and effect change.

The Fight for Jewish Chaplains

General Grant's outrageous Order no. 11 was the only official anti-Jewish directive ever issued by the United States government. Fortunately, it remained in effect for just several weeks before being repealed. Another event of the Civil War affecting Jews had a more lasting effect.

At the outbreak of the Civil War in 1861, the Jewish population in the United States was estimated at two hundred thousand, approximately 0.5 percent of the population.[19] During the war, approximately 3.2 million men fought for the North and the South, including perhaps eight to ten thousand Jewish men (efforts to reach a more accurate estimate are ongoing).[20] The horrors of war took a toll on soldiers, yet while most Americans opposed the appointment of military chaplains to provide spiritual support as a violation of the separation between church and state, Congress did not agree and made provisions to expand the chaplaincy early on in the war. For Jewish soldiers in the Union army, having the comfort of a Jewish chaplain was not a possibility since, by law, a recognized army chaplain had to be "a regularly ordained minister of some Christian denomination."[21]

In 1861 a Pennsylvania regiment known as "Cameron Dragoons," with a large Jewish enrollment and a Jewish commanding officer, chose one of its members, Colonel Michael Allen, a Hebrew teacher in civilian life, to be their regimental chaplain. As regimental chaplain, Allen served soldiers of all religions and held nondenominational services on Sundays. When a Young Men's Christian Association (YMCA)

Fig. 4. Union Captain Jacob Jacobs, Company F, Eighty-Third New York
Infantry Regiment. Library of Congress.

representative visited the camp in Virginia, he was astonished to learn that the chaplain was neither a Christian nor an ordained clergy member. His subsequent public complaint forced Allen to resign. In his place, the regiment chose Rabbi Arnold Fischel of New York's Shearith Israel Congregation. Not a Christian, of course, Fischel was nonetheless an ordained clergyman. Yet when Fischel applied to the War Department for a commission, he was denied. Legally he did not meet the requirement that a chaplain had to be Christian.

The Jewish community's reaction was swift. Jewish newspapers editorialized about the issue. The Board of Delegates of American Israelites asked Rabbi Fischel to go to Washington and, in a civilian role, serve Jewish soldiers recuperating in local hospitals—and, moreover, to begin lobbying President Lincoln to change the chaplaincy requirements.

When Fischel spoke to President Lincoln about the unfair requirements, Lincoln told him, "I shall try to have a new law broad enough to cover what is desired by you in behalf of the Israelites."[22] Attention then turned to Congress, where debate on the issue began. Final action came in July 1862, when Congress changed the chaplaincy requirements to read that any "regularly ordained minister of some religious denomination" could be appointed as a military chaplain.

Despite his hard work lobbying for the change, Rabbi Fischel did not serve as the first Jewish chaplain in the Union Army. Instead, Rabbi Jacob Frankel of Philadelphia's Rodeph Shalom Congregation was the first American rabbi appointed as a military chaplain. Other rabbis soon followed. Jewish chaplains have served both Jewish and non-Jewish soldiers in every American war ever since.

Judah P. Benjamin

Vilified and honored at the same time, the noted lawyer and orator Judah P. Benjamin was the best-known Jew during the Civil War. Born in St. Croix in 1811 when it was occupied by the British, he moved with his family to Charleston, South Carolina, as a child. He attended Yale College but mysteriously left before graduating and moved to New

Fig. 5. After the breakout of Civil War, the Louisiana senator and lawyer Judah P. Benjamin became attorney general and secretary of war for the Confederacy. Library of Congress.

Orleans, where he studied law and was admitted to the bar. He was also a successful plantation owner and a supporter of slavery.

The Louisiana legislature elected him as a United States senator in 1852. He thereby became the second Jewish U.S. senator (after David Levy Yulee of Florida, and before senators were elected by popular vote). In 1853 President Millard Fillmore offered him a seat on the Supreme Court, but he refused, preferring to remain in the Senate.

During his 1858 reelection campaign, Benjamin's opponent, Henry Gray, said of him, "His forefathers have crucified the Savior of the world," to which Benjamin was said to have quickly retorted: "It is true I am a Jew and when my ancestors were receiving the Ten Commandments from the immediate hand of Deity, midst the thunderings and lightnings of Mount Sinai, the ancestors of my opponent were herding swine in the forests of Great Britain."[23] Benjamin prevailed in a hard-won campaign.

In 1861, with war imminent, Benjamin left the United States Senate to join the Confederacy. His outspokenness in defense of slavery rights in the South led Senator Ben Wade of Ohio to refer to him as "the Israelite with Egyptian principles."[24] Senator Henry Wilson of Massachusetts used an antisemitic canard to denounce him as a traitor to "the Government of his adopted country, which gives equality of rights even to that race that stoned prophets and crucified the Redeemer of the world."[25]

Some considered Benjamin the "brains of the Confederacy" for the competent advice he gave to Confederate president Jefferson Davis. Over time, Benjamin held top positions as the Confederate States of America attorney general, secretary of war, and secretary of state. To this day he remains the only Jew whose image has appeared on American currency (the $2 Confederate bill).

His closeness with Jefferson Davis notwithstanding, Benjamin was not immune from antisemitic attacks. Called Judas Iscariot Benjamin, linked with the betrayer of Jesus, he became the scapegoat for all that went wrong for the South in the war. A minister referred to Benjamin as "a little pilfering Jew . . . one of the tribe that murdered the Savior."[26]

In 1928 the poet Stephen Vincent Benet would envision Benjamin's feelings in his epic Pulitzer Prize-winning poem, "John Brown's Body":

Judah P. Benjamin, the dapper Jew,
Seal-sleek, black-eyed, lawyer and epicure,
Able, well-hated, face alive with life,
Looked round the council-chamber with the slight
Perpetual smile he held before himself
Continually like a silk-ribbed fan.
Behind the fan, his quick, shrewd, fluid mind
Weighed Gentiles in an old balance. . . .

The mind behind the silk-ribbed fan
was a dark prince, clothed in an Eastern stuff,
Whose brown hands cupped about a crystal egg

That filmed with colored cloud.
The eyes stared, searching.
"I am the Jew. What am I doing here?"[27]

As the Confederacy faced defeat, many in the South blamed Benjamin. With the war over, fearing arrest by the Union army, Benjamin fled to England, where he lived out his life as an honored and successful barrister.

Jewish Contributions to American Life

After the war, amid charges from both sides that Jews had avoided military service, longtime attorney, diplomat, and Jewish communal leader Simon Wolf researched the names of Jews and the units they served in the Union and Confederacy. His four-hundred-page book, *The American Jew as Patriot, Soldier and Citizen,* listing over eight thousand Jewish names, was published in 1895 to refute the antisemitic charge. Today, scholars question Wolf's methodology in the selection of names, since many Christian soldiers of the era had biblical sounding names as well.

His was not the only attempt to provide facts about Jewish contributions to American life. In 1892, for example, the American Jewish Historical Society was formed to serve as a national scholarly resource. Its goal was to make American Jews more aware of their historical heritage by exploring, researching, documenting, archiving, and publishing works on every facet of American Jewish life.

By the Civil War's end in 1865, the German Jews who had arrived in the 1840s and 1850s had succeeded in establishing themselves in America. Their accomplishments were highly visible in retail merchandising and clothing manufacturing, and later in the world of finance. Pillars of society in their communities, they expressed their love of culture by participating in literary and theatrical activities, and their children studied in some of America's most prestigious universities. Yet even so, they felt excluded. As Rabbi Sabato Morais wrote, "The merchant who cheats his creditors, the criminal in the prisoner's dock, is a civil offender if he belongs to the Baptist or the Episcopal denomination, but if he comes of Hebrew blood, Judaism is made responsible for fraud and theft. *Jew, Jew, Jew* is the one all-comprehensive charge."[28] One writer snidely noted that a large percentage of attendees at German theatrical presentations were Jews. "Just look at Rebekka and Sarah! How they manage to lean out over the first balcony so that people will be sure to see them and know that they are there and that they have seats on the first balcony, seats that cost 50 cents apiece!"[29]

The growing Jewish population began to strengthen communal and educational life. Perhaps the most influential Jewish leader in America in the latter half of the nineteenth century was Reform Rabbi Isaac Mayer Wise. His newspaper, the *Israelite*, founded in 1854, had wide distribution. He also aimed to unite all American Jews in a union of congregations. Wise understood that because of jealousy among his colleagues, his idea could not come from a rabbi. Instead, he turned to a successful merchant, Moritz Loth, who in 1873, formed the Union of American Hebrew Congregations (today the Union for Reform Judaism), with thirty-four Reform congregations represented.[30] No Orthodox representatives attended. Two years later, Wise became president of Hebrew Union College, the first seminary to train American-born rabbis (up until then all rabbis in America, Orthodox and Reform, had been foreign born). Also under Wise's leadership, the *Union Prayer Book* was created for use in all Reform congregations.

When an argument about kosher food at the so-called Treyfa Banquet of 1883 split the Reform movement, a group broke away to eventually form Conservative Judaism in America. Melding traditional observance with innovation, in 1886 they created their own rabbinical school, the Jewish Theological Seminary, with the noted scholar Dr. Solomon Schechter accepting the school's presidency in 1902. Schechter founded the United Synagogue of America, which became the umbrella organization of the Conservative movement (which paralleled the Union of American Hebrew Congregations) in 1913. To serve a growing Orthodox community, the Rabbi Isaac Elchanan Theological Seminary (RIETS) was chartered in New York in 1897. Judaism now had its own religious and educational institutions on American soil.

To support and expand Jewish literacy in America, The Jewish Publication Society of America (JPS) was founded in 1888. From the beginning, the society aimed to provide lay Jews with easily accessible books on Jewish history, literature, and religion. One early JPS publication was an English translation of Heinrich Graetz's monumental six-volume *History of the Jews*. JPS also became known for its acclaimed English translations of the Hebrew Bible, *The Holy Scriptures* in 1917 and *The JPS Tanakh* in 1985, as well as commentaries on the Bible and other works of Jewish history and thought.

Jews and Hotels

As Jews became more conspicuous in American life in the years after the Civil War, some members of the white, Protestant majority began to view them as social and economic threats. Negative stereotypes led to restrictions in housing, employment, and education. Newspaper advertisements for employment, hotel, and resort accommodations clearly advised that Jews need not apply. When the *New York Tribune* ran an advertisement from a hotel that stated, "Jews are not admitted," a Jewish reader questioned whether "a newspaper of such high standing and influence as THE TRIBUNE should allow such an advertisement in its columns."[31] Responding that some Jews, like some Christians, may be undesirable guests, the newspaper criticized the hotel owner for targeting all Jews—but also advised Jews not to be so sensitive and did not ban discriminatory advertisements.

Jews proactively fought a national movement to officially declare the United States a Christian nation. They rejuvenated earlier attempts to eliminate "Blue Laws," which prohibited Jews from working on the Christian Sabbath (Sundays) even though they observed the Sabbath on Saturdays. Jewish newspapers were vocal in opposition to Christian prayers in public schools.

Joseph Seligman arrived in the United States in 1837 at age eighteen. He began as a door-to-door peddler; by the end of the Civil War he was a clothing manufacturer, banker, and financier. Yet his wealth and place in society were not enough to overcome the discrimination of the day. For ten years, Seligman and his family had summered at the Grand Union Hotel in Saratoga Springs, New York. Upon their arrival for their usual stay on June 13, 1877, the manager denied them entry, explaining that new hotel owner Judge Henry Hilton (no relation to the current Hilton hotel family) had instructed that "no Israelites shall be permitted in future to stop at this hotel."[32] Incredulous, Seligman responded, "Do you mean to tell me that you will not entertain Jewish people?" "That is our orders, Sir," was the reply.[33]

Returning home to New York City, a furious Seligman made the incident public. The *New York Times* covered it in a front-page story with the headline, "A Sensation at Saratoga."[34] In a public letter to Judge Hilton, Seligman asked why Hilton refused Jews at his hotel while welcoming them to shop in the A. T. Stewart department store he also owned.

So questioned by reporters, Judge Hilton responded, "There is a class of people whom I will not have in the hotel, and I have a right to say so. I don't see how this concerns the general public."[35]

Legally, Hilton was mistaken. One historian, Britt Tevis, has argued that Hilton violated at least three laws—federal, state, and common— when he denied the Seligmans entry into his hotel. At the federal level, Congress had enacted the Civil Rights Act of 1875 two years earlier, which prohibited discrimination in public places. While specifically designed to protect African Americans, essentially the law applied to all Americans regardless of background. (The law was loosely enforced, and the United States Supreme Court would declare it unconstitutional in 1883.) Despite his dubious legal standing, Hilton was not held accountable in court. Changing social and legal conditions made it unattractive for Jewish organizations to litigate the case.

Meanwhile, reaction was quick to follow. Newspapers editorialized against Hilton's action. Leading Jewish clothing manufacturers stopped doing business with A. T. Stewart while Jewish customers stayed away.

Hilton was not apologetic. Trying to make a distinction among Jews of various backgrounds, he disparaged Seligman as someone who had made money but "is of low origin, and his instincts are all of the gutter. . . . He is too obtuse or too mean to see his vulgarity. . . . People won't go to hotels where the Seligman Jew is admitted. And hotels if they would thrive must keep out those who would ruin their existence."[36]

Hilton's views about Jews were not his alone. A letter published in the *New York Times* proclaimed, "This cry of the Jews about equal rights under the Constitution is all sham; they know that the reason they are shut out from society . . . is because they are disagreeable and offensive, and being so, force themselves where their qualities disgust others, and being Jews, persist, though they know they are not wanted."[37] Another such letter stated, "The average Jew is disagreeable, obtrusive, gaudy, insolent, and not to be tolerated by persons who dislike those qualities. Add to these the lack of cleanliness which marks many of the race, and the petty avarice which has always distinguished it, it is not to be wondered at that Judge Hilton, preferring the custom of the better classes, should have attempted to banish from the Union a class whose presence made that better custom impossible."[38]

Two years later, Austin Corbin, owner of the Manhattan Beach Hotel on the easternmost end of New York's Coney Island, announced he would rather go out of business than admit a Jew to his first-class hotel. "They are contemptible . . . a pretentious class who expect three times as much for their money as other people. . . . As a rule they make themselves offensive to the kind of people who principally patronize our road and hotel and I am satisfied we should be better off without them with their custom."[39]

Even when states passed laws eliminating discrimination in public places, some Jews still found themselves unwelcome at hotels. In 1907 Bertha Frank, sister of United States Senator Isadore Rayner of Maryland, arrived at the Marlborough-Blenheim resort in Atlantic City, New Jersey. Apparently, the management did not know she was Jewish when she arrived. But when she tried to make reservations for her two nieces, she was asked if they were Jewish and then told that the hotel did not accept Jews. Much annoyed, she protested to the manager, who simply replied, "The policy of the house is opposed to Jews."[40] This was despite the fact that in 1884 New Jersey had passed a law "prohibiting discrimination based on race, color or previous condition of servitude."[41] Frank packed her bags and left.

Creating Their Own Resorts and Clubs

Exclusion from resorts, hotels, and private clubs led Jews to create their own. When Herman Cohen along with Charles and Sigmund Werner were denied membership in the prestigious Union Club of New York City, they helped found the Harmonie Club. In Memphis, Tennessee, Jews founded the Memphis Club. In Cincinnati, when the only Jewish member of the University Club proposed another Jew for membership, the entire club dissolved. In response, local Jewish businessmen founded the Allemania and Phoenix Clubs.

Jews were not immune from discrimination even in the realm of medicine. Jews who wanted to enter the medical profession faced discrimination and a strict quota system which prevailed well into the twentieth century. Doctor Edward C. Halperin, a medical historian, wrote, "Leaders of U.S. medical schools rationalized their objections to the admission of Jewish students on the grounds of proportional representation as well as the classic anti-Semitic canards of Jewish defensiveness, bookishness, poor manual dexterity, and avarice."[42] Jewish doctors who made it through medical school found themselves excluded from internship and residency opportunities at hospitals. Meanwhile, Jewish patients felt unwelcome in existing hospitals where missionaries attempted to convert them and where kosher food was unavailable.

As a result, Jewish-funded hospitals began appearing in the 1850s in cities around the country. Mount Sinai in New York City and the Jewish Hospital in Cincinnati were among the many Jewish hospitals founded in the United States.

Slowly, Jews were discovering ways to circumvent antisemitism while continuing to build their lives as Americans.

5

The Great Wave

It began as a trickle in the 1870s, but by 1914 over two million Eastern European Jews had arrived in the United States. Many came from the Pale of Settlement, the area set aside for Jews in the Russian Empire that included all or parts of present-day Belarus, Latvia, Lithuania, Poland, Ukraine, Romania, and Russia—indeed, Russian Jews constituted the largest group of immigrants—though significant numbers of Jews also arrived from Romania and Austria-Hungary. All of these Jewish immigrants were a part of a larger wave of immigration as people from southern and eastern Europe made their way to the United States.

Jews in the Pale typically lived in confined shtetls, little villages, where they worked as small merchants, in a community characterized by a Jewish majority who spoke the Yiddish language. In larger cities, Jewish professionals, students, and intellectuals often tried to assimilate into Russian life. Yet, no matter where they lived, suspicion of Jews abounded. All Jews were affected by a rise in pogroms during the second half of the nineteenth century, government-sanctioned physical violence. The hatred they faced, coupled with worsening economic conditions, led many Eastern European Jews to abandon the land they had lived in for generations.

Their arrival did not thrill established Jews whose families had migrated and set up roots in the United States generations earlier. Largely assimilated members of Reform congregations, the established American Jewish community had little in common with the newcomers, who were poor, usually practiced traditional forms of Judaism, spoke Yiddish, and were generally unfamiliar with American culture. While the new immigrants spread throughout the country, one million settled in New York City, particularly on Manhattan's Lower East Side. By sheer numbers they changed the image of American Jewry, and not always in ways their coreligionists viewed charitably.

The cultural and economic gaps between the acculturated and assimilated uptown Jews and the poor downtown Jews, stereotyped by appearance and language, were glaring. At first, the uptowners tried to distance themselves from the newcomers, afraid that other Americans would categorize all Jews together in a wave of deeper discrimination. But subsequently, for both self-protective and humanitarian reasons, the established Jewish community set to work to Americanize the latest wave of immigrants, in part by providing access to educational opportunities.

The new Jewish immigrants realized they also needed to help themselves. In 1881 newly arrived Jews from Eastern Europe created the Hebrew Immigrant Aid Society (HIAS) to assist other Jewish refugees fleeing Europe. Establishing offices in dozens of cities in the United States and Europe, HIAS helped thousands of immigrants negotiate the legal, medical, and employment hurdles they faced to gain admission to America. HIAS even established a bureau on Ellis Island, the immigrant processing station, providing financial aid, travel stipends, and legal assistance to help the newcomers establish themselves in their new land.

A prominent Protestant minister, A. E. Patton, summed up the feelings of Americans who did not welcome Jewish immigrants. "For real Americans to visit Ellis Island," he said, "and there look upon the Jewish hordes, ignorant of all patriotism, filthy, vermin-infested, stealthy and furtive in manner, too lazy to enter into real labor, too cowardly to face frontier life, too lazy to work as every American farmer has to work, too filthy to adopt ideals of cleanliness from the start, too bigoted to surrender any racial traditions or to absorb any true Americanisms, for a real American to see those items of filth, greedy, never patriotic stream flowing in to pollute all that has made

America as good as she is-is to awaken in his thoughtful mind desires to check and lessen this source of pollution."[1]

The distinctiveness of the new immigrants—the black coats, the Yiddish tongue, etc.—made them easy marks for name calling, beard pulling, and outright discrimination. Their pushcarts were overturned on the Lower East Side and young thugs targeted them with rocks. The reality of their poverty did not impede the perpetuation of myths regarding Jews' relationship to money. A backhanded compliment stated, "Of all the nations, which the world has known, the commercial instinct is strongest and most fully developed in the Jew. He never sacrifices future opportunity for present gain."[2] The stereotype of hook-nosed, grotesque looking, money-obsessed Jews was perpetuated on stage, in cartoons, and song. Nursery rhymes like *Jack and Jill* and *Old King Cole* were an accepted part of growing up in America, but another Mother Goose rhyme for children taught that Jews were not to be trusted:

> Jack sold his egg to a rogue of a Jew
> Who cheated him out of half his due.
> The Jew got his goose,
> Which he vowed he would kill.
> Resolving at once
> His pockets to fill.[3]

By the mid-twentieth century that rhyme had disappeared from schoolbooks but not before influencing generations of American children. Such insults hurt, of course, but were secondary to the newcomers' struggle to provide for their families and establish themselves in their new home.

Another challenge was the frequency of Christian missionaries trying to convert Jews. With so many immigrants arriving daily, the missionaries were hopeful of significant success in at least reaching some. In this they were mistaken. When in 1910 a clergyman of the Jewish Evangelical Society applied for a license to preach on the Lower

East Side, Jews objected and Mayor William Gaynor responded by denying the license. The mayor wrote him, "Do you not think the Jews have a good religion? . . . I do not think I should give you a license to preach for the conversion of the Jews in the streets in the thickly settled Jewish neighborhoods. . . . Would you not annoy them and do more harm than good? How many Jews have you converted so far?"[4]

Some New York citizens feared that the sudden influx of Jews to the city would lead to newcomers replacing Christians in business, politics, and culture. Cartoons in journals of the day depicted stereotypically long-nosed Jews as pawn brokers overtaking Christian-owned stores. Such replacement myths would resurface periodically through the years, including in our own times, with accusations that Jews and dark-skinned people aim to replace white Americans.

Employment

A great many Jews found employment in New York's garment industry. By 1897 sixty percent of Jewish workers in New York labored in the trade.

A few Jewish immigrants found opportunities in the newly emerging film industry. Without ever attending film school (and generally having worked in industries not related to film), former clothing salesmen and junk dealers Louis B. Mayer, Samuel Goldwyn, and the Warner Brothers (Harry, Albert, Sam, and Jack) moved to Hollywood and helped forge a new entertainment medium. They arrived in Hollywood as entrepreneurs and not as part of a Jewish plot to control an industry, as antisemites would later charge. Ironically, several of the early Hollywood films they produced depicted Jews in negative stereotypical roles.

The R. Hoe and Company Incident

Members of some Lower East Side Orthodox synagogues, trying to bring some unification to religious practice, invited a respected Lithuanian Torah scholar, Rabbi Jacob Joseph, to become the chief rabbi of New York City. The poor rabbi was doomed to failure from the begin-

Fig. 6. Louis B. Mayer, head of Metro-Goldwyn-Mayer, shown here with actor Clark Gable. Moviestore Collection Ltd / Alamy Stock Photo.

ning. Not all Orthodox synagogues honored his position and other Jews ridiculed the idea that there could be a chief rabbi in America. He soon found himself immersed in conflicts and was gradually ignored. Rabbi Joseph suffered a stroke in 1897 and died penniless on July 28, 1902. Only then did he receive the respect that had so long eluded him in life. On July 30 nearly fifty thousand mourners gathered in a procession through the streets of the Lower East Side to accompany the rabbi to his final burial place. In death, the good rabbi was about to receive fame as the object of antisemitic violence.

As the procession passed the large factory building of the R. Hoe and Company printing press factory, workers inside began jeering and throwing pieces of wood and iron, rubbish, and water-soaked rags out of the upper story windows onto the men, women, and children escorting the rabbi's hearse below. Some Jews hurled objects back at the workers while others charged the factory. Surprised by the turn of events, workers on the first floor aimed water hoses at the angry crowd of mourners and called the police. A large detachment of police arrived, and a riot ensued. Instead of going after the workers who instigated the violence, the police began beating, shoving, and arresting Jews. One of the mourners, Julius Reiter, later recalled the police rushing forward and yelling, "Kill those sheenies! Club them right and left! Get them out of the way!"[5] Adam A. Cross, the police inspector at the scene, blamed the mourners for initiating the riot.

Jews in New York City at the turn of the twentieth century numbered about six hundred thousand, or a fifth of the population. Jewish leaders, both uptown and downtown, cognizant of their latent political power, demanded a meaningful response from city officials. A newspaper confirmed, "One thing is self-evident, and that is, the politicians are all catering to the Jewish vote."[6] A vigilance committee was formed and mass meetings held on the Lower East Side called for a formal investigation. Mayor Seth Low appointed a citizen committee, which included two prominent Jews, to review the riot. The mayor also instructed Police Commissioner John Nelson Partridge to produce a full report on the incident. "Such an incident is discreditable to our city," the mayor wrote.[7] But the police commissioner was less than forthcoming in his investigation and, claiming he needed a rest, submitted his resignation at the end of the year.

The citizen committee report exonerated Jews of being the aggressors in the melee, blaming the Hoe employees for instigating the violence and the police for their negligence during the event. The report recommended immediate reforms in the police department, although one historian has noted, "Neither the Commissioner's departure, the report of the mayor's committee, nor the riot led to any significant changes."[8] Officers were charged for assaulting innocent Jewish bystanders but were exonerated. The police practice of using clubs indiscriminately against civilians was reviewed but did not change.

Nonetheless, the police understood that their actions would now be under public scrutiny. Jews had flexed their political muscle and used their numbers to obtain a certain level of satisfaction in response to an antisemitic attack.

A Legacy of Activism

All the while concerned with antisemitism at home, American Jews followed the increasing number of pogroms throughout the Russian Empire. The brutal attacks against Jews in Kishinev, Bessarabia, in 1903 and 1905 led a group of influential and philanthropic Reform Jews to form the American Jewish Committee (AJC) in 1906 "to prevent the infringement of civil and religious rights of Jews and alleviate the consequences of persecution."[9] Although originally focused on helping Jews abroad, the AJC soon became an important "defense organization" for American Jews. One of its first successes was the passage of a 1913 law in New York making all discrimination in public accommodations illegal.

Today, many look back with a glorified nostalgia of life on the Lower East Side, where they imagine poor but hard-working immigrants living in a tranquil Jewish environment. In truth, the Lower East Side at the turn of the twentieth century was plagued with poverty and disease and had a population density greater than Bombay, India. The newcomers came with little secular education or industrial experience. To survive, they depended on their wits and benefited from their light skin, which allowed them to slowly, if tenuously and incompletely, take part in mainstream society. While some immigrants opened pushcart businesses on the streets, other newcomers gravitated to employment in the growing garment industry. Working under terrible conditions in sweatshops—dirty, noisy, and unhealthy factories that were hot in summer and cold in winter—they barely eked out enough money to provide for their families.

At the same time, many new immigrants brought with them a legacy of activism in opposing the rule of the Russian czar. They used their organizing skills to create militant unions to fight for their worker rights. In 1900 the United Hebrew Trades Union joined together with smaller garment worker unions, creating the International Ladies' Garment Workers' Union and giving a voice to thousands of sweatshop workers.

By 1909 downtrodden workers could no longer bear the terrible conditions of toiling long hours with little pay or job security in dangerous shops. On November 22, 1909, thousands of shirtwaist workers, mostly young immigrant women, went on strike. The "Uprising of the Twenty Thousand" resulted in higher salaries and improved, but not perfect, working conditions, including fewer work hours and better lighting and safety conditions. Two years later, a fire at the nonunion Triangle Shirtwaist Company led to the tragic deaths of 146 workers, which captured national headlines and led to the establishment of stricter safety regulations for workplaces. Leading the charge for better working conditions was a Jewish immigrant from England, Samuel Gompers, the founder and first president of the American Federation of Labor. For nearly forty years, Gompers's leadership brought American workers better job security, higher pay, and a unified political voice. His advocacy led American workers of the first half of the twentieth century into the middle class, able to provide their families with decent living conditions and hope for their futures.

Education, Embarrassment, and Action

Jewish families in New York crowded into crumbling tenement apartments quickly realized that while they were severely handicapped by culture, language, and poverty, nothing would be impossible in America for their children. The route out of the Lower East Side was education, especially a college education.

Students began the journey by enrolling in New York's free public colleges. According to historian Max Dimont, "In 1908, though Jews constituted but 2 percent of the total [American] population, over 8.5 percent of the college population [in New York City] was Jewish."[10]

Jewish students throughout the country, especially in elite schools, did not always find a warm welcome. Some colleges and universities, fearing that an influx of Jewish students discouraged non-Jews from enrolling and negatively affected the social atmosphere of their institutions, imposed admission quotas (see chapters 6 and 7). Jewish students who were admitted tended to excel in their studies, but they were often barred from fraternities, extracurricular activities, and sports. In response, they formed their own Jewish fraternities.

A small number of Jews took another road out of poverty: crime. Unsupervised and left to their own devices, some youngsters became thieves and joined gangs. Pickpocketing, prostitution, extortion, and stealing—mostly nonviolent crimes—led to thousands of arrests yearly. Historian Moses Rischin wrote, "In 1909 some 3,000 Jewish children were brought before Juvenile Court."[11]

That said, journalists and elected officials often highlighted the Jewish identity of arrested perpetrators, leading readers to assume that a larger number of Jews were criminally involved than was really the case. As one writer put it, their parents "work early and late in the sweat-shops or in their miserable tenement rooms, while their children grow up in the streets."[12] To be sure, poverty, crowded living conditions, and lack of advancement did lead some Jews to criminal activity, but the vast majority of the new Jewish arrivals were peaceful and hard-working.

Public embarrassment led the "uptown Jews" to action. In the past, convicted Jewish boys had been sent to Catholic or Protestant reform schools, but Jews were embarrassed that they could not take care of their own and realized they needed their own institution. In 1902 Jewish community leader Louis Marshall and philanthropist Jacob Schiff helped found the Jewish Protectory and Aid Society to care for delinquent Jewish boys sentenced by the courts.

A few years later the Protectory and Aid Society established a modern juvenile detention facility called the Hawthorne School in New York's Westchester County. The school prepared boys for jobs in such fields as carpentry and plumbing while teaching standard classroom subjects and Jewish practice. At the dedication ceremony in 1907, Judge Samuel Greenbaum said, "We should stop and consider that twenty-five years ago it was a rare thing to see a Jew in a criminal court. Now thousands can be seen there, some of them illiterate and others poverty stricken."[13] In 1911 society president Mortimer L. Schiff proudly announced that in the few years since the school's opening, 155 boys had been paroled, with 137 leading productive lives. The women of the Protectory and Aid Society, who belonged to some of the most prominent Jewish families in the country, founded a similar school for girls after the Hawthorne School was established. The Cedar Knolls School, as it was known, moved to the Hawthorne Campus in 1917. Cedar Knolls educated girls in accordance with standards set by the New York City Board of Education while also providing vocational and religious training to its students. Both schools had an important, perhaps life changing, influence on these young boys and girls.[14]

Taking Dewey to Task

Lawyer and Jewish community leader Louis Marshall was not shy about defending the Jewish community's reputation whenever its antithesis surfaced—as it did with Melvil Dewey, who loved books but Jews, not so much. At Columbia University, where Dewey was the chief librarian, he established the first school of library science in the country. He was a founder of the American Library Association, a director of the New York State Library, and most famously, the inventor of the Dewey Decimal System (still used today in libraries around the world). But Dewey was also a land developer, and in 1895 he founded the exclusive Lake Placid Club resort, which did not allow Jewish members. The club's official circular stated, under the heading of "Objectionable Guests," "No one will be admitted as a member or guest whom there is physical, moral, social or race objection. . . . This invariable rule is rigidly enforced. It is found impracticable to make exceptions for Jews or others excluded, even though of unusual personal qualifications."[15]

Louis Marshall could not tolerate a public servant like Dewey manifesting public antisemitism. In 1904, in collaboration with a number of prominent Jewish men, he presented a petition seeking Dewey's removal from office to the New York State Board of Regents, which supervised the state library. He also represented the petitioners during the nine months of hearings, which were reported in the newspapers. In the end, the Board of Regents issued a formal rebuke of Dewey for his discriminatory practices but did not remove him from office. Dewey, however, stung by the negative publicity, resigned his position in 1905. In 2020 the American Library Association renamed the Melvil Dewey Medal—its top honor, established in 1952 for "creative leadership of a high order"—the "ALA Medal of Excellence."[16]

Bingham's Brutal Bungle

Despite the self-help undertakings of the Jewish community, negative views about Jews continued. In his 1906 antisemitic bestseller, *The Jewish Spectre*, George H. Werner claimed that Jewish immigrants did not want to become Americans but only to insulate themselves within a Jewish community. Using the ancient myth of Jews as financiers he contradicted himself by saying that Jewish bankers would soon disappear while at the same time charging that Jewish influence in America would be increasing in financial matters. He snidely added that "the Jewish question in New York will adjust itself, for the Jews of the lower east side will be more than half converted into Americans when they get their hair cut."[17]

Jewish anger exploded with the 1908 publication of an article by New York City's police commissioner Theodore A. Bingham alleging that while Jews comprised just one-quarter of New York's population, half of the city's criminals were Jewish: "Among the most expert of all the street thieves are Hebrew boys under sixteen, who are being brought up to lives of crime."[18] Jewish community reaction was swift in coming. Rallies held in the Lower East Side protested against the stereotyping of the entire Jewish population as criminals, and Yiddish newspapers refuted Bingham's wildly overestimated statistics. The commissioner later apologized, but damage to the Jewish community's image remained.

One positive result from the incident was the continued focus on social support within the Jewish community. Along with schools for juvenile delinquents, Jews established the Lakeview Home for Unmarried Mothers in 1910 (at the time, having a child out of wedlock was considered an embarrassment). Settlement houses provided educational, vocational, and recreational opportunities. Jewish Big Brother and Jewish Big Sister organizations also worked to curb the delinquency rates. All the while, news reports about Jewish criminal activities continued to occupy newspaper headlines, embarrassing both uptown and downtown Jews.

The Rosenthal Affair

Rabbi Judah Magnes of Temple Emanu-El, whose membership included many of the city's wealthiest and most influential Jews, realized it was time to create a single organization to represent all of New York's Jewish community, uptown and downtown, with one voice. In 1909 he was instrumental in gathering more than two hundred Jewish institutions to create the *Kehillah* (a Hebrew word that recalled the semiautonomous organized Jewish communities of Europe), an umbrella organization to coordinate educational and religious activities and to combat crime.

About three years later, early in the morning of July 16, 1912, Herman "Beansy" Rosenthal was shot to death on the steps of the Metropole Hotel, sending shock waves through New York's Jewish community and making headlines nationwide.

Rosenthal was a gambler in business with a corrupt police lieutenant, Charles Becker, who ironically was in charge of the antigambling squad. Upset that Becker had been forced by superiors to raid his gambling house, Rosenthal volunteered to testify about police connections with gamblers in front of a grand jury later that day. To prevent Rosenthal from testifying, Becker arranged for Lower East Side gangster "Big Jack" Zelig (Selig Harry Lefkowitz) to assassinate the gambler. "Big Jack" then assigned "Gyp the Blood" (Harry Horowitz), "Leftie Louie" (Louis Rosenberg), and "Whitey Louis" (Jacob Seidenshner)—all Jewish—and a non-Jewish gangster to do the actual killing.

As Rosenthal emerged from the hotel, a car pulled up and the four gunmen rushed out and began shooting. Bystanders witnessed their getaway, and the shooters were quickly arrested.

A new problem arose: Zelig, the gang boss, had to be prevented from testifying in court against Lieutenant Becker; another Jewish gangster, "Red Phil" (Philip Davidson), assassinated him. Rosenthal's killers, as well as Lieutenant Becker, were all found guilty and sentenced to death. "Red Phil" was sentenced to twenty years' imprisonment.

The killings put the crime problems of the immigrant Jewish community directly in the glare of newspaper headlines obsessed with police corruption. Aside from Becker and one gunman, everyone else involved in both murders was Jewish. A few New York papers referred to Rosenthal as "an undersized Jew" and his assassins as "East Side thugs" and "Jew gamblers."[19] Rabbi Magnes, writing on the Kehillah's behalf, protested to the *New York Evening Telegram*, "No one can have any objection to your condemning Jews who happen to be gamblers, and to pointing them out as Jews, if you see fit . . . What I want to know is, what prompted your sneer in speaking of 'Jew gamblers'?"[20] Most newspaper accounts did not specifically mention that the criminals were Jewish, but there was no mistaking their identity.

As much as the exciting misdeeds of the Jewish gangsters fascinated newspaper readers, they were a source of humiliation and concern to Jews. Over generations, the phrase "kol Yisrael arevim zeh bazeh" (Shevuot 39a)—all Israel are responsible for each other—had cautioned that an illegal or immoral act by one Jew could embarrass an entire Jewish community. Indeed, the misdeeds of individuals Jews throughout history had provoked antisemitic reactions blaming all Jews for their actions.

The Kehillah decided to go beyond issuing statements. To put their metaphorical "Jewish house" in order, they created a bureau of investigation to collect information about criminal activity on the Lower East Side and then pass on that information to law enforcement. They hired detective Abraham Shoenfeld who, together with his group of agents and informers, infiltrated, documented, and reported on Jewish gangs, prostitution houses, and gambling establishments to the police.

This proactive activity attracted positive reaction. In his November 17, 1912, sermon at Brooklyn's Christ Church, the Reverend William Sheafe Chase applauded the Kehillah's work by saying, "The officials of the Jewish community have adopted resolutions expressing sorrow at shocking degree of moral and political degeneracy in this city and saying that as citizens . . . they view with profound indignation the profanation of the Jewish name."[21] As immigration continued, Jews established communal infrastructure designed to reduce crime, help indigent Jews, and improve the community's reputation in the eyes of the white Protestant majority.

In time, Jewish criminal activity in the Lower East Side decreased, as did the negative publicity. In later years, Jews would manage to leave the densely packed tenements and slums where they had initially settled. Yet, despite their apparent success and economic mobility, antisemitism would continue.

6

A Lynching and a Lawyer

On the morning of January 5, 1895, in the shadow of the Eiffel Tower, a French army captain was publicly stripped of his military insignia and his sword unceremoniously split in two. Amid cries of "Death to the Jew! Death to the traitor!" the disgraced captain was then sent off to life imprisonment on Devil's Island off the South American coast.[1] His crime was high treason; he had allegedly passed secret documents to France's archenemy, Germany. His name was Alfred Dreyfus and he was a Jew.

From the beginning, Dreyfus insisted on his innocence. And as evidence later trickled out indicating that he was indeed innocent, France became a country divided. After all, a respected French military court had found him guilty, and amid growing antisemitism in France, it was not Dreyfus the army captain but Dreyfus the Jew who was on trial. In the eyes of many, his Jewishness was enough to make him guilty.[2] Although Dreyfus was later pardoned and fully exonerated, the legacy of antisemitism surrounding his famous case was not erased.

The Leo Frank Case

About twenty years later a similar event occurred in the United States.

Leo M. Frank, who was born in Texas and grew up in Brooklyn, moved to Atlanta in 1908 to manage the National Pencil Company. Frank's uncle was a partial owner of the company, but even without his family connections, young Leo was well qualified for a leadership position. He had studied at Cornell University, interned with two northern companies, and even traveled to Germany to become acquainted with the pencil industry.

Fig. 7. National Pencil Company manager Leo Frank was wrongfully convicted of killing a fifteen-year-old girl, hijacked from his jail cell, and lynched. The virulent antisemitism surrounding his case played a crucial role in the establishment of the Anti-Defamation League. Library of Congress.

In Atlanta, he became active in the Jewish community. He joined the city's leading Reform congregation, often known simply as "the Temple," and was elected president of Gate City Lodge no. 144 of the Jewish fraternal organization B'nai B'rith. Frank was also well integrated into the local Jewish community through his marriage to Lucille Selig, whose family was prominent among Atlanta Jews.

His promising future began to crumble on Confederate Memorial Day, April 26, 1913. As the city prepared for the annual parade, thirteen-year-old Mary Phagan headed toward Peachtree Street to join the celebration. On her way, she stopped at the pencil company to pick up her pay. Like many other children, to ensure her family's survival, she worked many hours a day—in her case, fastening rubber tips onto pencils for ten cents an hour.

She never saw the parade. Early the next morning, Newt Lee, the company night watchman, found her body in the pencil company's basement. She had been raped and strangled to death.

Police questioned several employees but quickly suspected Leo Frank. He was the last person to see the young girl alive. And he had two other strikes against him. He was a Jew, and more significantly, in Atlanta, less than half a century after the end of the Civil War, he was a Yankee Jew.

Two barely literate notes found near the body appeared to accuse Lee of the murder. When the police questioned Lee, an African American, and James Conley, another African American who worked as a sweeper in the factory, Conley said he had written the notes at the instruction of his employer, Leo Frank. Conley's story changed and was inconsistent, but the police proceeded to pursue Frank as the main suspect.

Frank's Jewishness became an important part of the case. As one Atlanta newspaper put it, "Our little girl—ours by the eternal God! Has been pursued to a hideous death and bloody grave by this filthy perverted Jew of New York."[3]

Emotions were high, as was the temperature, when the trial of Leo Frank began on July 28, 1913. Outside the courtroom, crowds strained to hear snatches of the testimony through the open windows. The trial, presided over by Judge Leonard Strickland Roan, lasted for almost thirty days. The solicitor general, Hugh M. Dorsey, presented a parade of three hundred witnesses, much of whose testimony, later recanted, proved damaging to Frank. Jurors heard of Frank's alleged cavorting with underage prostitutes and of orgies taking place in his office. James Conley's testimony, probably the first time in the South that the word of an African American was heard in a court against a white defendant, was particularly effective. Conley told the jurors that he helped Frank carry Mary Phagan's body into the elevator and down to the basement. It was later shown that the elevator was not used that day.

Frank's defense attorney, Reuben Arnold, told the jury that no evidence existed to prove his client's guilt. In his closing argument he said, "If Frank hadn't been a Jew, there would never have been any prosecution against him."[4] Throughout the trial, the populist politician and publisher Thomas Watson fanned the flames of hatred. His weekly newspaper, the *Jeffersonian*, and his monthly magazine, *Watson's*, spread disinformation about the case and antisemitic canards about Jews in general. Crude stories, suspicions, half-truths, and lies about Frank and Jews increased both his newspaper's circulation and mob hatred.

The trial's outcome was never in doubt. On August 25 the jury took less than four hours to deliver a guilty verdict. The *Atlanta Journal* reported, "The very atmosphere of the courtroom was charged with an electric current of indignation. . . . The courtroom and streets were filled with an angry, determined crowd, ready to seize the defendant if the jury had found him not guilty." Among those gathered outside, frequent comments along the lines of "innocent or guilty, we'll get the damn Jew!" could be heard.[5]

Four days later, Judge Roan sentenced Frank to death by hanging with an execution date of June 22, 1915. Outside the state capitol, onlookers danced with joy while Fiddlin' John Carson sang his *Ballad of Mary Phagan*:

> Little Mary Phagan
> She went to town one day;
> She went to the pencil factory
> To get her weekly pay. . . .
> Leo Frank he met her
> With a brutish heart and grin;
> He says to little Mary,
> "You'll never see home again . . ."
> Judge Roan passed the sentence;
> He passed it very well;
> The Christian doers of heaven
> Sent Leo Frank to hell . . .[6]

As Jews braced themselves for increased antisemitism because of the case, Frank's lawyers began a series of failed appeals to the conviction. They turned first to the Georgia courts, and when those appeals to set aside the verdict were denied, they appealed to the United States Supreme Court, with American Jewish Committee president attorney Louis Marshall representing Frank. On April 9, 1915, the Supreme Court rejected that appeal.

The antisemitic cloud hanging over Leo Frank led attorney Sigmund Livingston to establish the Anti-Defamation League (ADL) in 1913 under the auspices of the Jewish fraternal organization B'nai Brith. The mission of the ADL, later to separate from B'nai Brith, was "to stop, by appeals to reason and conscience and if necessary, by appeals to law, the defamation of the Jewish people . . . to secure justice and fair treatment to all citizens alike . . . put an end forever to unjust and unfair discrimination against and ridicule of any sect or body of citizens."[7] Meanwhile, the AJC, originally founded to combat antisemitism overseas, was also galvanized by the Frank case and turned its attention inward, toward hatred of Jews in America. A leader of both the AJC and the ADL, Adolph Ochs, publisher of the *New York Times*, increased coverage of Frank's case in his newspaper. He also led a successful campaign to discourage the use of objectionable references to Jews in newspapers such as appeared during the Frank trial.

Frank's supporters also hired a nationally known detective, William Burns, to investigate the murder. Burns concluded that "the conviction of Leo Frank was one the foulest perversions of Justice the United States has ever known."[8] His finding did not change the original court verdict. Leo Frank was scheduled to hang.

Georgia governor John M. Slaton, perhaps influenced by the negative popular opinion of his state outside of Georgia, reviewed all the original trial records and concluded that Frank was indeed innocent. Afraid of the consequences should he free Frank, he used his powers as governor to commute Frank's sentence from death to life imprisonment instead. The governor then ordered Frank moved from Atlanta to the state penitentiary farm in Milledgeville.

Response was quick in coming. Throughout the state the governor was hanged in effigy and threatening mobs attacked the governor's mansion. At that point the governor declared martial law, calling in the National Guard in an attempt to restore order. Fortunately for him, his term as governor was coming to an end a few days after he issued the commutation. He and his wife required a police escort to the train station, and the couple would not return to the state of Georgia for another ten years.

By contrast, Tom Watson experienced a revival to his fortunes after his earlier political career had resulted in a series of electoral failures. The governor's pardon set Watson on a mission of retribution. "In Georgia, the blood of Mary Phagan yet cries out in vain for vengeance," he wrote in the *Jeffersonian* on August 15, 1915, "and the Jew who atrociously assaulted her; and choked her to death, occupies luxurious quarters at the State Farm, where the heat is fanned from him by electricity, and where a rich carpet keeps his delicate feet off the bare floor."[9] Defending the mob that had attacked Governor Slaton's home and pushing the theme of vengeance, Watson now called for the lynching of Leo Frank. His readers' cries for blood intensified.

Watson formed a vigilante group called the Knights of Mary Phagan. On the night of August 16, 1915, a caravan of eight automobiles carrying Knights entered the prison in Milledgeville, overpowered the guards, and spirited Frank away. Then they drove 140 miles through the night to Marietta, Mary Phagan's hometown, and lynched Leo Frank from a tree. Local men, women, and children quickly gathered and began ripping pieces of the rope, buttons, and the hanging body's nightshirt as souvenirs. Photographs of the dead man were taken and widely distributed. That year, members of the Knights of Mary Phagan revived the Ku Klux Klan (KKK), a white supremacist group founded after the Civil War that mostly terrorized African Americans but also targeted Jews and Catholics.

In the next issue of the *Jeffersonian*, Watson cheerfully reported, "A Vigilance Committee redeems Georgia and carries out the sentence of the Law on the Jew who raped and murdered the little Gentile girl, Mary Phagan. . . . Let Jew libertines take notice! Georgia is not for sale to rich criminals."[10]

Responses from other parts of the country were not as gleeful. The *Boston Traveler* observed, "In this crowning demonstration of inherent savagery, Georgia stands revealed before the world in her naked, barbarian brutality. She is a shame and a disgrace to the other states of the Union."[11] The *Akron Beacon Journal* noted, "Georgia cannot plead a rush of passion, a hot blooded forgetting of normal impulses as responsible for this act. This hate that followed Frank through the prison bars was deliberate, premeditated, cool, organized."[12] The *Brooklyn Times Union* charged that the lynching of Leo Frank should make Georgia "blush with shame before the eyes of the world."[13] Louis Marshall bluntly stated, "Tom Watson is the murderer of Leo Frank."[14] Marshall went on to demand that the State of Georgia indict Watson for murder.

Instead, prosecuting attorney Hugh Dorsey rode his newfound popularity (and Tom Watson's support) into a successful bid for governor in 1916. Subsequently Dorsey and Watson competed to become the U.S. senator from Georgia; Watson won that contest. In other words, Dorsey and Watson's involvement in the Leo Frank Case did not ruin their reputations in voters' eyes; rather, it enhanced them.

For decades, the murder of Mary Phagan remained one of the country's most debated historical events. The case came to a dramatic end sixty-nine years later, in 1982, when Alonzo Mann made a startling death-bed confession: "Leo Frank did not kill Mary Phagan, she was murdered instead by Jim Conley."[15] Mann, then a fourteen-year-old office boy at the pencil factory, had witnessed Conley carrying the girl's body to the basement. Conley threatened the boy with death should he tell anyone. After living with this secret all his life, Mann finally came forward to set the record straight. Finally, in 1986, the Georgia Board of Pardons and Paroles granted Leo Frank a posthumous pardon.

Louis Brandeis

The vitriolic antisemitism surrounding the Leo Frank trial morphed into a less violent version a year after Frank's lynching, when Presi-

Fig. 8. Known as the "People's Attorney," Louis Brandeis was the first Jew appointed to the U.S. Supreme Court. Library of Congress.

dent Woodrow Wilson nominated Louis Brandeis to the United States Supreme Court.

Brandeis was born in Louisville, Kentucky, in 1856. His parents, who came from German-speaking Bohemia, instilled in him a love of learning. Educated in both Louisville and Germany, he entered Harvard Law School at age eighteen and excelled at his studies. Upon graduation in 1879, he and a Harvard classmate, Sam Warren, opened a law firm. The Boston firm quickly gained a reputation for fighting against monopolies, banking abuses, corruption in government, and the unfair business practices of railroads and insurance companies. Brandeis fought for social justice and civil rights. He also became known as an effective mediator, averting labor union strikes and industrial conflicts. The "People's Lawyer," as he was sometimes called, often defended poor clients in court without pay.

On more than one occasion, Brandeis saw how poor families were left penniless after the death of a working parent. Yet they could not afford life insurance to ensure their family's survival. Brandeis developed a plan which in 1907 led the Commonwealth of Massachusetts to pass legislation that allowed local savings banks to sell affordable life insurance. With its beginnings in Massachusetts, Saving Bank Life Insurance spread throughout the country.

While his professional work earned the respect of some Bostonians, it was not enough for Brandeis to enter certain corners of local upper-class society. Even when his law partner got married, Brandeis was not invited to the wedding since the future Mrs. Warren would not allow a Jew to be present.

Having grown up in a nonobservant Jewish home, for most of his early life Brandeis had only minimal formal connections to the Jewish community. By 1912 he started to take a more prominent role, however. What had changed for Brandeis was his involvement in the Zionist Movement, which advocated for a Jewish homeland in Palestine. A major turning point for Brandeis, as well as for the trajectory of the Zionist Movement in the United States, occurred in 1914: that August, Brandeis emerged from a conference held at the Hotel Marseilles in New York City as the leader of the Zionist Movement in America. Brandeis had come to Zionism not for religious reasons but because he related what he saw as "American ideals" to his vision for a Jewish state. "To be good Americans," he said, "we must be better Jews, and to be better Jews we must become Zionists."[16]

In politics, Brandeis supported Woodrow Wilson's candidacy in the 1912 presidential election. Impressed by Brandeis's progressive outlook and his work as a lawyer, the new president wanted to appoint the Boston lawyer to his cabinet, first as attorney general and then as secretary of the treasury, but given strong opposition from influential Bostonians and Democratic Party leaders in the business and financial communities, neither appointment happened. In 1916, however, Wilson, set off a great controversy in Washington when he decided to appoint Brandeis to a vacant seat on the U.S. Supreme Court.

Former president William Howard Taft, who was generally supportive of Jews but who had suffered politically at the hands of Brandeis a few years earlier, could hardly control his vitriol. Taft castigated Brandeis in his personal correspondence with a Washington reporter: "He is a muckraker, an emotionalist for his own purposes, a socialist, prompted by jealousy, a hypocrite . . . who is utterly unscrupulous . . . a man of infinite cunning . . . and in my judgement, of much power for evil."[17]

Historians do not agree on how much Brandeis's Jewishness influenced the opposition to his appointment to the Supreme Court. Most people involved with advocating for or against Brandeis's appointment refrained from publicly referring to the nominee as a Jew. Observers did notice Brandeis's religion and that he would be the first Jew appointed to the Supreme Court, but the controversy mostly centered on his outspoken positions on the political issues of the day. After all, Brandeis was a nationally prominent radical and progressive who had already locked horns with important people like President Taft.

Many of the deliberations over Brandeis's fitness to serve on the Supreme Court invoked his reputation in Boston, where he was a prominent attorney. Influential local businesspeople pressured both Massachusetts senators, Henry Cabot Lodge and John W. Weeks, to reject Brandeis's nomination. For his part, in private correspondence, Lodge told a friend he considered Brandeis an unqualified candidate and believed that Wilson had appointed him simply to influence the Jewish vote. "If it were not that Brandeis was a Jew, and a German Jew," Lodge wrote, "he would never be appointed."[18] Nonetheless, Lodge, concerned about his reelection in a state with a growing Jewish electorate, did not publicly refer to Brandeis's religion during the confirmation process.

Those opposed to Brandeis's nomination were not shy about making their opinions known to senators. A prominent Boston stockbroker, William Fitzgerald, wrote to Weeks, "The fact that a slimy fellow of this kind . . . together with his Jewish instinct, can almost land in the cabinet, and probably on the bench of the Supreme Court of the United States, should teach an object lesson to men who believe that for future generations manhood should be the test . . . rather than showing that shysters can reach the goal."[19] Abbott Lawrence Lowell, the president of Harvard University who would later attempt to restrict the number of Jewish students there, protested to Lodge, "Are we to put on our Supreme Bench a man whose reputation for integrity is not unimpeachable? It is difficult—perhaps impossible—to get direct evidence of any act by Brandeis that is, strictly speaking, dishonest; and yet a man who is believed by all the better part of the bar to be unscrupulous ought not to be a member of the highest court of the nation. Is there anything that can be done to make his confirmation less probable?"[20] (Ironically, except for one person who openly opposed the appointment and another who refused comment, all Harvard Law School faculty members supported Brandeis's confirmation.)

Opposition to Brandeis's appointment was not limited to his hometown. A group calling itself Southern Gentile Democrats sent a telegram to the Senate Committee on the Judiciary: "We protest to the end and resent vigorously the appointment of the Jew to the United States Supreme Court bench. We American gentiles feel bitter and will no longer support the President. Where he gained one Jew he will lose 10,000 gentiles. It is a disgrace and a shame."[21]

Negative responses to Brandeis's nomination did not dissuade President Wilson. "Many charges have been made against Mr. Brandeis," Wilson wrote. "They throw a great deal more light upon the character and motives of those with whom they originated than upon the qualifications of Mr. Brandeis."[22] An article in the *Washington Times* also spoke out in his favor: "If there is any Senator who opposes Mr. Brandeis because he is a Jew, that Senator ought to be whipped out of Congress."[23]

Finally, on June 1, 1916, the U.S. Senate confirmed Brandeis by a vote of forty-seven to twenty-two. While Lodge voted against the nomination, Weeks was conveniently absent and did not vote.

Two years later, Brandeis, along with Rabbi Stephen S. Wise of New York, helped found the American Jewish Congress, whose mission was "to safeguard the civil, political, economic and religious rights of the Jewish people wherever these rights may be threatened or violated."[24] Unlike the American Jewish Committee, which was viewed as an extension of "aristocratic" German Jews, the congress was created as a democratic institution which more widely reflected the larger Jewish community of recent immigrants. Rabbi Wise, one of the original founders of the National Association for the Advancement of Colored People (NAACP), served as American Jewish Congress president. Sharing Brandeis's devotion to progressive causes and to Zionism, Wise would become an unofficial spokesmen of the American Jewish community in the first half of the twentieth century.

The Great War

The *American Jewish Year Book* for 1918–19 estimated the growth of the American Jewish population from 400,000 in 1887 to 3.2 million in 1918. When the U.S. entered World War I in 1917, some two hundred fifty thousand Jews, many of them recent immigrants, were among the nearly three million men conscripted. Jews comprised 3 percent of the population, yet 4.5 percent of those serving in the United States Army and Navy.

For the first time, in barracks, mess halls, and the field, large numbers of Americans got to personally meet Jews and dispel ingrained stereotypes about them. For one, Christian soldiers who insisted on seeing the horns on their Jewish comrades' heads came to realize that Jews did not have horns—a belief that dated to the erroneous translation of a biblical passage in the fourth century CE. The Hebrew word for "rays" of light had been translated instead as "horns" and may have later influenced Michelangelo to place horns on the head of his famous statue of Moses.

The European war put thousands of European civilians, including Jews, in the war zones desperately in need of food, medicine, fuel, and clothing. As a discriminated group in Europe, particularly Eastern Europe, Jews were likely suffering in greater measure than their non-Jewish neighbors. In 1914 Jewish philanthropists in the United States created the Joint Distribution Committee (JDC) to coordinate and streamline the relief efforts of multiple Jewish organizations. Known simply as the Joint, the JDC began by raising money to help the impoverished Jewish population of Palestine. From then on, the JDC would continue to aid Jewish populations in need of economic, medical, and food support throughout Europe and the Middle East.

Meanwhile, in the United States, the War Department, unequipped to care for the social and religious welfare of millions of soldiers, turned to the YMCA to take charge. Their work, while well-meaning, made Jews apprehensive. How could a Christian organization understand the unique religious needs of Jews? Would Jews be subject to proselytization?

In response, the Jewish Welfare Board (JWB) was organized to coordinate with the War Department "to be with the Jewish soldier and sailor everywhere, aiding him, cheering him, inspiring him."[25] Serving Jews of all denominations, from Reform to Orthodox, the JWB created the *Abridged Prayer Book for Jews in the Army and Navy of the United States*. It was an emergency compromise bridging the different religious practices to unite all Jews in the military. They fought army regulations so Jewish military chaplains could wear insignias featuring the tablets of the Ten Commandments on their uniforms in place of crosses and saw to it that the Star of David, and not the cross, was placed over Jewish graves.

The "Red Scare"

The positive feelings about Jewish participation in the war effort were quickly diminished once the war ended. Nativism—the belief that native-born Americans, particularly those of white, Anglo-Saxon heritage, were superior to foreign-born Americans—overtook American thought.

The 1917 Bolshevik Revolution, which wrought a communist government in Russia, provoked a "Red Scare" in the United States, as many Americans feared that communism might spread to their country. The fact that some American Jews had participated in socialist and labor union activities and that some Jews were prominent in the Russian Revolution gave credence to the association of immigrants, particularly Jews, with socialists, anarchists, and communists, refueling the fires of American antisemitism.

In 1919 a U.S. Senate subcommittee led by Lee Overman of North Carolina opened a series of hearings to investigate Bolshevik influence in America. One witness stated that all Jews were Bolsheviks and that the Russian Revolution had in fact been planned on the Lower East Side of New York. To refute the wild charges, Louis Marshall of the American Jewish Committee issued a statement reprinted in American newspapers declaring that most Jews opposed the Bolsheviks. "Everything that real Bolshevism stands for," he wrote, "is to the Jew detestable. His traditions wed him to law and order. . . . The innuendo is also thrown out that the Jews are not patriotic. Let their record during this war speak for them. . . . Attack Bolshevism as much as you please, and the Jews of America are with you."[26] This was the beginning of a decades-long fight to combat the association of Jews with communism.

7

The Bigoted 1920s

The end of World War I saw an upsurge of nativism in America. Fear of communism and suspicion of foreigners led to a growth of antisemitism. The foremost purveyor of this hatred was Henry Ford.

Henry Ford

The founder of an automobile empire that bore his name, Henry Ford was obsessed with Jews. He had an idyllic and mythical image of America as an agrarian, rural, and Protestant country at a time when America was urbanizing with the arrival of millions of immigrants, including over two million Jews. In 1919 he bought a failing local Michigan newspaper, the *Dearborn Independent*, and required Ford automobile dealers around the country to sell it. In time it became a successful national weekly whose circulation rivaled that of large New York newspapers.

Almost immediately, Ford turned the paper's focus on Jews. Blame for everything that had changed his vision of America—jazz music, politics, entertainment, finance, literature—fell on Jews. A continuing series of unrelenting articles attacked Jews' patriotism and character. Street hawkers of the *Dearborn Independent* created fights on the streets by shouting out the latest anti-Jewish headlines.

To substantiate his false claims, Ford's newspaper gave credence to the pseudo-historical *Protocols of the Elders of Zion*. The paper also serialized many of its antisemitic articles and published them in a four-volume set that was sent to libraries and schools across the country. But the so-called proof was fake itself. In 1921 the London *Times* exposed the *Protocols* as plagiarized from a nineteenth-century French book. Researchers have since learned that the czarist Russian secret police forged the *Protocols* in 1903 in order to convince Russians of the existence of a secret international Jewish plot to control the world and destroy Christian civilization—and, they hoped, in so doing, to legitimize and strengthen the ongoing pogroms against Jews. In the alleged words of the *Protocols*, "When we establish ourselves as lords of the earth, we will not tolerate any other religion except that of our own, namely a religion recognizing God alone, with whom our fate is bound by His election of us and Whom also the fate of the world is determined."[1]

In popularizing the *Protocols* in the United States, Ford unleashed a hateful force that would empower antisemites for generations.

The first *Dearborn Independent* edition, headlined "The International Jew: The World's Problem," debuted on May 22, 1920. In subsequent issues headlines blared, "Will Jewish Zionism Bring Armageddon?," "The Economic Plans of International Jews," and "The Peril of Baseball—Too Much Jew." The constant inference was that all Jews were Bolsheviks or communist supporters intent on overthrowing American democracy. Meanwhile, the U.S. government was supposedly under the influence of Jewish interests. The paper quoted the *Protocols*: "For the time being, until it will be safe to give responsible government positions to our brother Jews, we shall entrust them to people whose past and whose characters are such that there is an abyss between them and the people."[2]

Popular culture was a frequent topic. The *Dearborn Independent* portrayed movies, sports, and music as some of the areas where Jews infiltrated American society. One article chided its audience, "Reader, beware! If you so much as resent the filth of the mass of the movies, you will fall under the judgment of anti-Semitism. The movies are of Jewish production. If you fight filth, the fight carries you straight into the Jewish camp because the majority of the producers are there. And then you are attacking the Jews."[3] Popular music also offended Ford: "Many people have wondered whence come the waves upon waves of musical slush that invade decent parlors and set the young people of this generation imitating the drivel of morons. . . . The mush, the lush, the sly suggestion, the abandoned sensuousness of sliding notes, are of Jewish origin."[4] Ford found jazz particularly offensive. A headline in his newspaper proclaimed, "Jewish Jazz—Moron Music-Becomes Our National Music."

For Ford, even the theater presented difficulties. Popular Jewish performers like Benjamin Kubelsky, Fania Borach, and Nathan Birnbaum had changed their names to Jack Benny, Fanny Brice, and George Burns; Ford outed their real Jewish-sounding names in the *Dearborn Independent*. When "Eli, Eli," a Yiddish song written in the 1890s, became popular on the vaudeville stage, Ford claimed the use of the song had been decreed by "Jewish headquarters which has ordered the speeding up of Jewish propaganda. The situation of the theater now is that American audiences are paying at the box office for the privilege of hearing Jews advertise the things they want non-Jews to think about them."[5]

Ford shamelessly accused Jews of fomenting anti-Christian hatred. "Not content with the fullest liberty to follow their own faith in peace and quietness," a *Dearborn Independent* article stated, "the Jews declare . . . that every sight and sound of anything Christian is an invasion of their peace and quietness, and so they stamp it out wherever they can reach it through political means."[6] The industrialist also accused the Kehillah in New York City of controlling the entire American Jewish community. By 1920, when the organization had fallen apart and was set to dissolve, Ford attributed to it overreaching powers it never had.

In the Jewish community, there was no unified plan to counter Ford's antisemitism. Ford, after all, was an iconic American entrepreneur, and antisemitism had taken hold on a large sector of American society. As a result, some Jewish leaders felt that any public response would backfire. Louis Marshall, president of the American Jewish Committee (AJC), wrote directly to Henry Ford, accusing him of fomenting "a libel upon an entire people who had hoped that at least in America they might be spared the insult, the humiliation and obloquy which these articles are scattering throughout the land and which are echoes from the dark middle ages" and asking that he disown the antisemitic content of his newspaper.[7] Ford did not respond; instead, a *Dearborn Independent* editor replied, "Your rhetoric is that of a Bolshevik orator."[8] Seeing that no dialogue was possible and fearing that personal attacks on Ford would only increase public debate about Jews, Marshall focused instead on monitoring and criticizing Ford's newspaper. That did not prevent Marshall from heading Ford's list of targeted Jews. Mocking Marshall personally, Ford stated, "It would be interesting to know how the name of Marshall found its way to the Jewish gentleman. It is not a common name, even among Jews who change their names."[9]

The ADL took a different tack, urging state legislatures to pass laws against libel. A few communities enacted rules restricting the sale of Ford's newspaper on the street, but courts quickly overturned those rules as violating the First Amendment.

From its inception, the ADL had also fought newspapers' indiscriminate use of the word "Jew" to identify Jewish lawbreakers. The *Dearborn Independent*, which had no limit on using that identifier frequently, mocked the ADL's efforts by commenting, "For the state of affairs, the Anti-Defamation League receives the credit . . . It has concealed the Jew where he wishes to be concealed."[10]

Local communities and families adopted other tactics in parallel to the ADL's efforts. Although a few Ford automobile dealers were Jewish, Yiddish newspapers refused to publish Ford advertisements. American Jews, many now in the middle class, boycotted Ford vehicles—a practice that would last for decades.

While Ford had many supporters nationwide, others disagreed with his pervasive attacks on Jews. Political writer John Spargo authored *The Jew and American Ideals*, a positive look of American Jews, which the American Jewish Committee proceeded to disseminate. The AJC also published "The Protocols: Bolshevism and the Jews. An Address to Their Fellow Citizens by American Jewish Organizations," an eighteen-page pamphlet signed by nearly all the major

Jewish organizations (including the American Jewish Congress, B'nai Brith, and Orthodox, Conservative, and Reform rabbinical groups) that factually refuted the false charges about Jews and communism in the *Protocols*. Referencing Ford, the pamphlet stated, "We have refrained from commenting on the libels contained in the *Dearborn Independent*. Ford, in the fulness [*sic*] of his knowledge, unqualifiedly declares *The Protocols* to be genuine, and argues that every Jew is a Bolshevist. We have dealt sufficiently with both of these falsehoods. It is useless in a serious document to analyze the puerile and venomous drivel that he has derived from the concoctions of professional agitators. He is merely a dupe."[11]

Spargo, whose book had attracted national attention, also issued a statement denouncing Ford, signed by one hundred prominent Christians, including former presidents William Howard Taft (who had opposed Brandeis's Supreme Court nomination), Woodrow Wilson, and president-elect Warren G. Harding; he also arranged for its publication in newspapers countrywide. In an interview, former president Theodore Roosevelt compared Ford with P. T. Barnum, the circus huckster. "Ford," Roosevelt said, "has no conception of what we mean by Americanism."[12]

Newspapers editorialized against Ford. The *Vicksburg Herald* (Mississippi) praised Taft for protesting "emphatically against the anti-Jewish propaganda of Henry Ford's organ, the *Dearborn Independent*. . . . The propaganda, with its weird charges, is an importation of the European dark ages."[13] The *Appeal*, a Minnesota paper, declared, "The Jews [do not] turn the other cheek when they are kicked and get another kick. Oh, no; they fight back when they are attacked. . . . That's the way to do it; fight back."[14] Leading with the headline, "Henry Ford—Pogromist," the *Butte Daily Bulletin* (Montana) said, "Mr. Henry Ford . . . is spending a great deal of money in an endeavor to fan the flames of religious and racial hatred in the United States."[15] The *Leavenworth Times* (Kansas) charged, "The attempt to create prejudice against the Jews is entirely reprehensible and one which is receiving—as it should receive—the severe criticism of the leading papers of the country."[16]

As Ford was slowly isolated, the *Dearborn Independent* continued with its vitriol. The newspaper finally met its match when it went after a Jewish lawyer, Aaron Sapiro, who had been working in California to organize farmers into cooperatives. Starting in the April 12, 1924, issue with the headline, "Sapiro's Dream—An International Wheat Pool," the paper began a series of articles accusing Sapiro and Jewish bankers of plotting to control all agriculture in the United States by exploiting farmers. Various articles alleged that he associated with communists and anarchists and was training farm children with communistic ideas.

Sapiro fought back. First, he sent Ford a letter demanding retraction of the printed false accusations. When Ford refused, and the *Dearborn Independent* continued to print defamatory articles about Sapiro and Jewish plots, Sapiro went into Federal Court in Detroit on April 25, 1925, and brought a libel suit against the automobile tycoon in the amount of $1 million dollars.

Ford's high-priced team of lawyers embarked on a delaying process utilizing legal loopholes. Their plan was to discourage Sapiro so much that he would drop the suit. They underestimated Aaron Sapiro.

When, on September 14, 1926, the judge assigned to the case finally announced he would open the case, Ford's lawyers objected and demanded the judge's replacement, accusing him of being prejudiced against Ford. The judge recused himself. A new judge, Fred M. Raymond, granted Ford another continuance that further delayed the proceedings and set a revised trial date of March 1, 1927. After yet another delay, the actual trial began on March 15.

By now, one major change was in effect. The court ruled that Sapiro could only sue for libel against himself personally and not on behalf of the larger Jewish community.

Over weeks, witnesses were called and questioned. Grilled under oath for three weeks by Ford's lawyers, Sapiro never faltered. Sapiro's lawyer then announced he would subpoena Henry Ford himself to testify under oath.

But before Ford could appear, he was allegedly involved in a suspicious automobile accident that his lawyers insisted made him unable to testify soon. When Sapiro's lawyer asked the court to permit impartial doctors to examine Ford, the trial took a sudden turn. Ford's investigators informed the court that one juror had been approached with a bribe attempt. In her denial to the press, the juror angrily stated that the charge was a ploy to have the case thrown out. Judge Raymond had no choice but to declare a mistrial and arrange a date for a new trial.

The public circus was too much for Henry Ford. With a new model automobile about to be released, he feared his antisemitic image would hurt sales. He wanted the embarrassing lawsuit to go away. To diffuse the situation, he sent two operatives to New York to speak privately with Louis Marshall, the head of the American Jewish Committee whom he had previously vilified in the *Dearborn Independent*. Ford, the operatives explained to Marshall, had meant no harm to Jews and was unaware of the newspaper articles written under his name. Marshall was unconvinced, but he used this meeting as an opportunity to stop the spread of the automaker's anti-Jewish propaganda. He told the emissaries that there would have to be a "complete retraction of all the false charges made, an apology, a discontinuance of the attacks and amends of the wrong."[17]

Ford accepted the terms completely. He even asked Marshall to draft a statement in the form of a letter which the automaker would then address to Marshall. Ford accepted Marshall's writing without any edits. The June 30, 1927, letter, excerpted here, was quickly made public and reprinted in newspapers across the country:

> It goes without saying that in the multitude of my activities it has become impossible for me to devote personal attention to their management or to keep informed as to their contents. . . . To my great regret I have learned that Jews generally, and particularly those of this country, not only resent these publications as promoting anti-Semitism, but regard me as their enemy. . . . I am deeply mortified that this journal . . . has been made the medium for resurrecting exploded fictions, for giving currency to the so-called Protocols of the Wise Men of Zion, which have been demon-

strated, as I learn, to be gross forgeries. . . . I deem it to be my duty as an honorable man to make amends for the wrong done to the Jews as fellow-men and brothers, by asking their forgiveness for the harm that I have unintentionally committed.[18]

Ford went on to promise that all the copies of the *International Jew* (his serialized *Protocols* series) in print would be withdrawn from circulation. On July 27, 1927, Henry Ford ordered all Ford dealers to stop accepting subscriptions to the *Independent*. The paper closed for good in December 1927.

But the genie could not be put back into the bottle. The damage was done and could not be undone. The *Protocols*, as well as the ideas they inspired, remain in existence. Despite repeated statements demonstrating that the *Protocols of the Learned Elders of Zion* are a forgery, antisemites continue to reprint them and they continue to influence antisemitic thinking worldwide.

As for Ford, when his assistant asked if the printing presses should be sold, Ford supposedly responded in the negative, saying, "I might have to go after those Jews again."[19]

Within the Jewish community, Ford's apology created a stir. Some Jews believed it was sincere; most were skeptical. A humorous parody song, "When Henry Ford Apologized to Me," was an instant hit in Jewish homes.

To avoid another trial, Ford quickly reached a private settlement with Aaron Sapiro purported to be $140,000 (today worth over $2 million). The July 17, 1927, headline of the English supplement to the Yiddish-language newspaper the *Daily Forward* was overly optimistic: "Dramatic Collapse of the Anti-Semitic Movement in the United States."

The KKK

The Ku Klux Klan, which had gone through a number of transformations since its founding in 1865 to fight Reconstruction in the South, was revived in 1915 to oppose not only African Americans but also

Catholics and Jews. As a white supremacist organization, the Klan sought to impose a social order that marginalized any groups that threatened its white, Protestant worldview. Because we are focused on antisemitism, we will explore the Klan's anti-Jewish history without forgetting that the Klan's hatred was more far-reaching.

It is not difficult to identify the revitalized Klan's general attitude toward Jews. Many of the same men who had formed the Knights of Mary Phagan, the group that lynched Leo Frank in Marietta, Georgia, likely attended the ritual at Stone Mountain that founded the modern Klan. A few years later, in 1923, Klan Imperial Wizard Dr. H. W. Evans proclaimed, "Already a fifth of the Jewish race is in this country . . . Their homes are not American but Jewish homes. . . . They will never emerge for a real intermingling with America."[20]

In the early 1920s the KKK claimed over four million members and exercised its political muscles publicly. In 1922 it helped elect governors in four states and may have influenced as many as seventy-five races in the United States House of Representatives. In 1925 the Klan demonstrated its power when some forty thousand Klan members dressed in their distinctive, white-hooded robes and marched down Pennsylvania Avenue in Washington. Although the Klan's power declined by the 1930s, its widespread influence made clear that minority groups were at risk of violence and not necessarily welcomed in their own communities.

Jewish organizations debated how to respond to the Klan. They feared that any call for violent response would only inflame Klan passions and lead to more problems. A Jewish newspaper editorial stated, "The Jew does not fear the Klan because much stronger forces have attempted to exterminate the Jew throughout history without success, and it certainly does not fall to a band of nightshirted gentry to complete the job left undone by czars, emperors, and Henry Flivver [Henry Ford]. . . . The only way Jews could fight Klanism, Fordism, and every other brand of anti-Semitism was for Jews to become BETTER JEWS."[21]

Flaming crosses on Jewish lawns and boycotts of Jewish businesses were part of the Klan's standard repertoire. One Ohio businessman,

Charles D. Levy, wrote to President Calvin Coolidge seeking help. The Klan had arranged boycotts on several of his stores; furthermore, "In front of thousands of spectators who had gathered to hear the speakers [at a mass meeting in Ashland, Ohio], the Ku Klux Klan openly told the audience they should not patronize any Jewish merchant. I think this is . . . very unfair to an American citizen or even a Non-American citizen. . . . All I am asking for is your protection in this matter."[22] Although the Klan almost certainly affected other minority groups like African Americans more acutely than it affected Jews, Levy's case demonstrates that the nativist rhetoric negatively characterized American Jews and targeted them for being different from the white Protestant majority.

Discrimination in Higher Education

While Jews were relieved that Henry Ford's source of hate against them had been silenced, they continued to experience antisemitism in other ways. In the 1920s they found themselves increasingly denied acceptance to prestigious universities, employment, private clubs, and public accommodations.

For immigrant Jews, education was their children's road to success. Deprived of a secular education in their home countries, children of immigrants quickly embraced the free—and legally required—public schools of America. Private schools were another matter. While some accepted Jewish students, others did not. An advertisement for Miss McClintock's School for Girls in Boston clearly stated, "Although the school is non-sectarian, it does not admit Hebrews."[23]

Higher education was a common goal within the Jewish community, and Jews soon constituted a larger percentage of college students than other groups. In 1922 the *Nation* magazine reported that in 1919, 90 percent of students at the public College of the City of New York were Jewish; and their enrollment in the privately run Columbia University's class that year may have reached as high as 40 percent. Harvard University's Jewish student numbers grew from 10 percent in 1912 to 20 percent a decade later. That statistic particularly concerned Harvard's president Abbot Lawrence Lowell, who felt that the increase in Jewish students would transform the traditional image of elite universities, such as Harvard, from a "gentleman's country club."[24] Many of the Jewish students from humble backgrounds, while academically eager and proficient, did not come to Harvard prepared to fit into the school's social life. "The anti-Semitic feeling among the students is increasing," Lowell wrote, "and it grows in proportion to the increase in the number of Jews. . . . When the number of Jews was small, the race antagonism was small. . . . If every college in the country would take a limited proportion of Jews, I suspect we should go a long way toward eliminating race feeling among the students."[25]

Although Lowell advocated for an explicit quota on the percentage of Jews at Harvard, the university's faculty voted against doing so. However, Lowell and his allies discovered other ways of keeping Jews out of Harvard. They introduced nothing short of a revolution in college admissions, inaugurating policies such as admissions interviews, personal essays, a preference for students from certain areas where few Jews lived, and new methods of evaluating applicants that focused more on character than academic achievement. They also changed the admissions paperwork so that Harvard could more easily identify the character traits it sought to include and exclude from its community. Following Harvard's lead, some schools established waiting lists for students, which made it easier to exclude Jewish applicants. One unidentified admissions director was quoted in the *Nation* at the time, "With a waiting list, you can do almost anything."[26] Certain schools even resorted to outright lying by telling Jewish applicants there was no more room or that the applicant did not meet academic requirements.

Columbia University President Nicholas Murray Butler tried to justify the school's newly instituted selective admissions policy: "[We have] not eliminated boys because they were Jews and do not propose to do so. We have honestly attempted to eliminate the lowest grade of applicant and it turns out that a good many of the low grade men are New York Jews."[27]

Another creative way of managing the number of Jewish students was through legacy admissions: giving children of alumni special privileges. Few Jews then were graduates of these schools. As Dartmouth College President Ernest Hopkins said, "Any college which is going to base its admissions wholly on scholastic standing will find itself with an infinitesimal proportion of anything else than Jews eventually," thereby totally upending the existing social character of the school.[28]

A big fear among college administrators was that having too many Jews on campus would make the school unappealing to students who came from the upper echelons of white, Protestant society. Throughout the country, other institutions of higher learning joined the elite "Big Three" of Harvard, Yale, and Princeton in reducing the number of Jewish students accepted.

To uncover who was Jewish and who was not, schools, beginning in the 1920s, began to ask invasive questions on application forms. Sometimes, prior to applying, Jews legally changed their names to less Jewish-sounding names, so some colleges then began asking if their family names had ever been changed. If the admissions committee was still unsure of a person's background, another question asked for the names of grandparents and their birthplaces. Some schools required submission of a photograph, as if it alone could reveal if an applicant was Jewish. Many colleges and universities began to simply ask students for their religious affiliation. Harvard even asked high school principals and headmasters about each applicant's religious preference.

Among Ivy League colleges, Columbia and the University of Pennsylvania maintained a comparatively high proportion of Jewish students. A nonflattering popular college song during the early part of the twentieth century sported the following lyrics:

Oh, Harvard's run by millionaires,
And Yale is run by booze,
Cornell is run by farmers' sons,
Columbia's run by Jews.
So give a cheer for Baxter Street,

Another one for Pell,
And when the little sheenies die,
Their souls will go to hell.[29]

Jewish students took antisemitic incidents in stride as they pursued their educational objectives. One example concerns an incident at the United States Naval Academy in Annapolis, Maryland. Despite endured insults and indignities over four years, Leonard Kaplan graduated in 1922 as the class salutatorian with the second highest grades in the class. That year's yearbook, *The Lucky Bag*, contained serious alphabetical biographies of each graduate, followed by a humorous characterization that poked affectionate fun at the student. What set Kaplan's biography apart from the others was an additional fake biography. In it, his nickname was given as Porky, his birthplace as "the township of Zion . . . educated in the Convent of Zion."[30] In addition, Kaplan's biography page was set apart from the others, without a page number, and placed at the end of the book. That page was perforated, allowing it to be detached without defacing the book. In the index of graduates, his name was missing.

Reaction was swift in coming and was the subject of discussion in the U.S. Senate. While the Naval Academy superintendent, Admiral Henry Braid Wilson, dismissed the event simply as "boy's cruelty to boys," the acting secretary of the Navy, Theodore Roosevelt Jr., son of the former president, formally reprimanded *The Lucky Bag* editor.[31] Captain Leonard Kaplan, later a recipient of the Legion of Merit, went on to a successful career in the United States Navy and finally retired in 1948.

Hyman Rickover

Another 1922 Jewish classmate of Kaplan's at Annapolis was Hyman Rickover, remembered as "the father of the nuclear Navy." Born in Poland, young Hyman arrived in the United States at age five. After graduation from the Naval Academy, he rose in the ranks, always confronting the ingrained antisemitism of other officers. Responsible for

Fig. 9. Admiral Hyman Rickover is credited with advocating for and creating America's nuclear navy. Volgi Archive/Alamy Stock Photo.

the creation of the atomic submarine, he was nonetheless passed over for promotion to admiral until his allies in Washington intervened on his behalf in 1953.

Outside the Navy, Rickover was popular for his accomplishments. One magazine wrote, "The real charge against Dreyfus was his religion. And it was because of his religion that Rickover was blacklisted by the Navy he had served so well."[32] A loud public and political response to Rickover's treatment led the U.S. Senate Armed Forces Committee to withhold approval of that year's admiral's list, which did not contain his name.

Secretary of the Navy Robert Anderson convened a new selection board which nominated Rickover, and he was promoted to admiral.

Discrimination in Employment

In the 1920s Jews were largely invisible in heavy industries such as steel, utilities, and railroads. They were also generally excluded from executive positions in America's largest industries: automotive, insurance, chemical, petroleum, and engineering. Additionally, despite the prominence of certain Jewish-led banking firms such Goldman Sachs and Lehman Brothers, few Jews held executive banking positions. While local Jewish insurance company agents did serve heavily Jewish areas, they were rarely promoted to higher corporate positions. Likewise, there were Jewish petroleum dealers, but very few could be found in management roles. There were Jewish auto dealers, but Jews were rarely represented in corporate headquarters.

As a result, Jews gravitated to businesses that did not require large sums to enter and where they could be in control of their own success. Many went into the garment and entertainment industries; others worked as shop owners.

Despite the belief that Jews controlled Wall Street and finance, *Fortune* magazine reported that Jews "do not run banking. They play little or no part in the great commercial houses."[33] In 1934 a list of eighty thousand American corporations listed in *Poor's Register* indicated that fewer than 5 percent had Jewish officials. This was a far cry from the total domination antisemites like Ford claimed.

When the American Jewish Congress investigated New York employment agency discrimination, it found "even the unprejudiced employer is given only the Christian applicant. When Jews are sent, it is because others do not qualify."[34] An investigator from the organization applied to New York agencies for one hundred jobs and reported that in over ninety cases, he was told that a Jew was unacceptable—all this in a city where Jews comprised 30 percent of the population. State laws forbidding discrimination were often circumvented or ignored.

Unwelcoming Places

"Refined American Jews are very cautious about choosing their residences as well as their summer resorts," wrote poet and writer Elias Lieberman. "They do not wish to invite insult."[35]

For Jews looking for a residence or a vacation spot in the 1920s and 1930s, careful reading of advertisements could avoid embarrassment.

They could automatically disregard advertisements with the admonishments, "Gentiles only," "Hebrew patronage not solicited," or the more coded phrase, "restricted clientele," a polite way of saying no Jews allowed. The Old Fort Inn in Maine advertised great cuisine and the fact that it "receives no Hebrew patronage."[36] The Sononsco House in Mt. Pocono, Pennsylvania, proudly stated, "Hebrews, consumptives and dogs not solicited."[37] Another resort plainly stated, "Altitude 1860 ft. Too High for Jews."[38] Some hotels, approached by a potential Jewish guest, quoted prohibitive rates or simply said they were fully booked.

Individual Jews protested about the discrimination, but aside from publishing reaction statements and issuing petitions, national Jewish organizations such as the AJC and the ADL chose not to publicly challenge them. Privately, people like Louis Marshall sent letters reminding offenders that their actions violated the law, urging them to comply, and threatening legal repercussions. Many Jewish leaders believed that publicly opposing discriminatory practices would only heighten antisemitic feelings. All in all, the existing antidiscrimination laws generally failed to correct the problem. Resorts often adopted coded language that did not significantly change how they conducted business but instead veiled their discriminatory practices.

Some Jewish publications posted warnings about unwelcoming places. In 1917 the Federation of Jewish Farmers of America issued *The Jewish Vacation Guide to Hotels, Boarding and Rooming Houses Where Jews Are Welcome*. A few years later, the *Wisconsin Jewish Chronicle* stated, "The Jewish people want to know WHERE THEIR PATRONAGE IS NOT DESIRED OR SOLICITED JUST BECAUSE THEY ARE JEWS.... They believe that America is big enough and broad enough and intelligent enough to contain good business institutions who desire to do business with MEN AS MEN."[39]

Within this context, Jews responded by building their own vacation spots, among them hotels featuring bountiful food, sport activities, and entertainment in the Catskill Mountains of New York, later known as the Borscht Belt.

When comedian Groucho Marx was denied membership in a country club, he is reported to have facetiously asked if his daughter, who was half-Jewish, could go into the swimming pool only up to her waist. When well-known Jewish leaders in the film industry were denied membership in local country clubs, they created their own: the Hillcrest Country Club in Los Angeles. To their delight, and possibly the chagrin of clubs that had denied them membership, oil was discovered on the property in the 1950s, generating a large amount of money that was shared among the members.

Fear of foreigners and communists and resentment toward the millions who had immigrated to the United States over the preceding three decades contributed to the 1924 Immigration Act (also known as the Johnson-Reed Act after the two politicians who guided it through Congress). The act severely limited the yearly number of immigrants to America to one hundred fifty thousand people and only accepted 2 percent of people from a country based on the number of people from that nation already present in the United States in 1890—a year selected on purpose, since it preceded the mass immigration of Eastern and Southern Europeans. In 1890 the overwhelming majority of Americans were descended from Great Britain, Germany, and Northern Europe.

This fact prompted one magazine to call the restrictive rules "the Nordic immigration policy."[40] The *Wisconsin Jewish Chronicle* commented, "America henceforth closes her doors to Jews, not because they are inferior by any physical or mental or moral test, but just because THEY ARE JEWS."[41]

Libel in Massena

In September 1928 the blood libel accusation, a key feature of European anti-Jewish violence for centuries, emerged on American soil in the upstate New York town of Massena. Although accounts of the incident vary, enough facts exist to reconstruct what happened there. On September 22, a day before Yom Kippur began the next evening, four-year-old Barbara Griffiths disappeared. While a search for her began, state trooper Corporal H. M. McCann apparently heard from a local café owner, possibly a recent immigrant from Greece, that Jews kidnapped and killed children before a major holiday to use their blood in their rituals. The usual myth involved use of Christian blood to make matzah for Passover, but in Massena one Jewish holiday was as good as another. Searchers for the little girl entered Jewish-owned stores looking for her.

McCann brought the suspicion to the attention of Mayor W. Gilbert Hawes, who arranged for the trooper to interrogate the local rabbi, Berel Brennglass of Congregation Adath Israel. Summoned to the police station on Sunday, with the *Kol Nidre* service to begin at sunset and a mob gathering outside, the incensed rabbi strongly refuted the accusations of human sacrifice and the use of Christian blood in Jewish rituals. Little Barbara emerged safely in the late afternoon from the woods where she had been lost. That, however, did not quelch rumors that the girl had been released only when her alleged kidnappers became frightened. The mayor launched a boycott of locally owned Jewish businesses.

That evening, at *Kol Nidre*, the rabbi informed his congregation about what had happened. "We must forever remind ourselves," the rabbi said, "that this happened in America, not tsarist Russia, among people we have come to regard as our friends. We must show our neighbors that their hatred originates in fear, and this fear has its roots in ignorance. We must show them they have nothing to fear from us. We must tell the world this story so it will never happen again."[42]

On the afternoon before services, local Jewish leaders had gathered and tried to forge a strategy to combat the brewing storm. The synagogue's president, Jacob Shulkin, contacted prominent local and national figures for assistance, including Louis Marshall of the American Jewish Committee and Rabbi Stephen S. Wise of the American Jewish Congress. Marshall wrote to Mayor Hawes, charging him with ordering the rabbi's interrogation "on the intolerable assumption that the Jews required the blood of Christian children for their holy days."[43] Rabbi Wise also wrote to the mayor, accusing him of fomenting a libel against the Jewish people.

Speaking out gave these leaders a chance to combat the charges of blood libel, in hopes that this would diminish the possibility that the false claims would surface elsewhere. Within days, newspapers around the country carried the story. Editorials expressed their indignation that such an event had occurred in the United States.

Mayor Hawes, who was running for reelection, responded to Rabbi Wise, "I regret exceedingly that this misunderstanding has arisen. . . . If I am chargeable with any act or word in this matter which has been offensive to the Jewish people, I certainly regret it."[44] Meanwhile, Governor Al Smith, then a presidential candidate, followed a suggestion from Wise and ordered the State of New York to investigate. The result was the reprimand and suspension of Corporal McCann, who issued his own apology to Rabbi Brennglass: "I am writing to say that I regret more than I can tell you and am very, very sorry for my part in the incident at Massena. . . . I realized, as I did not before, how wrong it was of me to request you to come to the Police Station at Massena to be questioned concerning a rumor which I should have known to be absolutely false."[45]

Governor Smith later wrote to Rabbi Wise, "I cannot believe that this libelous myth has been resurrected and credited even for a moment by any one [sic] connected with the service of the state, or any of its civil divisions. I can hardly believe that either the mayor or a state trooper summoned a rabbi to a police station on a religious holiday in connection with an absurd ritual murder charge."[46] Meanwhile, a group of interfaith scholars issued a statement affirming that "the blood accusation is a cruel and utterly baseless libel on Judaism . . . There is no custom, ceremony or ritual among Jews any where [sic] . . . which calls for the use of human blood for any purpose."[47]

While the Jewish community in Massena was able to escape without experiencing a great tragedy, a nightmare was looming across the Atlantic that would have a profound impact on Jews worldwide.

8

The Rising Storm

By the time Adolf Hitler came to power in Germany in 1933, his hatred of Jews was long known. Beginning in 1920s Bavaria, Hitler attracted followers to his National Socialist Party, often referred to as the Nazis, and spewed increasing vitriol against Jews. In 1923 the *Wisconsin Jewish Chronicle* quoted Hitler as saying in a public speech that problems in Germany will only be solved when Jews are expelled and "the anti-Semitic swastika cross waves from the roof of the Berlin castle."[1]

After the German elections of 1933, the Nazis began limiting the rights and freedoms of Jews. Beginning with a law that banned Jews and other political opponents from the civil service, Jews were increasingly subjected to harsh regulations. The German government targeted them, taking such actions as sponsoring a nationwide boycott of Jewish businesses and limiting the number of Jewish children in public schools. In 1941 Jews were forced to wear yellow stars on their clothing to identify themselves as Jews in public.

Public Protests

The rise of Nazism in Germany deeply affected American Jews. Defense organizations in the United States debated actions to be taken but could not reach consensus. The American Jewish Congress advocated public rallies and demonstrations while the American Jewish Committee and B'nai Brith preferred to monitor the situation and avoid a confrontational approach.

When the Jewish War Veterans called for a national boycott of German goods in March 1933, the American Jewish Committee rejected the idea, fearing that Nazis would only retaliate against German Jews.

Rabbi Stephen S. Wise of the American Jewish Congress initially rejected the proposal, but his organization changed its stance and endorsed an economic boycott. At the time, he argued, "The time for prudence and caution is past. We must speak up like men. How can we ask our Christian friends to lift their voices in protest against the wrongs suffered by Jews if we keep silent ... It is not the German Jews who are being attacked. It is the Jews."[2] Boycotters set up picket lines in front of department stores, and labor unions such as the American Federation of Labor protested against the purchasing of German-made goods. (In May 1933 the Nazis had prohibited German trade unions and strikes and sent union leaders to concentration camps.). Efforts to boycott German goods continued in subsequent years. In 1935 New York City mayor Fiorello La Guardia prohibited the use of German steel in the construction of the Triborough Bridge, declaring that "the only commodity we can import from Hitlerland now is hatred, and we don't want any in our country."[3]

Washington was cool to requests for official American action. In March 1933 Rabbi Wise of the American Jewish Congress and Dr. Cyrus Adler of the American Jewish Committee met with Secretary of State Cordell Hull in Washington to protest German treatment of Jews. In response, the secretary promised to consult with the American embassy in Berlin and subsequently sent a telegram to Wise and Adler that reported the mistreatment of Jews had been a temporary event. Hull's informants in Berlin suggested that violence had occurred but was probably exaggerated and was now over. Hull was hopeful that Germany was simply recalibrating in response to a political upheaval and that "the situation, which has caused such widespread concern throughout this country, will soon revert to normal." To Wise, however, as well as many Americans, "the enlightened opinion of America must watch with profoundest anxiety the development of events in Germany."[4]

On March 27, 1933, about one million people in cities across America gathered to protest the antisemitic actions of the Nazi government in Germany. The main event took place at Madison Square Garden in

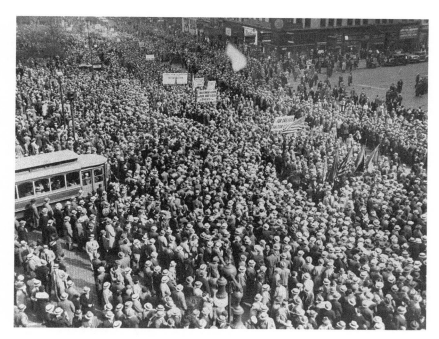

Fig. 10. More than a hundred thousand demonstrators gather in front of New York's Madison Square Garden to participate in an anti-Nazi march, May 10, 1933. United States Holocaust Memorial Museum, courtesy of National Archives and Records Administration, College Park MD.

New York, where the American Jewish Congress sponsored a mass protest rally. Nearly twenty-five thousand people packed the arena while thirty-five thousand filled the adjoining streets, listening through loudspeakers as speaker after speaker denounced the anti-Jewish actions in Germany. Former New York governor and presidential candidate Al Smith joined Senator Robert Wagner, Mayor John P. O'Brien, labor union head William Green, featured speaker Rabbi Wise, and many other religious and political leaders to denounce Hitler. Both the NBC and CBS radio networks broadcasted the event live to the country.

Elsewhere in New York and throughout the United States, protesters made their voices heard. Another ten thousand protesters marched in

Fig. 11. Addressing twenty-five thousand people crammed inside Madison Square Garden, Rabbi Stephen S. Wise pleads for an immediate end to the physical attacks and discriminatory measures against Jews in Germany. United States Holocaust Memorial Museum, courtesy of National Archives and Records Administration, College Park.

Brooklyn, and many pushcarts on the Lower East Side closed down as a protest. In Pittsburgh, five thousand people attended a mass meeting in Carnegie Hall while another twenty-five hundred stood outside. The main speaker there was the Right Reverend Alexander Mann, bishop of the Episcopal Diocese of Western Pennsylvania, who declared, "The moral and Christian faith of a multitude of German people is on trial . . . The Nazi government is riding for a fall and fall it will."[5] The protesters then passed a resolution calling on the United States government to intervene. In Chicago, four thousand persons filled an auditorium, with another two thousand outside, to hear Governor Paul McNutt of Indiana speak about the outbreak of violence against German Jews. Such "injustice is outrageous against morality and humanity," McNutt declared. "I rise to protest against acts of the German government."[6] The Chicago protesters then adopted their own resolution calling for restitution of Jews' rights in Germany, to be sent to Washington.

In Washington, congressman William Sirovich (D-New York) introduced a resolution condemning Hitler and Nazism. Thomas Blanton of Texas interrupted Sirovoch to add, "In this connection may I not call the attention of my friend to the fact that there is unreasonable, foolish, cruel persecution of the Jews right here in the Nation's Capital?"[7] Blanton was referring to housing discrimination against Jews specifically in Washington, but the reality was national: antisemitism in America was thriving. In employment, leading corporations discriminated in their hiring, and New York employment agencies displayed signs notifying prospective clients they did not accept applications from Jews. Throughout the 1930s, antisemites of all strains continued to spread hatred in the United States through publications, rallies, and radio broadcasts.

Franklin Delano Roosevelt, who assumed the presidency in 1933, inherited a country still mired in the Great Depression, with unemployment at an all-time high (25 percent) and many Americans worrying where their next meal would come from. Roosevelt had run on a set of policies he called "The New Deal," promising opportunities for struggling Americans, and within his first one hundred days in office, he created five sweeping programs, including Social Security for the elderly, projects that put people to work again, and unemployment insurance.

The New Deal would create a lifeline for many Americans, but Roosevelt drew criticism from many corners of the country, nonetheless. African Americans protested that the New Deal tended to exclude them from many of its key programs, like Social Security and the National Recovery Administration's efforts to guarantee a minimum wage in certain industries. Others disparagingly referred to it as the "Jew Deal." Roosevelt had appointed Jews to various positions within his administration (except for one cabinet member, all lower-level posts), and they became lightning rods to his antisemitic political opponents. Some even accused Roosevelt of being a secret Jew, purposely mocking his name as Rosenfeld.

Silver Shirts

In the 1930s, Italy had its Black Shirts, Germany its Brown Shirts, and the United States Silver Shirts. As Hitler seized power in Germany, William Dudley Pelley founded the Silver Legion of America, whose members wore silver shirts. Pelley's group aimed to create a Christian commonwealth that excluded Jews and to "save the United States from a state of Sovietism," which they alleged was promoted by Jews.[8] Additionally, Pelley called attention to what he saw as the undue influence of Jewish men in the American banking industry and charged that President Roosevelt had been drawn into a Jewish conspiracy. Of course, neither of these claims were true, but they convinced an aggrieved segment of the American population.

Congressman Louis T. McFadden of Pennsylvania, a Pelley supporter, inserted excerpts of the *Protocols of the Learned Elders of Zion* and blasts at "international Jewish bankers" into the Congressional Record. Accusing President Roosevelt of leading a Jewish-controlled administration, McFadden predicted that unless the president reverted to Christian values, there would be a fascist revolution in the United States.

The Silver Shirts aligned with European fascists and organized themselves into paramilitary units trained for a takeover of the United States and the deportation of all Jews. Their weekly newspaper, *Liberation*, featured attacks on Jews and reprints of articles from Henry Ford's defunct *Dearborn Independent*. Referring to Hitler's attacks on Jews, the American Jewish Committee quoted Pelley, "But Hitler is not going to finish that work. THE FINISH OF IT COMES RIGHT HERE IN AMERICA."[9]

The Silver Shirts generated a lot of publicity but did not attain a large following. Their national membership never reached over fifteen thousand. Perhaps more telling is that fact that when Pelley decided to run for president in 1936, he only managed to get on the ballot in one state and received only about fifteen hundred votes. Due to its fascist roots, the group drew plenty of negative attention from the press and federal government, which caused it to fall apart after the United States entered World War II.

Other Advocates against Jews

Pelley was not alone in advocating against Jews. Robert Edward Edmondson, an antisemitic pamphleteer, distributed about five million printed leaflets during the 1930s. A 1935 leaflet he published used a Star of David to identify "sinister" figures within the Roosevelt administration. Edmondson also maligned two influential Jewish lawyers, Professor Felix Frankfurter of Harvard Law School and Supreme Court Justice Louis D. Brandeis, associating them with communism. As World War II approached, he issued a circular claiming, "The American people have no quarrel with Germany or Japan. They do not want to fight either nation. And neither do the Germans nor the Japanese want to fight us. The only people who want war are— THE JEWS!"[10]

James True amplified the news out of Nazi Germany by predicting that American Jews would experience their own pogrom in 1936. Influential Jews, including Frankfurter, he said, "should be bumped off and put in their graves."[11] To prepare for the pogrom, he invented and patented a special police truncheon he called the "Kike Killer" to use on Jews. In the end, the pogrom never materialized.

Around this same time, a loose alliance of so-called patriotic groups with antisemitic agendas emerged to fight communism. In 1938 Congress created the House Committee on Un-American Activities (HCUA), later called the House Un-American Activities Committee (HUAC), to investigate fascist, communist, and pro-Nazi operations in the United States. The following year, retired U.S. Army general George van Horn Mosely delivered an inflammatory speech in Philadelphia claiming the existence of a secret Jewish organization bent on bringing communism to America. After the general's testimony before the HCUA, committee chair Congressman Martin Dies of Texas said, "The examination of the witnesses in this plot to foment anti-Semitism has convinced me and the members of the Committee that the real goal of the instigators of this plot was to influence the American people to a point where they would succumb to a military dictatorship."[12]

Meanwhile, George Deatherage resurrected a white supremacist group that had been founded by a former Confederate military officer after the Civil War, the Knights of the White Camelia. Deatherage hoped to foster antisemitic activity and create a fascist, Christian-nationalist political party. To thwart the international Jewish "kehillah" supposedly plotting a revolution to take over the country, he strove to unite the approximately eight hundred pro-fascist organizations in America to prepare for the violence to come; the plan consisted largely of recruiting fifty million Americans into the fascist movement by 1940. He recruited General van Horn Mosely to lead the fight against the alleged Jewish plot. However, like others mentioned in this section, Deatherage never realized his goal. By 1942 Pelley, Edmonson, True, Deatherage, and other fascist sympathizers had been arrested and charged with sedition. Two years later, the government tried and failed to prosecute thirty more right-wing individuals on charges of sedition. Although the "Great Sedition Trial of 1944" never materialized into convictions, Americans would no longer tolerate fascism in public the way they had in the years before World War II. American fascism would not permanently disappear, but it never regained the influence and acceptability in public that marked the years before World War II.

Coughlin, Kristallnacht, and the Christian Front

By the 1930s technological advances had created a new way to reach a national audience: radio. While uses of the radio varied, Catholic priest Father Charles E. Coughlin recognized its potential to bring his message into American homes. Initially a Roosevelt supporter, Coughlin became disillusioned when he did not gain access to the administration and began rallying against Roosevelt and the New Deal. His agenda also included isolationism, anti-communism, opposition to banking, and, later, antisemitism.

Coughlin's weekly broadcasts from the Royal Oak, Michigan, National Shrine of the Little Flower attracted as many as forty million listeners at the peak of his influence. In 1938 he ignited two controversies. First, he drew the ire of the Jewish press for reprinting the already discredited *Protocols of the Learned Elders of Zion* in his news publication *Social Justice*. Then, he incited an even larger debate for his response to the infamous Kristallnacht pogrom in Germany.

On the evening of November 9–10, 1938, the Nazi government organized a national pogrom in German cities. It became known as Kristallnacht, or the Night of Broken Glass, because shards of glass lined the streets after the Stormtroopers and Hitler Youth attacked over 7,500 Jewish institutions, businesses, and homes, destroying 267 synagogues. Nazi police agencies arrested as many as thirty thousand Jews, marking the first time the regime used mass incarceration against Jews. In short, Kristallnacht marked a major turning point for the Nazi regime. Although German officials were still years from deciding on the Final Solution to eliminate the Jewish people, Kristallnacht represented a turn toward harsher, more extreme measures to alienate Jews from German society.

On his radio program of November 20, Father Coughlin minimized the effect of Kristallnacht by claiming that the Nazis were only acting to combat the spread of communism, which he closely associated with Jews, from spreading in Germany. His comments were so vicious that one major radio station in New York refused to air his next broadcast, but most stations continued to transmit his show. Within the Catholic Church, Cardinal George Mundelein of Chicago issued a statement that Coughlin did not speak for the church; nor did any of his statements reflect its teachings. When the war broke out in 1939, at least one of Coughlin's articles in *Social Justice* was found to be a translated copy of the writing of Nazi Minister of Propaganda Joseph Goebbels. In 1939 the General Jewish Council (formed five years earlier by the American Jewish Committee, American Jewish Congress, B'nai B'rith, and the Jewish Labor Committee as a unified voice to combat antisemitism) published a booklet, *Father Coughlin: His "Facts and Arguments"*, which challenged the antisemitic tirades of the radio priest, and also sent a confidential letter to Jewish leaders around the country, enlisting them in monitoring Coughlin's misstatements.

Coughlin's largest base of support came from working-class, largely Irish Catholics in large cities joining others who feared communism and were suspicious of Jews. An organization called the Christian Front drew support from Coughlin's followers and moved incitement from the airwaves to the streets. Front members hawked copies of Coughlin's *Social Justice*, distributed leaflets urging shoppers to only buy from Christian-owned stores, and went on the attack, assaulting Jews and people they thought looked Jewish. Sympathetic Irish-Catholic police officers sometimes took the hooligans' side and let the assaults continue without interruption. In 1939 and 1940 New Yorkers experienced around forty or fifty raucous Christian Front street meetings "at which crowds have been exhorted to liquidate the Jews in America."[13]

The Fronters' rowdy behavior moved from New York City, where they counted an estimated twelve thousand followers, to other cities. In Philadelphia, Fronters broke synagogue windows and terrorized Jews on the street. In New York and Boston, roving gangs of Irish-Catholic youths attacked young Jews in heavily Jewish areas. In Minneapolis, Coughlin supporters distributed leaflets warning that Jews were planning to rule the world. In Terre Haute, Indiana, the windows of Jewish-owned stores were smeared with antisemitic slogans.

In early 1940 FBI agents arrested seventeen Christian Fronters plotting an armed revolution to eradicate Jews and overthrow the U.S. government; they were charged with sedition. The Fronters had planned to attack communists and Jews, which they viewed as synonymous; then, they expected, members of the National Guard would join with them to seize control of the government and install a government friendly to their cause. In short, they had hoped—but failed—to incite a revolution.

During an eleven-week trial, the courthouse was filled with people who supported the accused plotters. Others peddled Coughlin's publication *Social Justice* outside the courtroom. The sympathetic jury acquitted the defendants. In response to the verdict, Father Coughlin stated that the resentment built up during the trial would only increase antisemitism throughout the country.

Historian Oscar Handlin estimated that "at least four million, and perhaps as many as ten million Americans enlisted in such organizations as the Ku Klux Klan, the Silver Shirts, and the Christian Front."[14] Antisemitic violence remained a threat, and many American Jews felt powerless to respond. Jews did not have an important political voice at the time and did not want to provoke further violence. They feared being viewed as too pushy if they advocated for their rights. Prior to the United States entering World War II in 1941, most Americans were against interfering in another European war, and Jews did not want to be cast as warmongers. Meanwhile, a homegrown Nazi organization flexed its support for Germany.

German American Bund

The German American Bund, formed in 1936 by Americans of German ancestry, publicly supported the Nazi agenda while creating a mirror image of the German Nazi Party in the United States. Members across the country numbered in the thousands, an estimated twenty-five thousand at the Bund's peak, most of them ethnic Germans and immigrants who had arrived in the United States after World War I. Bund leaders operated youth training camps that indoctrinated young people with Nazi philosophy and served as meeting places for their parents. Sympathizers freely exhibited their support of the Nazi cause. Parades, rallies, and meetings featured antisemitic speeches amid swastika flags and uniformed stormtroopers giving "Heil Hitler" salutes.

On February 20, 1939, the Bund held a giant "Americanism" rally in New York City's Madison Square Garden. Many of the twenty-thousand participants wore full Nazi-style storm trooper uniforms. A giant full-length portrait of George Washington was flanked by American and swastika flags. Huge banners on the balcony proclaimed, "Stop Jewish Domination of Christian America" and "Smash Jewish Communism." Vendors sold Father Coughlin's *Social Justice* newspaper while speaker after speaker denounced Jews, President Roosevelt (who they referred to as Rosenfeld), and New York City mayor Fiorello LaGuardia, whose mother was Jewish. Ironically, the mayor had been under pressure not to permit the demonstration, but the American Jewish Committee had sent a letter to the Madison Square Garden management saying it was opposed to "any action to prevent the bund from airing its views. . . . We believe that the bund is completely anti-American and anti-democratic [but] nevertheless we believe that the basic right of free speech and free assembly should never be tampered with in the United States."[15] Reporter Dorothy Thompson, in the audience, later remarked how comical it was that speakers who spoke with heavy German accents made fun of "un-American" Jews who spoke with Yiddish accents.

Outside, a larger crowd of more than twenty-five thousand demonstrated against the Nazi event. Over sixteen hundred police officers, some on horseback, worked to keep the protestors in order. At least one Jew, Isadore Greenbaum, made it inside. As the evening's last presenter, Bund leader Fritz Kuhn, thundered about Jews seeking world domination, Greenbaum lurched onto the stage. Uniformed stormtroopers beat him savagely before the police could intervene.

Greenbaum was then arrested and sentenced to ten days in jail. "I went to the Garden without any intention of interrupting," Greenbaum told the judge. "But they talked so much against my religion and there was so much persecution, I lost my head."[16]

Wagner-Rogers Bill

From 1933 to 1938 the Roosevelt administration suppressed Jewish refugee immigration below what the law permitted by refusing to allow the existing quota from Germany to be filled. Concerned for the safety of European Jews as war loomed, national Jewish organizations urged the government to administer the immigration laws less harshly, but their calls went unheeded. On February 9, 1939, shortly after the November 1938 Kristallnacht pogrom, Senator Robert Wagner (New York) and Representative Edith Rogers (Massachusetts) introduced the Wagner-Rogers Bill, which would have allowed twenty thousand Jewish children from Germany entry outside of the annual quota from Germany. Famous Hollywood actors Henry Fonda and Helen Hayes, and political figures such as former president Herbert Hoover, 1936 Republican presidential nominee Alf Landon, and former first lady Grace Coolidge were among those advocating for Wagner-Rogers (Hayes testified for admitting the children at the hearings, and Coolidge announced that she and her neighbors in Northampton, Massachusetts, would personally care for twenty-five of them). They faced strong headwinds, however. Around that time, Laura Delano Houghteling, President Roosevelt's first cousin and wife of the United States Commissioner of Immigration, remarked at a Washington DC social occasion that "20,000 charming [Jewish] children would all too soon grow up into 20,000 ugly adults"—a sentiment that seemingly reflected the tenor of the times.[17] According to a public opinion poll, 67 percent of Americans opposed the idea of bringing Jewish refugee children from Germany into the United States.

The drama played out during the hearings. A few weeks later, senators opposing the bill drafted an amendment to the bill that would apply the twenty thousand child immigrants to the existing German quota, which was already full for the year, thereby nullifying the bill's entire purpose to save the children now. The Senate Immigration Committee adopted the amendment on June 30, 1939. Opposing this amendment, Senator Wagner withdrew the legislation before it could be put to a vote in the committee, a prerequisite for it to be voted on by the entire Congress.

According to the United States Holocaust Memorial Museum,

> On September 1, 1939, Nazi Germany invaded Poland, beginning World War II. In June 1940, many members of the Non-Sectarian Committee for German Refugee Children became active in a new organization, the United States Committee for the Care of European Children (USCOM). After bringing British children to the United States, USCOM also secured passage for refugee children in France, Spain, and Portugal. Through USCOM's efforts, several hundred refugee children were admitted to the United States during the war, far fewer than the 20,000 children proposed by the Wagner-Rogers Bill.[18]

SS *St. Louis*

Meanwhile, in Germany, the noose tightened. There were few escape routes for Jews. In a cynical move by the Nazis, 930 Jewish men, women, and children with Cuban visas were allowed to board the Hamburg-Amerika Line ship SS *St. Louis* on May 13, 1939. When the ship docked in Havana, the Cuban president, Federico Laredo Bru, influenced by German agents, denied entry to all but twenty-two of the refugees. Nazi propagandists used the incident to highlight world apathy toward the Jews.

The American Jewish Joint Distribution Committee stepped in to negotiate with the Cuban government to permit the remaining 907 passengers to land. With no success, the ship left the port. To delay the return to Germany with hope that the United States would admit the passengers, Captain Gustav Schroeder cruised the ship off the Florida coast. American Jewish organizations, several newspapers, and the

St. Louis passengers themselves appealed to U.S. government leaders, foremost among them President Roosevelt, to permit a humanitarian conclusion, but the administration would not make an exception to the country's rigid immigration laws. Newspaper readers nationwide followed the drama surrounding the hapless passengers. One headline from an Oregon newspaper blared, "Jewish Refugees on German Ship Seek Divine Aid in Finding Home."[19] During the ship's return to Europe, the American Jewish Joint Distribution Committee conducted negotiations with European governments, arranging for passengers to disembark in England, France, Belgium, and the Netherlands. The 287 passengers fortunate enough to land in England survived. After Nazi troops invaded the other countries, many of the *St. Louis* passengers were eventually killed. Of the 620 passengers who were sent on to countries other than England, only half survived the war.

The *Quanza*

A year after the *St. Louis* incident, another ship, the *Quanza*, carrying over three hundred Jewish refugees, left Lisbon, Portugal. After disembarking most of the Jews with valid visas in New York, it sailed to Mexico with the eighty remaining refugees who held valid Mexican visas, but Mexico refused to honor the visas and allow the passengers ashore. From there the ship had to return to Europe. When Jewish attorney Jacob Morowitz learned that the ship had docked in Norfolk, Virginia, to refuel, he filed suit against the ship's owners for failing to honor their legal obligations to the refugees on board. The eighty passengers' plight was splashed across U.S. newspaper headlines. First Lady Eleanor Roosevelt intervened with her husband, who in this case reluctantly sent Patrick Malin, a representative of the President's Advisory Committee on Political Refugees, who arranged to have the refugees released despite strong State Department objections. While the *Quanza* refugees landed safely in the United States, the State Department tightened already strict immigration policies to assure such action could not again occur.

In 1940 Assistant Secretary of State Breckinridge Long, reflecting the administration's immigration policy, sent a secret memo to American consulates in Europe directing them to "resort to various administrative devices which would postpone and postpone and postpone the granting of visas . . . We can effectively control non-immigrants by prohibiting the issuance of visas."[20]

Charles Lindbergh and the Defense of American Isolationism

When World War II broke out in Europe on September 1, 1939, the United States adopted an officially neutral position toward Germany and England. Since 1933 Roosevelt's position had been to maintain friendly diplomatic and trade relations with Nazi Germany, and until Kristallnacht in 1938 he never publicly criticized Hitler's persecution of German Jews. American public opinion was overwhelmingly against entering the fight. When asked in a 1938 public opinion poll if persecution of Jews in Europe had been the fault of Jews, 55 percent of Americans polled answered "entirely or partly."[21]

A year later, the America First Committee was created to defend American isolationism and lobby against any American military support of foreign countries. The committee grew into a national membership of eight hundred thousand—a motley following of Roosevelt haters, German American Bundists, Christian Fronters, and assorted antisemites. Henry Ford and Father Charles Coughlin were staunch supporters.

The group's leading spokesperson was an American hero, Charles A. Lindbergh. In 1924 "Lucky Lindy" had become the first person to fly across the Atlantic. When he visited Germany in 1938, Hermann Goring awarded him a Nazi medal on Adolf Hitler's behalf. By 1940–41, Lindbergh was traveling around the United States, delivering antiwar speeches to huge crowds and radio broadcasts that reached millions.

His nationally broadcast speech in Des Moines, Iowa, on September 11, 1941, inflamed the country. "The three most important groups who have been pressing this country toward war," he told the crowd, "are the British, the Jewish and the Roosevelt administration."[22] As for Jews, he claimed, "their greatest danger to this country lies in the their large ownership and influence in our motion pictures, our press, our radio and our government . . . and for reasons which are not American, [they] wish to involve us in war."[23] Lindbergh threatened that if Jews did not stop "agitating for war . . . they will be among the first to feel its consequences."[24]

In her syndicated newspaper column, Dorothy Thompson refuted Lindbergh's claims about Jewish influence. "In fact," she wrote, "if every American Jew died tomorrow it would make not the slightest difference in the policy of the movies, the radio, the government, or the press."[25] She explained that few Jews held important government positions. Secretary of the Treasury Henry Morgenthau Jr. was the only Jewish member of the president's cabinet. Although Jews had been pioneers in the movie and radio industries, non-Jewish boards of directors controlled those businesses. For example, while the *New York Times* was owned by Jews, it had a largely Christian board. The major news services such as the Associated Press and the large newspaper chains such as Hearst and Scripps-Howard were not Jewish.

Jewish groups were also quick to respond to Lindbergh. The American Jewish Committee and the Jewish Labor Committee jointly denounced the "unsupportable charge impugning the patriotism of Americans of the Jewish faith" and noted that Lindbergh was adopting the same divisive language the Nazis were using in Germany to stir up religious and racial hatred.[26] The American Jewish Congress, for its part, declared that American Jews "will neither be bribed nor blackmailed into renouncing their full and equal status as citizens of the United States."[27]

Newspapers around the country editorialized about Lindbergh's speech. The *Omaha World Herald* said, "Many an American must have turned from the radio sick at heart . . . [Lindbergh] took up the slimy weapons of hate and prejudice."[28] The *San Francisco Chronicle* wrote, "The voice is the voice of Lindbergh, but the words are words of Hitler."[29] The *Duluth News Tribune* (MN) added, "Hitler used the technique in Germany of arousing opposition to Jews by charging that they owned the press and radio. . . . It was an untrue charge in Germany. It is a far more vicious falsehood in America."[30] The Hearst chain of newspapers, which had previously supported Lindbergh and his isolationist views, now denounced him as being unpatriotic and un-American.

Politically, the White House response came from the president's press secretary, Stephen Early, who told reporters, "You have seen the outpourings of Berlin the last three or four days. You saw what Lindbergh said last night. I think there is a striking similarity between the two."[31] When Senator Burton Wheeler, speaking to an audience in his home state of Montana, defended Lindbergh, he was met with boos and thrown eggs.

War and Antisemitism

On December 7, 1941, the Japanese attacked Pearl Harbor, leading the United States to declare war on Japan. A few days later, Germany, supporting its Japanese ally, declared war on the United States. Isolationism was no longer up for debate; the United States was now a World War II combatant. Within days, the America First Committee disbanded and the German American Bund was outlawed.

Yet, even as the war progressed, antisemitism did not diminish. In 1942, when asked if Jews have too much power or influence in the United States, 45 percent of polled Americans responded, "Yes." By 1944 the number had increased to 50 percent, and in 1945 to 56 percent.[32]

While over five hundred thousand Jewish men and women served in the armed forces, in a percentage greater than their 3.7 percent of the general U.S. population, rumors flourished that Jews were shirking their military obligations. Making its way through military bases was a parody of "The Marine Hymn," which included the lines, "From the shores of Coney Island looking Eastward to the sea, stands a Kosher Air Raid Warden wearing V for Victory," "Only Christian boys are drafted," and "They will find us Jews selling boots and shoes to the United States Marines."[33]

Knowledge of the "Final Solution"

Rumors of atrocities committed by the German army in Poland against Jewish civilians began surfacing shortly after the war began in 1939, but verification of these facts did not become public knowledge until 1942.

On November 28, 1942, Rabbi Stephen S. Wise held a news conference revealing the Nazi plan to murder all the Jews of Europe—a plan that was by that point well under way. His information came directly from Gerhardt Riegner, a World Jewish Congress representative in Switzerland who had received undisputed confirmation from a reliable Nazi Party member. The telegram stated, "Received alarming report that in Fuhrers headquarters plan discussed and under consideration all Jews in countries occupied or controlled Germany number 3–1/2 to 4 million should after deportation and concentration in East at one blow exterminated to resolve once for all Jewish question in Europe."[34] Rabbi Wise had actually received the telegram in August but Undersecretary of State Sumner Welles had asked him not to publicize the information until it could be officially verified. On November 24 Welles invited Wise to the State Department to "confirm and justify your deepest fears."[35]

The *New York Times* reported on the announcement but buried it on page 10 above a Macy's advertisement. It was apparently too fantastical to believe that a government, even Nazi Germany, could undertake the mass extermination of a people. Three weeks later, the U.S. government, together with the other Allies, publicly acknowledged the truth of Rabbi Wise's report: the Nazi-designed program to eliminate the "Jewish Problem" was being carried out in gas chambers set up in death camps in Nazi-occupied Poland.

Rabbi Wise and other Jewish leaders turned to President Roosevelt for help in saving the remaining Jews of Europe. On December 8, 1942, a delegation representing a cross-section of American Jewish organizations, including the American Jewish Congress, the American Jewish Committee, B'nai B'rith, Agudath Israel, and the Jewish Labor Committee, arrived at the White House. Rabbi Wise, speaking on the group's behalf, appealed to the president "to do all in your power to bring this to the attention of the world and to do all in your power to make an effort to stop it."[36] Roosevelt broadly responded by confirming the horrors taking place in Europe and stating that the government vehemently opposed the attacks on Jews. "We shall do all in our power," Roosevelt concluded, "to be of service to your people in this tragic moment."[37] His words never translated into direct action to save the millions of Jews facing certain death in Europe. The position of the president and his aides was that the only way to end the murder of Jews was to win the war as quickly as possible. But Jewish leaders pointed out that there might not be any Jews left alive in Europe by the time the war was over.

The Bergson Group

While mainstream Jewish organizations adhered to private diplomatic tactics, afraid to inflame antisemitism, a smaller activist organization emerged, determined to publicly challenge government leaders to take action: the Bergson Group. Zionist activist Hillel Kook, who assumed the pseudonym of Peter Bergson to protect his family in Palestine, enlisted the support of well-known entertainment figures, including playwright Moss Hart and Academy Award-winning screenwriter Ben Hecht (*Gone with the Wind, Scarface*), to raise awareness about European Jews. They staged a pageant in Madison Square Garden, featuring a cast of hundreds, including famed actors Edward G. Robinson, Paul Muni, and Stella Adler. The event, which included the emotionally laden "We Will Never Die," written by Ben Hecht, attracted forty thousand viewers on opening night. Then the pageant traveled to five other cities, always with overflowing audiences. In Washington, First Lady Eleanor Roosevelt and over three hundred members of Congress were among the attendees. The Bergson Group created and purchased full-page provocative advertisements in leading American newspapers. When in 1942 the Romanian government offered to free Jews with the payment of travel expenses only, Ben Hecht's full-page advertisement, printed in the *New York Times*, displayed the provocative headline, "For Sale to Humanity 70,000 Jews. Guaranteed Human Beings at $50 a Piece."

Bergson's group initiated imaginative public relations events. In October 1943 they organized the only public rally in Washington for rescue: a group of four hundred Orthodox rabbis marched to the Capitol, the Lincoln Memorial, and then Lafayette Park across the street from the White House to deliver a petition to the president calling for the creation of a special agency to save Jews "on a large scale." Vice President Henry Wallace met with the delegation. President Roosevelt claimed to be too busy and refused. The next day, photos of the four hundred bearded rabbis dressed in their distinctive black clothing standing on the steps of the U.S. Capitol served as a visual statement of defiance in American newspapers.

Some mainstream Jewish leaders were uncomfortable with such protests. Rabbi Stephen S. Wise called the march a "stunt." He and likeminded Jewish officials feared that outspokenness by Jews could lead to increased antisemitism.[38] Shaped by his strong loyalty to President Roosevelt and his policies, Wise was discomfited by Bergson's independence and his willingness to publicly challenge FDR on the Jewish refugee issue.[39] Wise's effectiveness was also affected by his advanced age, his health struggles, and his reluctance to think outside the box.[40] Yet the conventional protest tactics Wise favored in the prewar era were not as effective as the more unorthodox approach adopted by the Bergson Group in response to mass murder in the 1940s.[41] Years later, Marie Syrkin, an official of a small American Jewish organization during that period, recalled the sentiment then common within the Jewish leadership: "We felt we were good American citizens and we had to do what the American government wanted us to do, and the last thing the American government wanted was disturbance, uproar, change in immigration quotas, anything they thought would impede the war effort. We did nothing to rock the boat."[42]

War Refugee Board

In late 1943 Treasury Department officials discovered that their colleagues in the State Department were quietly blocking assistance for European Jews. This became apparent after a Jewish organization's application to send funds to Europe to aid refugees went unanswered. It had first gone to Treasury, where it was approved, and then met with delays when the State Department was asked to authorize it. Investigating the delays, Treasury staffer Josiah E. DuBois Jr. uncovered evidence that State Department officials were suppressing news about the mass killings and obstructing opportunities to rescue refugees. To hamper the Treasury Department's inquiries, Assistant Secretary of State Breckinridge Long doctored a telegram (sent by the State Department to U.S. diplomats in Switzerland) that revealed State's suppression of atrocity news, but DuBois discovered the subterfuge. When he alerted Secretary of the Treasury Henry Morgenthau Jr., Morgenthau instructed DuBois and his colleagues to prepare a report documenting what they had uncovered.

DuBois delivered the report to Morgenthau at the end of December. Provocatively titled *Report to the Secretary on the Acquiescence of This Government in the Murder of the Jews*, it directly accused the State Department of intentionally blocking the rescue of European Jewry. Morgenthau changed the document title to the less provocative *Report to the President*, and brought it to President Roosevelt. Meanwhile, members of Congress had been pressing the president to create a government agency to rescue refugees, and the Bergson Group had been sponsoring full-page newspaper ads likewise calling for the establishment of such an agency. Concerned by the growing controversy— especially in an election year—FDR agreed to create the War Refugee Board (WRB) "to take action for the immediate rescue from the Nazis as many as possible of the persecuted minorities of Europe."[43] The new board was given only meager funding; 90 percent of its budget came from two Jewish organizations, the American Jewish Joint Distribution Committee, and the World Jewish Congress. Often at great personal risk, WRB representatives in Turkey, Switzerland, North Africa, Portugal, and Italy used those funds to bribe border officials, create forged identification papers and other documents to protect refugees from the Nazis, and other lifesaving activities.

At the WRB's request, Swedish businessman Raoul Wallenberg traveled to German-occupied Budapest, the capital of Hungary, to aid Jews there; in the spring and summer of 1944, the Nazis deported hundreds of thousands of Hungarian Jews to the Auschwitz death camp.. With the WRB's assistance, Wallenberg created protective passports that helped save the lives of many tens of thousands of Hungarian Jews. The WRB also tried to convince the Allies and neutral countries to create temporary havens—which they called "free ports"—for Jewish refugees, but President Roosevelt was willing to admit just one such group: 982 refugees who were housed at Fort Ontario in upstate New York. "To avoid a conflict with existing strict immigration laws, the president made it clear that the refugees 'will be brought into this country outside the regular immigration procedure . . . [and] at the end of the war they will be returned to their homeland.' In effect the refugees would the personal guests of the president without the right to immigrate to the United States."[44]

Historians estimate that about two hundred thousand Jews and twenty thousand non-Jews were rescued through the War Refugee Board's efforts. While numerically this was a small percentage, given that six million Jews were killed during the war, the board's unflagging work in a relatively short time period (January 1944–May 1945) undermined the Roosevelt administration's longstanding claim that there was no way to rescue Jews except by winning the war.

Assaults on American Jews

Meanwhile, as the war raged in Europe, antisemitic activities persisted in the United States. Father Coughlin and the Christian Front continued to incite hate, blaming Jews for every ill in society. Jews were physically assaulted and synagogues and Jewish cemeteries desecrated around the country. Swastikas were painted on Jewish-owned storefronts. Antisemitic literature was freely circulated, leading to the introduction of a congressional bill that would allow the Postmaster General to stop the distribution of hateful propaganda through the mail. The ensuing hearings revealed a widespread use of the postal service to spread Nazi and anti-Jewish messages, but the bill never passed due to constitutional concerns regarding free speech.

In cities with large Jewish populations, particularly New York City and Boston, marauding gangs of mostly Irish-American youths viciously attacked Jewish children on the streets. This continuing violence received newspaper coverage but little reaction from local police. In 1943 a reporter for New York's *pm* newspaper, investigating events in Boston, documented "an organized campaign of terrorism against Jewish boys and girls in the city's Dorchester section" in which older boys and girls went hunting for Jews to attack while smashing windows of synagogues and Jewish-owned shops.[45] The governor, mayor, and police were maintaining a "hands off policy, despite numerous protests from Dorchester residents while gangs of marauders roam the streets of Dorchester at night, screaming imprecations against its residents."[46] At a news conference the next day, Massachusetts Governor Leveritt Saltonstall called the article's allegations untrue and ordered the reporter out of the State House. In response, the editor of *pm* sent a telegram to the governor explaining that the article "told how Jewish children are beaten and abused by gangs of toughs because they are Jews and how Christian Front anti-Semitism has led to vandalism, also directed against Jews. . . . We printed these things, Governor, because they go to the heart of American Fascism."[47]

Boston's mayor, Maurice Tobin, excused the violence as simply "a matter of juvenile hoodlumism" and not as hateful events. "This hoodlumism," he stated, "must be eliminated at once."[48] Methodist Bishop G. Bromley Oxnam of Boston responded, "The beating of Jewish boys is not the work of hoodlums. . . . It is not a prank that can be passed by with complacency. . . . Far from home our sons are fighting to destroy fascism. It must not be allowed to exist at home."[49] Governor Saltonstall later apologized to the reporter, saying the article was a rude awakening for him, and issued a statement decrying antisemitism as a menace to democracy. He and local leaders tried to control the violence without much success. The attacks continued.

In New York City, there was widespread desecration of Jewish cemeteries. Orthodox men, including rabbis easily identified by their clothing, were attacked on the streets. Even Jewish air raid wardens were attacked while on duty. Yet, Mayor Fiorello LaGuardia viewed the incidents as unorganized incidents while the city's largely Irish-American police often described them as simply boyish pranks.

Jewish Responses to American Antisemitism

American Jewish organizations frequently appealed to government authorities to intervene against antisemitism. In 1944, for example, the Anti-Defamation League of B'nai Brith (today known simply as the Anti-Defamation League) called on New York City's mayor to investigate and take steps to stop the antisemitic violence and vandalism there. "The assault incidents have a uniform pattern," the league explained. "In each case the hoodlum demands to know the religion of his intended victim. If the victim admits he is Jewish . . . an assault ensues. . . . The situation cannot be described as ordinary juvenile delinquency."[50] The ADL presented signed affidavits from Jewish children who were attacked and rabbis whose synagogues were desecrated.

The American Jewish Congress organized the National Conference to Combat Anti-Semitism. For two days in February 1944, one thousand delegates gathered in New York City's Pennsylvania Hotel to hear from prominent political and religious leaders. Senator Alexander Wiley of Wisconsin told the assembly, "We must make sure that in America there is no room for class persecution, race persecution, anti-semitism, or tauting [sic] of class tensions."[51] President Roosevelt wrote to the conference attendees, "Whoever condones or participates in anti-Semitism plays Hitler's game. There is no place in the lives or thoughts of true Americans for anti-Semitism."[52] The governors of twenty states sent supportive messages. While the American Jewish

Congress and the ADL took public stances supporting governmental responses to antisemitism, some national Jewish groups such as the American Jewish Committee preferred quieter approaches. They did not want to be portrayed as disloyal, concerned only with Jewish issues while America was at war. By keeping out of the public limelight, they believed they would not provide yet other targets for attack.

The Four Chaplains

Other groups focused on interfaith efforts. The National Conference of Christians and Jews (NCCJ), founded in 1928 to counteract Henry Ford's antisemitic publications, held meetings nationwide during the 1940s, including "Brotherhood Week" programs gathering together clergy and lay people from all religions with messages of mutual understanding.

The ideal of Jews and Christians linked in religious harmony and shared patriotism was illustrated by a dramatic incident in early 1943. A German submarine torpedoed a troop ship, the *Dorchester*, as it crossed the Atlantic, ultimately drowning more than six hundred of the nine hundred soldiers and sailors aboard. Also on board were four army chaplains: Catholic priest John Washington, Methodist minister George Fox, Reformed Church minister Clark Poling, and Rabbi Alexander Goode. As the *Dorchester* began to sink, the four chaplains maintained order and handed out life jackets. When they ran out of jackets, the chaplains removed their own and handed them to soldiers. Survivors later related how the four chaplains linked arms and prayed aloud as the ship went down. The story of the chaplains' heroism and unity resonated strongly with the American public. The four were posthumously awarded Purple Hearts, Distinguished Service Crosses, and a Congressional Medal of Valor. In 1948 the Post Office released a stamp depicting the four men with the words "interfaith in action." Memorials, chapels, and stained-glass church windows at military bases were dedicated in their honor. In 1988 Congress passed a resolution making each February Third "Four Chaplains Day" in the United States.

Fig. 12. U.S. stamp commemorating the heroism of four chaplains, including Rabbi Alexander Goode, who gave up their lives to save sailors aboard the sinking *S.S. Dorchester*. Alexander Mitrofanov / Alamy Stock Photo.

The Postwar Climate

In the aftermath of World War II, antisemitism declined in the United States. Americans now associated antisemitism with the hated enemy whom they had just defeated on the battlefield. In addition, the better economic conditions that prevailed in the postwar era eased social strains and conflicts. "Tribute for the turnabout in American anti-Semitic feelings," wrote historian Leonard Dinnerstein, "must be given both to Jews and Gentiles. Anti-Semitism did not disappear by 1950 but a larger segment of the American public realized that bigotry and discrimination were not in the national interest. Hence many American Gentiles joined organized Jewry's attempt to blot our manifestations of intolerance."[53] Even so, Jews continued to face discrimination in employment, housing, education, and social settings.

Looking back on the fight against antisemitism in the 1930s and 1940s, many Jewish leaders decided they would need to be more proactive in combatting prejudice in the years ahead. A new generation of social workers, lawyers, and trained Jewish communal professionals gradually replaced the older generation of organizational officials. Their efforts often emphasized scholarly research into the causes of prejudice and educational and public relations materials to combat bigotry through the mass media. Now that overt antisemitism had diminished, the fight for full legal and social equality was about to begin.

9

Into the Mainstream

The end of World War II in 1945 marked the beginning of a new era for American Jews.

On the whole, Jewish and non-Jewish soldiers had experienced positive interactions during the war. In the proceeding years, in the minds of many Americans, Judaism became elevated to one of America's three major religions, and Americans began to refer to "Judeo-Christian" values. Returning Jewish soldiers took advantage of government aid to attend college, favorable loans to buy new homes, and suburban housing developments on former agricultural fields. Jewish families left crowded, urban, Jewish ghettoes for sprawling suburbs where lawns were green and the air was clean. Urban neighborhoods had provided close-knit, cohesive community—kosher shops, synagogues, and Jewish neighbors, all within walking distance. In the suburbs, while connecting with their new non-Jewish neighbors, Jews began to reinvent their Jewish environments, building synagogues and cultural centers.

Discrimination in Housing

In the 1940s United States, one of the largest housing development builders was a father-and-son company called Levitt and Sons, whose iconic "Levittowns" have become synonymous with the growth of suburbs in the postwar era. Led by William Levitt, the company's earliest homes were sold with racially discriminatory deed covenants that precluded African Americans from becoming homeowners. This was not an unknown practice. For years, restrictive covenants of other homebuilders had also been used to keep Jews, African Americans, and other racial minorities from purchasing property in particular neighborhoods.

In January 1948 the issue surfaced at the level of the Supreme Court. Attorneys presented their arguments in *Shelley v. Kraemer*, a case on the legality of restrictive covenants; the case actually involved four similar cases, among them that of the Shelleys, an African American family sued by their new neighbors after buying a house in a St. Louis neighborhood which had a restrictive covenant. Various advocacy organizations, including Jewish groups, understood *Shelley v. Kraemer*'s implications for other minorities as well, and submitted amicus curiae, or "friend of the court," briefs on the Shelleys' behalf. The American Jewish Committee, Anti-Defamation League, Jewish War Veterans, and Jewish Labor Committee submitted a joint brief stating in part, "Organizations dedicated to the defense of American democracy cannot stand by silently while the residential areas of our cities and towns are overrun by a spreading flood of restrictive covenants banning occupancy by members of specific racial or religious groups."[1]

The Supreme Court ruled that while restrictive covenants were not necessarily unconstitutional, state enforcement of them violated the Equal Protection Clause of the Fourteenth Amendment. In other words, the case represented a hollow victory for African American activists and their allies. Restrictive covenants could continue as long as they were enforced in private.

As already mentioned, restrictive covenants also affected Jews. About a decade later the United States Commission on Civil Rights would declare, "In practically every large city in the United States and in its suburbs there is discrimination against Jews in housing."[2] As an example, the Commission reported that the New York City suburb of Bronxville had achieved the status that "Hitler called Judenrein — free of Jews."[3]

Discrimination in Employment and College Admissions

Discrimination in employment also persisted. Newspaper help wanted ads still could advertise that an employer wanted only Christian applicants. In 1945 New York State passed the Ives-Quinn Bill, which prohibited bias in employment—the first state to do so. By 1949 seven other states followed suit, but regulations were haphazard and weak if they existed at all.

During a 1949 hearing to create a fair employment bill, Rep. Clare Hoffman of Michigan (who also distributed anti-Jewish literature through the Congressional Record) stated, "There is no such thing as discrimination against Jews. In this country, if I understand the situation clearly, the Jews have the world by the tail. They are on top."[4] Stronger antidiscrimination rules would only emerge on the federal level with the passage of the landmark Civil Rights Act of 1964 and the Fair Housing Act of 1968 (see chapter 10).

Although discrimination in higher education began to ebb in the years after the war, some colleges and universities continued to discriminate against Jewish applicants, particularly in the graduate fields of medicine and law. The American Jewish Congress and other organizations documented the problem to provide government agencies with proof of discrimination. Many schools did not readily admit to discrimination, but data supplied by the Jewish organization B'nai B'rith showed the number of Jews in law and medical schools had decreased between 1935 and 1946 even though the overall number of students in those professions rose over the same period. In 1947 the Truman administration published this data as a part of a larger report entitled "Higher Education for American Democracy."

In 1948 New York State barred religious and ethnic discrimination for admission to any college or university in the state. A few other states, including Massachusetts and New Jersey, followed that example, but such legal action varied from state to state. It would take several decades before federal antidiscrimination laws applied to the entire country.

Discrimination in Admitting DPs to America

After the war, the United States and its allies had another major issue to resolve: thousands of Holocaust survivors were now stateless, their former homes gone, their families and friends dead. These people, known as "displaced persons" or DPs, became the subject of a prolonged debate over emigration from Europe and immigration to new homes. Aided by American funding, many DPs managed to clandestinely reach British-controlled Palestine. In 1948 they were integrated into the newly created State of Israel.

In the same year, Congress passed the Displaced Persons Act. Provisions in the law allowed over two hundred thousand DPs to enter the country, but in an ironic twist, the bill favored non-Jews. Preference was given to ethnic Germans, with 40 percent to come from Baltic countries newly under communist rule, and 30 percent of those admitted had to be farmers. (Jewish farmers were a rarity in Europe.) With tongue-in-cheek, the *Wisconsin Jewish Chronicle* reminded the bill's opponents that the Jewish arrivals were "biblical descendants of David the Sheepherder." President Truman stated plainly, "The bill discriminates in callous fashion against displaced persons of the Jewish faith."[5] He argued that the main discriminatory mechanism in the bill—a clause that opened immigration to DPs who had been in the war zone before a certain date—also discriminated against Catholics.

Jews did not have to look too far to understand why the Displaced Persons Act had been written in this way. West Virginia Senator Chapman Revercomb told colleagues, "We could solve this DP problem all right if we could work out some bill that would keep out the Jews."[6] Congressman Ed Gossett of Texas called the Jewish DPs "an injection of virus in our national bloodstream which is already becoming polluted."[7]

Jewish organizations, as well as President Truman, appealed to Congress to amend the law by raising the entry number of displaced persons to four hundred thousand and removing the regulations that blatantly discriminated against Jews. Conversely, opponents of accepting DPs offered a number of ongoing arguments. In 1948 during debate about the first law, one member of the Daughters of the American Revolution defended a resolution opposing any immigration outside the quotas by arguing the United States had as many immigrants as could possibly be integrated. Two years earlier, Senator Chapman Revercomb (West Virginia) of the Immigration Subcommittee of the Senate Judiciary Committee had drawn a connection between DPs and communism, writing in a report: "Certainly it would be a tragic blunder to bring into our midst those imbued with a communistic line of thought when one of the most important tasks of this government today is to combat and eradicate Communism from this country."[8] The leading antisemitic pamphleteer and speaker Gerald L. K. Smith, an avowed racist with a following in the thousands, declared, "We are aware of the fact that there are many fine Christian people in Europe who should permitted to enter the United States . . . These fine specimens of responsible citizens have been kept out, while the Jew-Communist herds have been allowed to flood in. This situation must be corrected."[9]

Ultimately, however, the opposition would not carry the day. On June 16, 1950, President Truman signed a new Displaced Persons law that wiped out the discriminatory provisions in the 1948 law and expanded the number of people admitted to the country. Although it had taken five years, U.S. immigration law finally facilitated the entry of more Jewish DPs into America.

Going Public to Combat Hate

In the shadow of the war, Jewish defense organizations began working with non-Jewish religious groups, the media, and government to combat hate. Popular magazines featured articles about everyday barriers ordinary Jews faced and how average Americans could help overcome hate. In 1948, the ADL produced a series of radio programs on civil rights that aired countrywide on the National Broadcasting Company network.

Two popular films also highlighted the pervasiveness of bigotry and hate. *Gentleman's Agreement*, winner of the 1947 Oscar for Best Picture, told the story of a Christian reporter who went undercover as a Jew to reveal the social discrimination affecting Jews in their daily lives. *Crossfire*, also released that year, exposed the pervasiveness of antisemitism in American life. On a more positive note, best-selling novels about World War II by Jewish writers such as Norman Mailer's *The Naked and the Dead* and Irwin Shaw's *The Young Lions* brought out the bravery and contributions of Jewish soldiers during World War II, countering the myth that Jews had shirked military responsibilities.

Jews and the House Un-American Activities Committee

Following World War II, the U.S. engaged in a "Cold War" with its former wartime ally, the Soviet Union. As Winston Churchill famously declared in 1946, an "Iron Curtain" descended across Europe, separating the communist-led bloc in Central and Eastern Europe from its Western counterparts.

In 1949 the Soviet Union announced possession of an atomic bomb, thereby joining the United States as the world's only other atomic power. Fear and disbelief gripped America. Many thought the Soviet Union could only have achieved such a scientific advance with help from American traitors. Similar to the early 1920s, another "Red Scare" gripped the United States in a vise of paranoid fear. Many Americans feared that communists were infiltrating the United States and its institutions.

The belief that Jews and communism were intertwined persisted. In Congress, as the HUAC swung into action to expose alleged pro-communist activities in government and the media, committee member Rep. John Rankin of Mississippi, perhaps the most avowed antisemite in Congress (though he did not limit his prejudices to Jews, voting against policies meant to benefit African Americans and Asians as well), accused Jews of trying to "enslave the white people of America, to destroy the American way of life and to wreck everything for which the great mass of the American people stand."[10] Without any evidence, he called Albert Einstein a communist and urged his deportation from the United States. He used words like "Jew" or "Yid" in pejorative ways, such as "Jew boy," "Jew lawyer," and "Jew reporter" (a denigrating antisemitic tactic to this day). In 1943, at the height of World War II, he had declared before the House of Representatives, "I hesitate to use the word 'Jew' in any speech in this House, for whenever I do a little group of communistic Jews in this country howl to high heaven. They seem to think it is all right for them to abuse gentiles and stir up race trouble all over the country, but when you refer to one of them, they cry 'anti-Semitism' or accuse you of being pro-Nazi."[11] Later, during a HUAC hearing, Rankin stated, "The information we have is that 75 percent of the members of the Communist Party in this country are Jews."[12] When the committee chair protested that the committee had no such information, Rankin responded emphatically, without any proof, "I do."[13]

HUAC's investigation into communism in America targeted Hollywood—particularly Jews who worked in film. Hollywood was not altogether a new place for antisemites to look for Jewish influence; Charles Lindbergh, for one, had alluded to Jews' supposed influence in the film industry in 1941. Now, committee chair Martin Dies bluntly charged, "There are too many Jews in Hollywood" while his colleague John Rankin ranted that the film industry was "insidiously trying to spread subversive propaganda, poison the minds of your children, distort the history of our country and discredit Christianity."[14] Rankin, like Henry Ford decades earlier, gleefully revealed the birth names of famous Jewish entertainers who had changed them in order to succeed in show business at a time when being Jewish could be a handicap.

The most famous of the witnesses brought before HUAC were the "Hollywood Ten": ten screenwriters and film directors hauled before the committee in 1947 to testify about their so-called connections to the Communist Party in the United States. Six of the ten—John Howard Lawson (born Levy), Alvah Bessie, Herbert Biberman, Lester Cole, Albert Maltz, and Samuel Ornitz—were Jewish, thereby conflating "communist" and "Jew" in the public eye. Indeed, an American Jewish Congress survey the following year found that 21 percent of Americans believed "most Jews are Communists."[15]

The "Hollywood Ten" refused to cooperate, citing their constitutional rights against self-incrimination. All ten were sentenced to brief prison sentences and fined $1,000 each for being in contempt of Congress. More importantly, shortly after their refusal to testify, film industry leaders, among them the Jewish heads of major studies, including Warner Brothers, Paramount, and Columbia, met at the Waldorf-Astoria Hotel in New York City in order to denounce the ten. The so-called Waldorf Statement issued by the Motion Picture Association of America tried to distance the industry from the accused and set the precedent for how the industry would navigate the new political climate. Torn from their professions and isolated from former friends, members of the Hollywood Ten took decades to recover. Some continued to work under pseudonyms, and others found employment abroad.

Additionally, hundreds of other entertainment professionals, including many Jews—Zero Mostel, Arthur Miller, Leonard Bernstein, Gypsy Rose Lee, Judy Holliday, and Artie Shaw, among others—were blacklisted and denied employment simply by having been accused of disloyalty.

Fear of communist infiltration into American institutions continued to grip the country. Many Americans saw communists and traitors lurking everywhere. People simply accused of liberal views lost their jobs or were blacklisted from their professions.

In 1950 the junior United States senator from Wisconsin realized the political potential of hunting alleged communists. Joseph McCarthy shocked Washington when he claimed that fifty-seven "card-carrying communists" were working in the State Department. This began a period characterized by McCarthy's bombastic style and unrelenting pursuit of communists, even in cases where he had little evidence to support his claims. Three years later, McCarthy used his position as chair of the Government Operations Committee and the Permanent Subcommittee on Investigations to carry on televised, circus-like hearings. McCarthy branded anyone who invoked their Fifth Amendment rights under the U.S. Constitution a "Fifth-Amendment communist." Millions watched as he accused hundreds of Americans of disloyalty, subversion, and/or treason without evidence, destroying their reputations and lives in the process.

These hearings also caused apprehension among Jews. However, McCarthy's record on Jews was more ambiguous than John Rankin's blatant antisemitism. He had Jews on his staff even as most American Jews disapproved of his actions in Washington. Yet, McCarthy never repudiated the support he received from notorious antisemites, including Gerald L.K. Smith and William Dudley Pelley.

In 1954, as McCarthy's influence in the Senate was waning, Albert Einstein observed, "America is incomparably less endangered by its own Communists than by the hysterical hunt for the few Communists that are here."[16]

Julius and Ethel Rosenberg

In this environment of fear, news of a spy ring that had given secret American atomic bomb information to the Soviet Union during World War II ratcheted up anti-communist fervor and deep concerns in the American Jewish community. That the ring was purportedly composed entirely of Jews created anticipation of an increase in antisemitism. FBI agents arrested Julius Rosenberg in July 1950, and then his wife Ethel a few weeks later. Involved in the plot were Soviet informant Harry Gold, alleged coconspirator Morton Sobell, and Julius Rosenberg's brother-in-law David Greenglass.

The trial of Julius and Ethel Rosenberg began on March 6, 1951. Gold had already pleaded guilty and received a thirty-year jail sentence. Greenglass also pleaded guilty but had not yet been sentenced. The Rosenbergs, the alleged organizers, were charged with conspiracy to commit espionage. Greenglass and his wife Ruth were the main witnesses against them. Harry Gold confirmed their testimony. On March 29, the jury found the Rosenbergs guilty. A week later, Judge Irving Kaufman sentenced them to death. After two years of failed legal appeals, they were executed at Sing Sing Prison on June 19, 1953. While some considered the trial an antisemitic plot, since the jury that

Fig. 13. Speaking at a November 23, 1953, B'nai Brith dinner celebrating the fortieth anniversary of the Anti-Defamation League's founding, President Dwight D. Eisenhower delivers a nationally televised address stressing the importance of supporting civil liberties for all. Everett Collection Historical / Alamy Stock Photo.

convicted them had no Jewish members, the judge, the prosecuting attorney, and the principal witnesses were Jewish. Even to this day, many aspects of the trial, including the alleged involvement of Ethel Rosenberg in the plot, remain contested.

Concerned about how the trial would affect Jews, Jewish American leaders went out of their way to demonstrate that they were loyal Americans and did not support communism. In 1952 Jewish organizations, including the American Jewish Committee, the American Jewish Congress, the Anti-Defamation League, the Jewish Labor Committee, the Jewish War Veterans, and the Union of American Hebrew Congregations, responding to a communist-affiliated group's efforts to inject antisemitism into the Rosenberg trial, issued a joint public statement denouncing the communists in the Rosenberg case: "We condemn these efforts to mislead the people of this country by unsupported charges that the religious ancestry of the defendants was a factor in the case. We denounce this fraudulent effort to confuse and manipulate public opinion for ulterior political purposes."[17]

The Jewish community could only have breathed a sigh of relief when the Rosenberg case ended without any meaningful backlash. Although American Jews continued to face antisemitic challenges, they were now comfortable enough to move on to the next chapter: the fight against racial and religious discrimination in America.

10

Civil Rights and Legal Rights

In the late 1940s into the 1950s, many Jews realized they needed to become more proactive, and in new ways, in fighting against discrimination and for civil rights. They had to broaden the fight against bigotry and intolerance to include everyone, not just Jews. They had to work with other minorities to overcome prejudice. They also needed to join among themselves to provide a united approach. In 1944 the American Jewish Committee, American Jewish Congress, and Anti-Defamation League joined the Jewish Labor Committee to create the National Community Relations Advisory Council (NCRAC), aimed at securing equality in education and civil rights for all. Their lawyers joined in many legal cases. They won some. They lost some, but each case sought to erode the seemingly solid wall of prejudice and discrimination.

Prayer in Public Schools

The First Amendment to the United States Constitution lay at the heart of many legal fights. Adopted in 1791 as part of the Bill of Rights, it stated, "Congress shall make no law respecting an establishment of religion, or prohibiting the free exercise thereof, or abridging the freedom of speech, or of the press, or the right of the people peaceably to assemble, and to petition the Government for a redress of grievances." For Jews, it came to mean that the U.S. government could not promote one religion over another or restrict an individual's religious practices, including the wearing of religious clothing such as a kippah or tallit.

In the twentieth century, a series of legal conflicts over religious rights would lead the U.S. Supreme Court to gradually overturn a number of accepted practices that infringed on First Amendment rights.

For many Jewish children attending public school in the early part of the century, the day began with a teacher-led prayer and Bible reading. Often the prayers and readings reflected majority Protestant beliefs, but Jewish parents largely kept quiet, not wanting to stir up antisemitic feelings in their communities. By the 1940s, however, Jews began to insert themselves into the debate about the role of religion in public schools. "Experience has shown," the American Jewish Congress later wrote, "that whenever religion intrudes into the public school, sooner or later Jewish children will be hurt."[1]

In 1940 the Champaign, Illinois, school board established a released time program similar to other public-school initiatives elsewhere in the country. Each week, representatives of various religions entered the public schools to provide religious instruction to students of their respective faiths. James McCollum's parents, who were atheists, sued the school board for violating the Establishment Clause of the First Amendment, which said, "Congress shall make no law respecting an establishment of religion." In December 1947 the McCollums's case made its way to the Supreme Court. In response, NCRAC and the Synagogue Council of America, another organization founded to unite different factions of American Jews, joined in the case with an amicus curiae brief supporting the McCollums, which stated, "As Americans and as spokesmen for religious bodies, lay and clerical, we . . . deem any breach in the wall separating church and state as jeopardizing the political and religious freedoms that wall was intended to protect."[2] In a landmark decision issued in the new year, the court ruled against the school board, saying that public schools could not aid religious groups by requiring student attendance in school to receive instruction from them.

School systems found a way around the court's ruling. Instead of inviting religious teachers into the schools, they now sent students out of their buildings to local religious institutions and prohibited teachers and administrators from making announcements or comments about the program in class. This version of released time required nonparticipating students to remain in school while the other students left the building. In New York City in 1948, two parents, Tessim Zorach, a Protestant, and Esta Gluck, a Jew, filed a suit against Andrew G. Clauson and other members of the New York City Board of Education, citing "utilization of the state's tax-established and tax-supported public school system to aid religious groups to spread their faith."[3] Again, with assistance from the American Jewish Committee, the American Jewish Congress, and the Anti-Defamation League, the case reached the U.S. Supreme Court. This time, in *Zorach v. Clausen*, the court upheld the idea of released time, since the religious instruction in question took place outside a school building and students were not forced to attend.

But that did not end the fight. Seeking to maintain a daily prayer in classrooms, the New York State Board of Regents created and directed public school teachers to lead students in a nonsectarian prayer they thought would satisfy the major religions: "Almighty God, we acknowledge our dependence upon Thee, and we beg Thy blessings upon us, our parents, our teachers and our Country."[4] Although saying the prayer was optional, some parents in New Hyde Park, New York, still objected on the grounds that New York State was violating the First Amendment by directing *any* prayer in the public schools. Organizing and filing suit, they gained American Jewish Committee and Anti-Defamation League support as the case, *Engel v. Vitale*, worked through the legal system.

Other religious groups did not always respond favorably to Jewish support for the *Engel* case. The Catholic journal *America* warned that Jewish support for the ban could increase antisemitism among Catholics by painting Jews "into a corner of social and cultural alienation."[5] Another Catholic journal, *Commonweal*, responded, "The Jew has to be perfectly free to argue for this or that constitutional or political position."[6] The two Jewish organizations persisted, and two other Jewish organizations, the Synagogue Council of American and NCRAC, joined the case with amicus curiae briefs when *Engel v. Vitale* finally made its way to the Supreme Court. In 1962 the court ruled on the matter in another landmark decision: all school prayers were indeed unconstitutional. American Jews, who had locked arms in order to combat prayer in public schools and advocate for a strict wall of separation between church and state, applauded the decision. The ruling was another step in removing religious practices from public schools.

In recent years, however, U.S. Supreme Court rulings appear to be whittling away at First Amendment rights. For example, a 2022 case involved a situation in a rural part of Maine without public secondary schools. In Maine, some "school administrative units" (similar to school boards) do not operate their own secondary schools and instead arrange for local children to attend private schools. However, state law specified that approved private schools had to be "nonsectarian in accordance with the First Amendment."[7] Three sets of parents—David and Amy Carson and Alan and Judith Gillis (whose children attended the Bangor Christian Schools) and Troy and Angela Nelson (whose child attended Temple Academy)—sued Pender Makin, Maine's education commissioner, alleging that the state's nonsectarian requirement violated another constitutional principle: the right to freely exercise (i.e., practice) one's own religion. This time, the Supreme Court ruled 6–3 in *Carson v. Makin* that when a state subsidizes private schools, it must allow families to use those taxpayer funds to pay for religious schools as well. In a dissent, Justice Sonia Sotomayer warned that the court had "upended constitutional doctrine" and expressed "growing concern for where this Court will lead us next."[8] Yet, not all American Jews viewed this decision negatively. Some within the Orthodox Jewish community welcomed the possibility of governmental support in funding yeshivot and Jewish day schools.

Shortly thereafter, the court heard a case involving Joe Kennedy, an assistant high school football coach in Bremerton, Washington, who began a practice of kneeling in prayer at the fifty-yard line after games. Players began joining him. The school board asked the coach not to pray in his official capacities as a coach and later declined to renew his contract. He sued, arguing that he was not acting in his role as a coach when he prayed after games. Accepting his argument, the Supreme Court ruled 6–3 in *Kennedy v. Bremerton* that the school system was preventing the coach from praying privately, thereby affecting his religious rights. Commenting on the case, American Jewish Committee general counsel Marc Stern warned, "The Court's see-no-evil approach to the coach's prayer will encourage those who seek to proselytize within the public schools to do so with the Court's blessing."[9]

Jews and the NAACP

In 1896 the U.S. Supreme Court in *Plessy v. Ferguson* had declared that segregation by race did not automatically mean racial discrimination. The court held that so long as separate facilities were equal, they did not violate the equal protection clause of the Fourteenth Amendment. "Separate but equal"—the complete separation of the races—became a way of life, particularly but not exclusively in the South, into the middle of the twentieth century. In reality, some Jews drew on their own experiences and traditions to realize that separate but equal meant separate and unequal. They pointed to the basic equality of human beings created in the image of God as taught in Genesis; the core teaching to "love your neighbor as yourself" (Lev. 19:18); the multiple commandments to pursue justice; and the historical memory of the Exodus, which included repeated admonition not to oppress others because "you were strangers in the land of Egypt."

The 1909 founding of the NAACP—in response to a major race riot in Springfield, Illinois (home of Abraham Lincoln), on August 14–16, 1908, that involved a mob of some five thousand white men and resulted in sixteen deaths and extensive property damage—was a milestone in the struggle for civil rights. Founded by African American activists and liberal whites, including several Jews, the NAACP aimed to expose racial prejudice and promote the equality of Black Americans. Jews were involved with the NAACP from the beginning. According to historian Nancy Weiss, four Jews signed the call for a meeting that is often seen as the organization's founding moment, and at least four Jews (only one of whom had signed the initial call) were on the NAACP's first board of directors. Perhaps more importantly, Jews served in prominent positions within the NAACP. Two brothers, Joel and Arthur Spingarn, served in various executive positions, including that of president; Kivie Kaplan served as president from 1966 until his death in 1975.

From its inception, the NAACP realized the importance of legal action. One of its early campaigns tried to criminalize lynching nationally, rather than leave it to state and local officials, who frequently turned a blind eye to racially motivated violence. Jewish lawyers played an important part in early legal activities, especially Nathan Margold, who set the NAACP's long-term plan and established the legal strategy the organization would follow to challenge segregation. Later, from the 1930s onward, African Americans lawyers like Charles H. Houston and Thurgood Marshall led the organization's legal battles. In 1940 leaders established the NAACP Legal Defense and Educational Fund (LDF), with Marshall, later to become the first African American Supreme Court Justice, as chief counsel. Continuing the legal work that already occupied much of the NAACP's attention, the LDF began bringing pivotal cases before the Supreme Court, including *Shelley v. Kraemer*, which declared that restrictive and discriminatory housing covenants could not be enforced (see chapter 9).

A number of civil rights lawyers also worked for the major Jewish defense agencies. As Rabbi David Saperstein, director of the Religious Action Center for Reform Judaism, explained on the fiftieth anniversary of the landmark *Brown v. Board of Education* decision, there "was an implicit recognition that Jews wouldn't be safe in America until they created a country with no room for discrimination."[10] In like vein, Supreme Court Justice Felix Frankfurter, an Ashkenazi Jew born in Vienna, once wrote in a dissenting opinion, "One who belongs to the most vilified and persecuted minority in history is not likely to be insensitive to the freedoms guaranteed by the Constitution."[11]

Julius Rosenwald was president of the mail-order giant Sears, Roebuck, and Company. He was also a great philanthropist, partially responsible for building more than fifty-three hundred schools for African American children in the Deep South from 1913 to 1932. Rosenwald worked with African American educator Booker T. Washington to create a grant-matching program, where local communities needed to raise their own funds in order to receive Rosenwald's. In effect, he enabled thousands of African American children to attend school and helped narrow the education gap between white and Black children in the South. When asked what prompted him to act, he responded, "I belong to a people who have known centuries of persecution, or whether it is because I am naturally inclined to sympathize with the oppressed, I have always felt keenly for the colored race. . . . The two races must occupy one country."[12] His Julius Rosenwald Fund also awarded scholarships that helped promising young Black students—among them artist Jacob Lawrence, singer Marian Anderson, and many future scientists and writers—receive higher education. Some today consider Rosenwald's philanthropy paternalistic, claiming that he made decisions for others, but for a generation of African Americans, it provided much-needed assistance. Many Black leaders of the civil rights movement credited their later successes to Rosenwald's generosity.

Nonetheless, it cannot be said that there was a single, universal Jewish response to the civil rights moment. In as much as many Jews were involved, other Jews and some of the businesses they owned played roles in enforcing racial norms throughout the country.

Fighting Discrimination in Graduate School

Overturning the Supreme Court's 1896 "separate but equal" ruling required a prolonged series of smaller cases that would provide legal precedents. In each instance, the Jewish "defense" organizations submitted friends of the court briefs to the Supreme Court.

Two African American men, George McLaurin and Heman Sweatt, sought admission to graduate schools in the late 1940s—McLaurin to a doctoral program in education at the University of Oklahoma and Sweatt to law school at the University of Texas. Both were denied and went to court. A state court found that Oklahoma violated McLaurin's right to equal protection under the law by denying him an education afforded to other students. The university then admitted McLaurin but required him to sit in a row specially designated for African American students, study at a special table in the library, and eat at his own table in the cafeteria.

In Sweatt's case, the University of Texas had created a separate, smaller, less equipped law school for African Americans: five full-time professors, twenty-three students, and a 16,000-volume library, in comparison to the main law school's sixteen full-time professors, 850 students, and 65,000-volume library. Eventually, the Supreme Court would have to rule whether those facilities qualified as "separate but equal."

Both McLaurin and Sweatt sued to be treated equally with whites and their cases ended up in the U.S. Supreme Court. In a friend of the court brief in the *Sweatt* case, the AJC and the ADL argued, "Inequality is an inevitable concomitant of segregation of racial groups in public educational facilities and as such violates the 'equal protection of the laws' provision of the Fourteenth Amendment."[13] In 1950 in two landmark decisions, *Sweatt v. Painter* and *McLaurin v. Oklahoma State Regents*, the court ruled that treating students of different races differently violated the Constitution. In the unanimous McLaurin decision, the court stated, "Having been admitted to a state supported graduate school, appellant must receive the same treatment at the hands of the State as students of other races."[14]

Although the two decisions applied specifically to graduate school education, they provided precedent for subsequent education-related cases. In particular, the cases made clear that the Supreme Court would no longer tolerate segregation based on race, setting the stage for the watershed 1954 *Brown v. Board of Education* decision.

Fighting Discrimination in Public School

Now it was time to remove the ostensibly "separate but equal" distinction from K–12 public schools. In an effort to challenge school segregation, the NAACP recruited thirteen parents whose children attended segregated public schools in Topeka, Kansas, to challenge the practice. Oliver Brown headed the list of parents (alphabetically, his was the first male name). After making its way through lower courts, *Brown v. Board of Education* reached the U.S. Supreme Court, with NAACP chief counsel Thurgood Marshall representing the parents, assisted by Jack Greenberg, a young Jewish lawyer (who would succeed Marshall at LDF when Marshall was named to the Supreme Court in 1961).

In 1954 the Supreme Court unanimously sided with Brown to overturn *Plessy v. Ferguson.* Dr. Kenneth Clark, an African American psychologist who had presented Black children with both black and white dolls and found the children believed the white dolls were "nice" and the black dolls "bad," is often credited with helping to sway the court. Clark's research, funded in part by the AJC, demonstrated that the self-esteem of black children suffered in a segregated society by generating feelings of inferiority.

Although "separate but equal" was no longer the law of the land, segregated schools remained the reality for many African American children. In its initial ruling, the Supreme Court had not provided a timetable for the integration of segregated schools. When it offered one the following year, ordering that the *Brown* decision be implemented "with all deliberate speed," many southern opponents of school desegregation interpreted the court's phrase in their own favor. As late as 1964 fewer than 22 percent of all segregated school districts had moved to desegregate.

Meanwhile, post-*Brown*, white leaders in Indianola, Mississippi, organized the "White Citizens' Council" to oppose the changed legal and social landscape. White Citizens' Councils quickly spread to other communities and formed a respectable, white opposition to desegregation. At the same time, the KKK used its typical scare tactics and intimidation to halt integration in their communities. Additionally, governors of southern states implemented a continuing succession of legal tactics to delay school integration.

As during the Civil War, many if not most southern Jews publicly identified with the views of their neighbors. Regardless of their personal feelings about segregation, they wanted nothing more than to blend into the background and avoid calling attention to themselves. In some cities, such as Dallas and Birmingham, southern Jews used their connections to quietly move toward desegregation. Despite the efforts to remain outside the conflict, however, several Jewish communities, especially in the South, became targets for antisemitic attacks because many northern Jews and national Jewish organizations were active in the civil rights movement.

Fighting for Civil Rights in the Streets

A year after *Brown v. Board of Education*, the fight for civil rights took a dramatic step out of the courtrooms and into the streets. Rosa Parks's 1955 arrest in Montgomery, Alabama, sparked a thirteen-month long boycott of the Montgomery bus system—and heightened civil rights activity. Hundreds of thousands of whites and Blacks dissatisfied with the status quo spearheaded a series of mass nonviolent protests, led by the words and actions of the Reverend Martin Luther King Jr., Rosa Parks, and others. Marches and tests of desegregation laws ensued on buses and in public spaces. In the early sixties, Freedom Riders, civil rights activists who boarded interstate buses in the North, faced violence and jail as they moved further into the South. A Black Freedom Rider, Hank Thomas, recalled decades later, "Jews played a very significant part in our human rights struggle. Half of the freedom riders were white, and of those whites, a very significant portion of them were Jews."[15] In some places, including a famous incident in Birmingham, segregationists greeted the Freedom Riders with violent mobs that assaulted and injured the riders. Nonetheless, the Freedom Riders managed to garner the sympathy of many Americans, who saw the images of violence in the press.

Demonstrations against segregated facilities were not limited to the Deep South. In 1960 in support of sit-ins to desegregate restaurants in southern department stores, American Jewish Congress president Rabbi Joachim Prinz urged department stores to integrate the lunch counters at their southern stores. In sympathy, members of Congress picketed a New York City Woolworth's store, demanding equal treatment of Black customers in their southern stores. Blacks were not allowed at the Gwynn Oak Amusement Park in Baltimore, a favorite amusement and picnic destination for white families. On July 4, 1963, the Congress of Racial Equality coordinated a large protest at Gwynn Oak involving clergy, including Rabbi Morris Lieberman of Baltimore Hebrew Congregation, who was arrested and subsequently explained, "I think every American should celebrate the Fourth of July."[16] The amusement park agreed to desegregate later in July and welcomed its first Black customers the following month.

Bombings of Jewish Buildings

In the South, where Black churches were frequent targets for bombings and other forms of racial violence, Jewish institutions were not immune from attacks. Between 1957 and 1960, synagogues in Miami and Atlanta and the Jewish Community Center in Nashville were all bombed. Jewish communities in other southern cities, including Birmingham, Gastonia (North Carolina), Charlotte (North Carolina), Jacksonville (Florida), and Little Rock (Arkansas), faced either failed attempts or threats of violence that never materialized. Jewish buildings were also bombed in Peoria (Illinois), Kansas City (Missouri), and Chicago.

On October 12, 1958, white supremacists detonated fifty sticks of dynamite at the entrance to the Hebrew Benevolent Congregation, better known simply as "the Temple," in Atlanta. The congregation's rabbi, Jacob Rothschild, was an outspoken supporter of African American rights. Atlanta's mayor, William Hartsfield, spoke amid the rubble: "My friends, here you see the end result of bigotry and intolerance, and whether we like it or not, those practicing rabble-rousing and demagoguery are the godfathers of the cross burners and the dynamiters."[17] President Dwight David Eisenhower publicly deplored the bombings.

Antisemitic Incidents

Even as Jews gained increased acceptance and antisemitic vandalism seemed to decrease, disturbing incidents continued. Swastikas appeared on tombstones in Jewish cemeteries, on synagogue doors, and even on churches, store fronts, and public buildings. Jews could hear phrases such as "Jews get out," "Heil Hitler," and "Jew die." Some vandalism was traced to teenagers and some to committed antisemites. In 1966 a group known as the Rat Finks, an ultra-right faction of the Young Republicans in New Jersey, created a songbook featuring this antisemitic lyric, which they unabashedly sang to the tune of "Jingle Bells" at state and national Republican conventions:

> Riding through the reich [*sic*] in a Mercedes Benz,
> Shooting all the kikes, making lots of friends.
> Rat-tat-tat-tat-tat-tat, mow the bastards down,
> Oh, what fun it is to have the Nazis back in town.[18]

Ultimately, multiple Republican groups denounced and distanced themselves from the hate group.

Civil Rights Act of 1964

Jews were involved with activist African American civil rights organizations such as the Student Nonviolent Coordinating Committee (SNCC), a student group dedicated to peaceful direct action. Jewish donors provided substantial amounts of financial assistance to these groups while also assisting as speech writers, lawyers, fund raisers, and activists.

In 1963 leaders of major civil rights organizations, including Dr. Martin Luther King Jr., advised President John F. Kennedy about a protest march they were planning, its first stated goal being "a comprehensive civil rights bill from the present Congress, including provisions guaranteeing access to public accommodations, adequate and integrated education, protection of the right to vote, better housing, and authority for the Attorney General to seek injunctive relief when individuals' constitutional rights are violated."[19] Ultimately receptive to the cause, President Kennedy introduced civil rights legislation in June. Still, it faced daunting opposition from southern members of Congress, who insisted that the legislation would infringe on states' rights. It would take over a year of activism and lobbying, as well as the jarring assassination of President Kennedy, for the bill to finally become law.

The planned march, named the "March on Washington for Jobs and Freedom," took place later that same summer. Some two hundred fifty thousand people crowded onto the National Mall on August 28, 1963, to hear the Reverend Martin Luther King Jr. deliver his "I Have a Dream" speech urging his listeners not to despair: through non-violence, the goal of equal rights in all aspects of American life was possible. Often forgotten because of King's iconic speech is that he was preceded at the microphone by Rabbi Joachim Prinz, the same rabbi who had protested outside of Woolworth's and had been a rabbi in Hitler's Berlin. "The most important thing I have learned in my life is that bigotry and hatred are not the most urgent problems," Rabbi Prinz told the crowd. "The most urgent, the most disgraceful, the most shameful and the most tragic problem is silence."[20]

On July 2, 1964, after months of political maneuvering, President Lyndon Johnson signed the Civil Rights Act of 1964 into law. Among its various mandates, the far-reaching law strengthened voting rights, outlawed segregation in public places, called for the desegregation of public schools, and made it illegal for employers to discriminate based on race, religion, or gender. On its heels came the Voting Rights Act of 1965, which removed some of the major barriers that prevented southern Blacks from voting, and then the Fair Housing Act of 1968, which outlawed discrimination in the sale or rental of housing based on race, religion, national origin, or sex.

Remarkably, both the Civil Rights Act of 1964 and the Voting Rights Act of 1965 were drafted in the conference room of the Religious Action Center of Reform Judaism building in Washington DC, which also housed the Leadership Conference on Civil Rights (LCCR).The legendary Black leaders A. Philip Randolph and Roy Wilkins had founded the Leadership Conference with a Jewish leader, Arnold Aronson, in 1950. As conference secretary, Aronson helped map legal and political strategies to pass multiple civil rights laws, including the Civil Rights Act, the Voting Rights Act, and the Fair Housing Act.

Jewish coalition building had helped give rise to these landmark pieces of legislation.

Freedom Summer

While events in Washington pushed the country toward government action that would help protect the rights of African Americans, students flocked to Mississippi. They hoped to help oppressed Black Americans exercise their constitutional rights and lay the foundation for grassroots activism once they returned to school. Their projects, which included creating community centers and "Freedom Schools," mostly focused on education and political activism that challenged the status quo in the Deep South.

During that summer of 1964, which became known as Freedom Summer, over one thousand volunteers, many of them Jewish, set up schools for Black children in Mississippi and organized health clinics to fill needs that separate but unequal public facilities had failed to address.

In June, three young volunteers, two Jewish and one African American, disappeared. Andrew Goodman, Michael Schwerner, and James Chaney had set out to help Blacks register to vote. On June 21 they were returning from Longdale, Mississippi, after investigating a Black church burning there, when they were pulled over and arrested near Philadelphia, Mississippi. After being held in jail for a few hours, they were released, but the police soon pulled them over a second time. The three were never again seen alive. When their disappearance became national news, it led to a massive manhunt. After an intensive FBI investigation, their bodies were found buried beneath a dam near Philadelphia.

The activists' murder sparked national outrage and an extensive federal investigation. In 1967 the federal government charged eighteen individuals with civil rights violations related to the disappearance/murder of the three young men (the state government had refused to prosecute). Seven were convicted and received relatively minor sentences.

Freedom Summer succeeded in gaining national media attention not just for Mississippi, but also the entire South's disenfranchisement of African Americans. A formative experience for many of the student participants, more immediately, it helped garner support for voting rights legislation. It focused attention on the experiences of Blacks in Mississippi who attempted to exercise their constitutional rights and prepared local activists to continue fighting for civil rights after the students returned to school.

Jews and Martin Luther King Jr.

Rabbis marched with Martin Luther King Jr. throughout the South. Some were beaten and many jailed.

After Freedom Summer, other major demonstrations for voting rights took place in Selma, Alabama, in March 1965. On March 7, a date better remembered as "Bloody Sunday," state troopers and local police brutally beat an interracial group of protestors led by John Lewis of the SNCC and Hosea Williams of King's Southern Christian Leadership Conference (SCLC) when they refused to disperse after crossing the Edmund Pettis Bridge. The protestors had already been the victims of violence, marching in response to the death of twenty-six-year-old Jimmie Lee Jackson. King, who had been in Atlanta, returned to Selma to lead follow-up protests, and many Jewish students and concerned clergy joined King in protest. Jewish participation in the protests was conspicuous because many of the rabbis, including Reform rabbis who typically did not cover their heads, wore yarmulkes. Additionally, a now-iconic photograph captured Rabbi Abraham Joshua Heschel, a friend and colleague of King, marching arm-in-arm with important African American leaders at Selma. Heschel later commented, memorably, "I felt my legs were praying."[21]

Still, not all Jews embraced King and the civil rights movement, and for his part, King recognized some of the schisms within the Jewish community, reflecting in 1958, "The national Jewish bodies have been most helpful, but the local Jewish leadership has been silent. Montgomery Jews want to bury their heads and repeat that this is not

Fig. 14. Rabbi Abraham Joshua Heschel presents the Judaism and World Peace Award to Rev. Martin Luther King Jr. at a Synagogue Council of America dinner in New York, December 7, 1965. Archivepl / Alamy Stock Photo.

a Jewish problem. I want to go on the record and agree that it is not a Jewish problem, but it is a fight between the forces of justice and injustice. I want them to join with us on the side of justice."[22]

On March 25, 1968, shortly before his assassination in Memphis, King spoke to the annual convention of the Conservative movement's

Rabbinical Assembly. He acknowledged Jews' many contributions to civil rights: "Probably more than any other ethnic group, the Jewish community has been sympathetic and has stood as an ally to the Negro in his struggle for justice."[23] But he also hinted at the rift which lay ahead: "On the other hand, the Negro confronts the Jew in the ghetto as his landlord in many instances. . . . I think our responsibility in the black community is to make it very clear that we must never confuse *some* with *all*."[24]

Splintering of the Jewish-African American Coalition

Jews had played a prominent role in the civil rights movement right from the beginning. Yet, by the mid-1960s a new group of Black civil rights leaders emerged who were more militant and less patient with the progress of integration. Calls for "Black Power" reflected the belief that African Americans needed to control their own futures. Moreover, conflicting agendas—especially conflicts over movement leadership, Israel, racism, and antisemitism—considerably weakened the spirit of cooperation that had marked the civil rights movement to that time. Black writer James Baldwin reflected the tension when he said, "One does not wish, in short, to be told by an American Jew that his suffering was as great as the American Negro's suffering."[25]

By the mid-1960s decades of built-up African American frustration with minimal educational and economic advancement, police brutality, and urban decay erupted with riots in the ghettos of major cities, including Los Angeles, New York, Newark, and Detroit. Just a generation earlier, some of these ghettos had been home to vibrant Jewish communities. While Jews had largely left the cities for the suburbs, the Jewish businesses that remained—often the only white stores in the community—were sometimes burned and looted in the violence.

What began as a labor dispute in New York City in 1968 marked another negative turning point in Black-Jewish relations. To improve education in the predominantly Black and Hispanic Ocean Hill-Brownsville section of Brooklyn, the school board had established a new school district under community control, with the power to choose its own personnel. In May the community-controlled board decided to transfer thirteen teachers and six administrators out of the district, but the teachers' union objected and led a walkout of 350 teachers throughout the district. Ninety percent of New York City's public-school teachers were white, and two-thirds of them were Jewish (years of discrimination had blocked Jews from professional careers in other sectors). In September, the new school board fired nineteen teachers, eighteen of whom were Jewish. In late September, at the beginning of the academic year, the union led a longer strike, which lasted through November. Altogether, this was the longest public-school strike in American history—six months—drawing a wedge between the predominantly Jewish teachers union and the mostly Black and Latin community. As one historian put it, "The Ocean Hill-Brownsville crisis brought out the unrealistic expectations each [community] had for the other."[26]

Inflammatory antisemitic literature and taunts spread throughout the Black community. An anonymous, widely distributed leaflet disparaged "the so-called liberal Jewish friend with his tricky, deceitful maneuvers, the Middle East murderers of colored people, the money-changers and bloodsucking exploiters who were responsible for the serious educational retardation of our black children."[27] Julius Lester, a Black activist and the host of a WBAI radio talk show, encouraged a Black teacher to read on air a student's strident poem that began, "Hey, Jew boy, with that yarmulke on your head. You pale-faced Jew boy—I wish you were dead."[28] He later defended the airing of that statement, saying, "I think it's important for people to know the kinds of feeling being aroused in at least one black child because of what's happening in Ocean Hill-Brownsville."[29] Instead, many accused Lester of antisemitism. (Lester, whose great-grandfather was Jewish, later converted to Judaism and became head of the Jewish Studies Department at the University of Massachusetts.)

The strike ended on November 17, when the New York State Education Commissioner asserted state control over the Ocean Hill-Brownsville district and the dismissed teachers were reinstated. But the acrimony of the strike left a scar in relations between American Jews and Blacks.

Around the same time, in January 1969, the Metropolitan Museum of Art in New York opened a photographic exhibit about Harlem. A recent local high school graduate, Candace van Ellison, wrote an introduction to the exhibit catalog that further inflamed relations with Jews: "Behind every hurdle that the Afro-American has yet to jump stands the Jew who has already cleared it. Jewish shopkeepers are the only remaining 'survivors' in the expanding black ghettos. . . . The lack of competition allows the already exploited black to be further exploited by Jews."[30]

Affirmative action—programs and policies designed to remedy systemic inequalities in education and employment by giving special consideration to historically excluded groups, like African Americans and women—and the related issue of admissions quotas also fomented tension between the Black and Jewish communities. Black groups supported specific targets or quotas, but most mainstream Jewish groups opposed them. At that time in the 1960s, some 15 percent of all students at American colleges—and sometimes 23 percent of students at major schools—were Jewish. Jews vividly remembered the discrimination they had worked hard to overcome and did not want to revert to the past. Nonetheless, Jewish groups worked to find other ways of helping minority applicants attend universities, by encouraging funding of remedial education, increasing scholarships, and offering special preparatory training for qualified individuals.

In the 1970s Marco DeFunis, a Jew, applied to a law school and Allan Bakke, a white Christian, applied to a medical school. Both were denied admission. They sued on the grounds that the schools violated their rights under the same Equal Protection Clause that had been instrumental in securing the *Brown* decision—in essence, that they had not been treated fairly under the law. Both cases reached the U.S. Supreme Court, where Jewish groups submitted friends of the court briefs on their behalf. The court declined to rule in the *DeFunis* case, since the law school had admitted him in the interim and he had nearly completed his studies; but did rule, in 1978, in the *Bakke* case, essentially banning the use of racial quotas while allowing race consideration in university admissions. Many Jewish groups were relieved, while their Black counterparts were incensed. Detroit mayor Coleman Young said, "Jews and blacks used to be part of a great coalition on many social causes. But it's fallen apart. Affirmative action divided them."[31]

Jesse Jackson, Louis Farrakhan, Leonard Jeffries

By the time the *Bakke* decision was issued, more Black Americans held antisemitic attitudes than their white counterparts, driven in part by the inflammatory rhetoric of some Black community leaders. A 1970 study ranked 73 percent of Blacks in their twenties, as opposed to 35 percent who were fifty and older, as high on its index of antisemitism. Unlike during the civil rights movement, by 1978 a survey of "black leaders" found that 81 percent agreed that "Jews chose money over people" and a 1975 poll found two-thirds of Blacks "indifferent to whether Israel existed as a state."[32]

In 1984 the African American civil rights leader Reverend Jesse Jackson ran to become president of the United States, but his campaign derailed after he referred to Jews as "Hymies" and New York as "Hymietown" during an interview. Coming to Jackson's defense—"If you harm this brother," he threatened Jews, "I warn you in the name of Allah, this will be the last one you harm"—was Louis Farrakhan, the fiery leader of the Nation of Islam, a militant group supporting Black self-reliance and separation from whites with considerable antiwhite sentiment.[33] The lightning rod for much of the antisemitic furor in America, Farrakhan praised Hitler as "a great man" and disparaged Judaism as a "gutter religion."[34]

Inventing wild-eyed theories, extremists accused Jews of such evils as infecting African American babies with AIDS and introducing drugs to youth in the Black ghettos. One of the most repeated lies was that Jews had been the main force behind slavery in the United States (In fact, while some Jews had been involved in the eighteenth-century slave trade, scholars have shown that they were not a driving force.) Another was the Jews' supposed control of the U.S. government. "The Jews," Farrakhan declared, "control the movement of this great nation, like a radar controls the movement of a great ship in the waters. . . . The Jews got a stranglehold on the Congress."[35] (In fact, in 1990, when Farrakhan made that allegation, of the 535 members of Congress serving both the House of Representatives and the Senate, thirty-four were Jews.)

Meanwhile, Leonard Jeffries, a tenured professor and chair of the Black Studies department at the City University of New York (CUNY), delivered an inflammatory speech on July 20, 1991, charging that Jews controlled the slave trade and were conspiring to portray African Americans negatively in Hollywood films. "For years I grew up as a youngster just like you did going to movies where the African peoples were completely denigrated," Jeffries said. "That was a conspiracy, planned and plotted and programmed out of Hollywood, where people called Greenberg and Weisberg and Trigliani and what not. It's not being anti-Semitic to mention who developed Hollywood. Their names are there. MGM, Metro Goldwyn Mayer. Adolph Zukor. Fox. Russian Jewry had a particular control over the movies, and their financial partners, the Mafia, put together a system of destruction of black people."[36] He also claimed that "The white boy can't be trusted . . . These white folks, even the good ones, you can't trust. There's a devilishness out there when it comes to this African thing."[37] Calls for his dismissal led CUNY officials to remove him from his role. After a long legal battle, Jeffries remained barred from his leadership position.

Chaos in Crown Heights

Relations between Blacks and Jews were especially wary and tense in Crown Heights, a Brooklyn, New York, neighborhood home to a large Black population and the worldwide headquarters of the Lubavitch Hasidic movement (known often by the Hebrew acronym Chabad). At about 8:20 p.m. on August 19, 1991, a police-escorted motorcade was bringing Rabbi Menachem Mendel Schneerson, leader of the

Lubavitch movement, home to Crown Heights after a visit to the cemetery where his wife and father-in-law were buried. Although the precise details of what happened next are murky, the relevant details are clear enough. The last car in the procession, trying to keep up with the procession, ran through a red or yellow light, hit another car, and ultimately struck two children on the sidewalk. Seven-year-old Gavin Cato was killed and his younger cousin severely injured. The driver of the car was a Lubavitch Hasid; the children were African Americans.

Angry bystanders quickly gathered. While some attended to the children, others attacked the Hasidic driver and his passengers, who had to be protected by the police before they were taken away in an ambulance.

A few hours later, an Orthodox but not Lubavitch student visiting from Australia, Yankel Rosenbaum, who had no connection to the accident, was beaten and stabbed to death while walking in Crown Heights. A young Black man, Lemrick Nelson, was charged with the murder. Upon his arrest the police had found a bloody knife and three bloody dollar bills in his pocket. Despite the evidence, a largely Black jury would later acquit Nelson of the murder, further outraging the Jewish residents of Crown Heights.

Cato's death triggered three days of rioting during which Crown Heights Jews were targeted for assault. Gangs of young Black youths roamed the neighborhood torching cars, breaking windows, and throwing rocks. "Jewish homes were being attacked, windows broken," the *Jewish Daily Forward* reported on August 21, 1991. "Jewish residents were cowering in the safest rooms in their homes. . . . Marauding bands of outside agitators were roaming around blaming Jews. This was taking place not in, say, prewar Poland or the Pale of Settlement back in an even earlier time. This was taking place in the Crown Heights section of Brooklyn."[38]

Fearful of stirring up further trouble, New York City mayor David Dinkins, who was Black, and police officials decided to keep a low profile so as not to further inflame the situation. Nonetheless, over the three-day period, 38 civilians, mostly Jewish, and 152 police officers were injured. Jewish homes and businesses were damaged: windows shattered, automobiles burned, and stores looted. One Jewish resident later recalled, "I was a prisoner in my house for 72 hours. I was forced to hide in the bedroom with my six children. Our house was attacked twice, and the police wouldn't come to my family's aid. The mayor must answer the question. Even if he didn't hold back the police, he must answer for what happened."[39]

Inciting the anti-Jewish actions was an emerging Black spokesperson, the Reverend Al Sharpton, who maintained relationships with Leonard Jeffries and Louis Farrakhan. Sharpton fomented Black anger at rallies where he called Gavin Cato's death a murder and never mentioned the actual murder of Yankel Rosenbaum. The Hasidic Jews of Crown Heights, he said, were "diamond merchants," a reference to the prominence of Jews in the diamond trade. On Saturday, August 24, at the height of the riots, Sharpton led a protest march through Crown Heights featuring antisemitic signs and cries of "No Justice, No Peace!," "Death to the Jews!," and "Whose Streets? Our Streets."[40]

Incident in Harlem

In 1995 Sharpton was involved in another Jewish-related incident in New York City's heavily African American Harlem neighborhood. An ongoing dispute between the Jewish owner of Freddy's Fashion Mart and his subtenant, a Black man named Sikhulu Shange who owned a store called the Record Shack, led to day after day of raucous picketing by African Americans shouting, "Get out, Jew bastards!," "Burn down the Jew store!," "Bloodsucking Jews!," "Kill the Jew bastards!"[41] Inflaming the picketers were Al Sharpton, who referred to the Jewish store owner as a "white interloper," and the rhetoric of Louis Farrakhan, who called non-Black businesses owners in Black areas "bloodsuckers."[42]

On December 8 one of the demonstrators, Roland Smith Jr., rushed into Freddy's Fashion Mart, ordered all the customers to leave, set the store on fire, and blocked the only exit. Smith shot four people who managed to escape the building, but another seven people were found dead after the attack. Police also recovered Smith's body from the building, after he killed himself.

Incidents like these fanned the flames of antisemitism in the African American community to the point that the percentage of Blacks holding antisemitic views doubled that of the larger white community. Anti-Defamation League polling showed that between 2007 and 2016 antisemitic views among all Americans hovered around 12 percent, but among African Americans, that figure ranged from 23 percent to 29 percent.[43] A 2019 ADL poll found Black respondents considerably more likely to believe antisemitic stereotypes than whites. A 2021 survey by the market research company YouGov found that "about 15% of self-identified white liberals believed in one of the three stereotypes included in the survey, compared to 42% of Black liberals. Likewise, about 30% of white conservatives believed one of the stereotypes, compared to more than 50% of Black conservatives."[44] Despite these high numbers, the survey pointed out that the majority of African Americans were not antisemitic.

Coming Together

On November 19, 2020, the University of Pennsylvania's Katz Center for Advanced Judaic Studies hosted an event titled "Then and Now: Black-Jewish Relations in the Civil Rights Movement." The featured speaker, professor of religious studies and Africana studies Anthea Butler, told the crowd, "What I think is important to all of us living in America right now, both American Jews and African American people alike, is the fact that our communities are being threatened by white supremacy and anti-Semitism, and people are dying because of these things. We need to figure out a way to talk about this, first of all, and secondarily to reestablish alliances between our communities, so that we are able to fight against the perils that are coming at us from the outside."[45]

Although cooperation between Blacks and Jews had weakened considerably in the latter part of the twentieth century, leaders of both groups have realized the need to repair the breech. In communities around the country Jews and Blacks have sought to heal the rifts that divide them. The ADL's World of Difference Institute, which helps educators, students, and others of all backgrounds to challenge racism, antisemitism, and prejudice, is now active in nearly thirty American cities. In 2018 the Council of Baptist Pastors and the Jewish Community Relations Council/AJC established a coalition to promote solidarity between Jews and Blacks in Detroit. In Philadelphia, the ADL created the Black-Jewish Alliance, and in Atlanta, the AJC formed the Black/Jewish Coalition. Similar efforts exist in other cities. In Washington DC and Philadelphia, Operation Understanding helps African American and Jewish high schoolers recognize and challenge antisemitism and discrimination. Civil Rights trips for Jewish youth to the South by groups such as Etgar36 provide participants with an understanding of oppression.

In 2018 the late U.S. Representative John Lewis of Georgia, who attended a Rosenwald School as a child, emphasized that Blacks and Jews have long shared a common cause. "Our foremothers and forefathers," he said, " all came to this great land on different ships, but we're all in the same boat now. We must look out for each other and care for each other. And never, ever give up . . . until we reclaim the soul of America. If we get it right here in America, maybe this country can emerge as a model for the rest of the world."[46]

11

Zionism = Judaism?

The United States was born in 1776, the State of Israel in 1948. Although the United States is nearly four times older than the nation of Israel, the history of the Jewish homeland began thousands of years earlier.

Exile and Return

Before the Romans captured Jerusalem and destroyed the Holy Temple in 70 CE, the area of ancient Israel known as Judea had been the focal point of Israelite and Jewish life. King David unified the tribes of Israel into a state with Jerusalem as its center around 1000 BCE. In 957 BCE his son Solomon built the First Temple, which stood for four centuries until its destruction in 586 BCE during the Babylonian conquest. The Second Temple, built under the leadership of Ezra and Nehemiah beginning some seventy years later, stood for more than four centuries until its destruction by the Romans in 70 CE. The Roman Empire then expelled most of the Jews from Judea, dramatically expanding the Jewish diaspora: a millennia-long exile from their Holy Land. Over the centuries, as Jewish life spread across the world, a small but continuous Jewish presence remained in that land, which came to be known as Palestine.

In the nineteenth century, the Zionist movement, which became a political movement under the leadership of Theodor Herzl (among others), began working for the reestablishment of a Jewish homeland in Palestine as a way to solve the problem of European antisemitism. Although by then Jews had generally been legally emancipated in Western Europe (receiving full legal rights of citizenship), antisemitism was still rampant. Herzl, a noted journalist, witnessed this personally. As a reporter covering the Dreyfus Affair, Herzl watched as the French Jewish army captain Alfred Dreyfus was falsely convicted of treason because of antisemitism. Meanwhile, pogroms in Russia physically threatened Jews living there. A particularly virulent outbreak in 1882 led to an exodus of Jews to Palestine and elsewhere. Zionism, Herzl envisioned, would establish the Jews' right to free themselves from unceasing antisemitism and govern themselves in their ancient homeland.

A half-century later, after World War II, Britain's hold over Palestine became increasingly difficult to maintain, given the continued conflict between Arabs living there and the growing Jewish population, as well as increased Jewish resistance to British control. Eventually, Britain turned to the United Nations for help. On November 29, 1947, the United Nations voted to partition Palestine into a Jewish and an Arab state. While Arab and Palestinian leaders rejected the proposed partition plan (which, being a General Assembly suggestion, was in actuality not binding on any of the parties), Zionist leaders formally (albeit warily) accepted it and Britain stated that it would end the Palestine Mandate on May 15, 1948.

Zionist leader David Ben Gurion declared the establishment of the State of Israel on May 14, 1948, the day before the British were scheduled to leave Palestine. The exhilaration felt by many Jews worldwide after two thousand years of longing now faced the reality of a war that threatened the nascent country with annihilation before it could even begin.

The combined and vastly numerically superior armies of six Arab nations invaded Palestine, yet the military of Israel succeeded in holding them back. In 1949 the Arab states finally agreed to sign a ceasefire with Israel (the 1949 Armistice Agreement) in which Israel's borders extended to 78 percent of the territory of Mandatory Palestine, beyond the 55 percent of the territory originally recommended by the UN partition plan.

Diverse Zionist Visions

After the creation of the state, Zionism as an ideology supported the right of Jews to continue living there. Yet Zionism held different meanings for different Jews. Some Jews, like Herzl, believed in political Zionism: there needed to be a safe haven, such as a state, for Jews in the world. Religious Zionists advocated for a country grounded in Judaism and its religious practices. Labor Zionists combined Zionism with their socialist beliefs in the quest to build an equitable society in the Jewish state. Cultural Zionists envisioned the Jewish homeland as a national cultural center, typically with the Hebrew language at its center. Outside of Israel, Diaspora Zionists supported Zionism in economic, political, and other ways while choosing to remain in the Diaspora.[1]

The Six-Day War

Even after the 1949 armistice agreement ending the 1948 war, *fedayeen*, armed guerrillas, crossed borders to take Jewish lives. Between 1949 and 1953, a significant number of Jews, mostly civilians, were killed. This period also witnessed multiple actions by the Israeli military amid circumstances that continue to divide historians, political leaders, and others today.

Gamal Abdel Nasser, Egypt's leader, adopted a hardline attitude toward Israel, closing the Gulf of Aqaba to Israeli shipping and supporting increasing *fedayeen* attacks. When Nasser nationalized the Suez Canal, England and France secretly planned with Israel to seize the canal and destabilize the Nasser regime. During the 1956 war that followed, Israel seized and occupied the Sinai Peninsula and the islands from which Egypt had closed shipping to the port of Eilat. Under sharp U.S. protest, Israel withdrew from the captured territories, with the guarantee that UN peacekeeping troops would safeguard those areas. With help from France, Israel secretly began to build a nuclear reactor, resulting in Israel joining the exclusive club of nuclear-armed nations.

Relative calm prevailed on Israel's borders in the years following the 1956 war. But gradually, small-scale violent attacks and incursions by the Palestinian Liberation Organization (PLO) and Arab states increased in size, frequency, and death toll. As tensions mounted, the Soviet Union moved to directly influence the Arab world. With Soviet encouragement, Egypt and Syria federated into a single state, the United Arab Republic (UAR). Israel's Foreign Minister Golda Meir warned that the UAR's subsequent anti-Israel hate campaign "cannot be considered harmless, since it is backed by great military forces and by the violent ambitions of a dictator who is out to make the Middle East his back yard [*sic*], and strangle Israel in the process."[2] On May 16, 1967, Egypt requested the withdrawal of all United Nations troops, and the UN agreed. Gone were the assurances given Israel a decade earlier.

War broke out on June 5, 1967, as Arab troops from Egypt, Syria, Iraq, and Jordan, armed with sophisticated Soviet weaponry, massed on the border of the Jewish state. Around the world, there was much sympathy for Israel but little tangible aid. Many in Israel, especially in the public at large, felt isolated. Some in Israel and in the Diaspora feared the end of the state. Rabbi Abraham Joshua Heschel represented the feelings of these Jews when he said, "Terror and dread fell upon Jews everywhere. Will God permit our people to perish? Will there be another Auschwitz, another Dachau, another Treblinka?"[3]

But in a series of preemptive surprise attacks against Egyptian air bases, Israel destroyed the Egyptian Air Force within hours, while it was largely on the ground. And in six days, the Jewish state, tiny but far superior in tactics, stunningly defeated the combined armies of five heavily armed Arab nations—and added a huge chunk of territory to its borders. Israel was now in possession of the entire Sinai Peninsula right up to the Suez Canal, the Gaza Strip, the Golan Heights, and the West Bank of the Jordan River, including the now unified city of Jerusalem. At the end of the Six-Day War, the public perception in many circles was that Israel had achieved a miraculous victory. Yet, ironically, that victory would bring two seismic changes that in the course of time would fuel anti-Zionism. The position of underdog was now increasingly perceived as shifting to the Arabs. And the occupation of Palestinians in the newly acquired territory shifted Israel from victim to aggressor.

The Occupied Territories

With the new territory, Israel inherited authority over the Palestinian population that lived there. Despite some dispute among its political and military leadership, Israel proposed to negotiate with the Arab states and return nearly all of the captured land in return for a guarantee of true peace. Arab leaders gathered at a conference in Khartoum, Sudan, in August 1967 and roundly rejected the offer.

This decision formed the basis of Arab policy toward Israel for much of the next decade: no peace with Israel, no recognition of Israel, and no negotiation with Israel. Nonetheless, in 1978 Israel, Egypt, and the United States signed the Camp David Accords, which set the stage for a historic Egypt-Israel peace treaty in 1979; other agreements, such as the 1994 treaty between Israel and Jordan, followed. The first of the Oslo Accords between Israel and the PLO, signed in 1993, aimed to initiate a process that would result in a final peace agreement between Israel and the Palestinians, but for multiple reasons, the process never produced a final agreement. The Palestinians rejected a peace offer in 2000, and all of Israel's peace proposals since, including a proposed withdrawal from over 95 percent of Judea and Samaria and sharing Jerusalem. Meanwhile, Israeli government policy encouraged Jewish settlement in the newly occupied territories of the West Bank and Gaza under Israeli military administration. Palestinians faced military checkpoints, road blocks, zoning restrictions, security regulations, and more.

Today, Israel is home to considerable internal divisions about the future of the West Bank (the Gaza Strip was returned to Palestinian control in 2005), with many Israelis opposing Jewish settlements throughout Judea and Samaria (which Israeli governments from across the political spectrum have continued to build and expand since 1967), and others supporting these efforts. Israel's larger political parties have generally needed to forge coalitions with the country's sizable Orthodox minority, especially the religious Zionist parties, many of which believe that God gave all of biblical Israel, including the West Bank, to the Jews, and support building Jewish settlements there. Joining them are other Israeli factions, from the ultra-Orthodox to secular nationalists, who view Israel's increasing control over the area as a necessity to protect the security of the Jewish state.

Equating Zionism with Racism

After the Six-Day War, some left-wing groups in Western countries and developing nations increasingly portrayed Israel as the new Goliath: a colonial-style aggressor against an indigenous people. In their eyes, the Palestinians were an oppressed dark-skinned minority up against an imperialist, racist Israel.

In November 1975, due in large part to support from Arab and Soviet Bloc countries and developing nations, United Nations resolution 3379 equating Zionism with racism passed by a vote of 72 to 35 with 32 abstentions, mainly from Western countries. Referencing various other anti-Zionist statements, the official resolution declared that "Zionism is a form of racism and racial discrimination":

> *The General Assembly, Recalling its* resolution 1904 (XVIII) of 20 November 1963, proclaiming the United Nations Declaration on the Elimination of All Forms of Racial Discrimination, and in particular its affirmation that "any doctrine of racial differentiation or superiority is scientifically false, morally condemnable, socially unjust and dangerous" and its expression of alarm at "the manifestations of racial discrimination still in evidence in some areas in the world, some of which are imposed by certain Governments by means of legislative, administrative or other measures,"
>
> *Recalling also* that, in its resolution 3151 G (XXVIII) of 14 December 1973, the General Assembly condemned, *inter alia*, the unholy alliance between South African racism and zionism,

Taking note of the Declaration of Mexico on the Equality of Women and Their Contribution to Development and Peace, 1/ proclaimed by the World Conference of the International Women's Year, held at Mexico City from 19 June to 2 July 1975, which promulgated the principle that "international co-operation and peace require the achievement of national liberation and independence, the elimination of colonialism and neo-colonialism, foreign occupation, zionism, *apartheid* and racial discrimination in all its forms, as well as the recognition of the dignity of peoples and their right to self-determination,"

Taking note also of resolution 77 (XII) adopted by the Assembly of Heads of State and Government of the Organization of African Unity at its twelfth ordinary session, 2/ held at Kampala from 28 July to 1 August 1975, which considered "that the racist regime in occupied Palestine and the racist regimes in Zimbabwe and South Africa have a common imperialist origin, forming a whole and having the same racist structure and being organically linked in their policy aimed at repression of the dignity and integrity of the human being,"

Taking note also of the Political Declaration and Strategy to Strengthen International Peace and Security and to Intensify Solidarity and Mutual Assistance among Non-Aligned Countries, 3/ adopted at the Conference of Ministers for Foreign Affairs of Non-Aligned Countries held at Lima from 25 to 30 August 1975, which most severely condemned zionism as a threat to world peace and security and called upon all countries to oppose this racist and imperialist ideology,

Determines that zionism is a form of racism and racial discrimination.[4]

Public condemnation of this UN resolution in America was swift. A Harris public opinion poll taken a few weeks later indicated that only 9 percent of Americans approved of the vote while 49 percent disapproved and 42 percent were unsure.[5] The public agreed that the

Jewish people were entitled to their own homeland and that the resolution was targeted more at Jews than Zionism. Forty-three percent favored the United States leaving the United Nations if such prejudice against Israel occurred in the future.

The U.S. Congress adopted a nearly unanimous resolution opposing the UN vote. Daniel Patrick Moynihan, American ambassador to the United Nations, stated memorably, "A great evil has been loosed upon the world. The abomination of anti-Semitism has been given the appearance of international sanction by the UN."[6] State and local governments also decried passage of the resolution, as did such disparate groups as the National Education Association and the League of Women Voters. Catholic and Protestant clergy from twenty-one states sent the UN Secretary General a statement calling the resolution "a revival of the all too familiar anti-Semitism which has plagued mankind through the centuries. It is, moreover, a falsehood without historical justification."[7]

Vernon Jordan, executive director of the National Urban League, a mainstream African American organization, lashed out at the UN resolution. "Smearing the 'racist' label on Zionism is an insult to the intelligence. Black people, who recognize code words like 'forced busing,' 'law and order,' and others, can easily smell out the fact that 'anti-Zionism' in this context is a code word for anti-Semitism."[8]

Lasting damage was done to Israel's reputation, even though on December 16, 1991, the UN General Assembly repealed Resolution 3379 by a vote of 111 for, 25 against, and 13 abstentions. Dramatic changes in the world political order contributed to the repeal. The breakup of the former Soviet Union led to former communist countries establishing diplomatic relations with Israel. Continued United States condemnation of the 1975 resolution persuaded other countries to vote for a repeal. Many developing nations that had voted for the original resolution now voted in favor of repeal, while Arab countries including Kuwait, Tunisia, and Egypt abstained. The negative votes came mostly from other Arab and Islamic states, along with certain anti-Western regimes like North Korea and Cuba.

U.S. Aid, OPEC, and the Jews

When Israel faced the worst crisis since the War of Independence—possible defeat in the 1973 Yom Kippur War—President Richard Nixon ordered a massive airlift of desperately needed military equipment for political and diplomatic reasons despite some of his advisors' strong opposition. Evidence would later surface that, personally, he did not like Jews. In recordings eventually made public, Nixon told aides, "The Jews are irreligious, atheistic, immoral bunch of bastards. . . . Most Jews are disloyal, you can't trust the bastards. They turn on you."[9] Yet Nixon put great faith in his Jewish secretary of state Henry Kissinger and came through for Israel in an hour of great need.

The Organization of Petroleum Countries (OPEC) retaliated against the United States for aiding Israel by imposing an oil embargo on America. Long lines at gas stations infuriated many Americans, some of whom publicly or privately blamed Israel and Jews for the shortages. Cars displayed bumper stickers reading "Oil Yes, Jews No" and "We need oil—Not Jews." Signs at several gas stations around the country proclaimed, "Don't blame us for high prices, blame the Jews" and "The Zionists have put us out of business."[10]

The end of the twentieth century then saw antisemitism reemerging in a different form. Some people who had used the word "Jew" negatively now supplemented their negativity with pejorative usage of the word "Zionist." Not all opposition to Israel and its policies would equate to antisemitism, but the line sometimes became exceedingly thin.

Ironically, political support for Israel has not necessarily indicated a positive opinion of Jews. Some evangelical American Christians have championed the Jewish state out of the belief that Israel's establishment is linked to the end of days and return of Jesus—and hold that when those end of days arrive, Jews and others who do not convert to Christianity will be judged unfavorably. At the same time, Christian support of Israel is considerable and valued by many Americans and Israelis alike. Many Americans also support Israel because they see it as the only true democracy in the Middle East—even as this point has itself become a source of contention among other Americans (both Jewish and non-Jewish).

The UN Durban Conference

In fall 2001 the United Nations World Conference against Racism, Racial Discrimination, Xenophobia and Related Intolerance met in Durban, South Africa. Its lofty agenda—to curtail worldwide discrimination—quickly fell apart as the focus zeroed in on accusing Israel of being an apartheid state inflicting genocide on Palestinians. As anti-Israel demonstrators distributed fliers with images of Hitler and vendors sold copies of *The Protocols of the Elders of Zion*, nations opposing Israel pressed to include a resolution equating Zionism with racism, leading both the United States and Israel to withdrew from the conference.[11] In the end the resolution was deleted from the final document. Yet a simultaneous conference of nongovernmental organizations (NGOs) in Durban resolved that Israel was "a racist apartheid state guilty of the systematic perpetration of racist crimes including war crimes, acts of genocide and ethnic cleansing . . . and state terror against the Palestinian people."[12]

The Apartheid Accusation

Since the 1990s accusing Israel of being an apartheid state has become a recurring motif within liberal and progressive groups. The term "apartheid" itself had emerged in South Africa in 1948. An Afrikaans word, apartheid referred to the institutional racial segregation that not only separated whites from native Blacks in housing and schools but also allowed minority whites to exert repressive control over the majority Black population by requiring passes restricting the movement of the Black populace.

Many individuals have criticized the application of the term apartheid to Israel and its policies. "Those who conflate the situations in Israel and the West Bank and then liken both to the old South Africa do a disservice to all who hope for justice and peace," said Richard

Goldstone, a Jew who served on the South African Constitutional Court. "The charge that Israel is an apartheid state is a false and malicious one that precludes, rather than promote, peace and harmony."[13] For example, the ADL has argued that whatever challenges and problems exist, accusations of apartheid overlook legal and institutional protections for Israel's Jewish and Arab inhabitants, as well as the role of Israeli Arabs in Israeli political, civic, and cultural life; moreover, while apartheid was intended to be permanent, Israeli policies remain, in principle, open to negotiation.[14]

This view, that there are pronounced differences between the old South Africa (before apartheid was abolished and Nelson Mandela was elected president in 1994) and Israeli rule of the West Bank, remains the prevailing view in many circles, especially in the United States. Still, some human rights groups, like Amnesty International and B'Tzelem in Israel itself, defend using the term and continue highlighting what they see as Israeli injustices in the occupied territories.

The BDS Movement

In 2005 Palestinian groups headed by Omar Barghouti created the Boycott, Divestment and Sanctions movement (BDS) to pressure Israel to end its occupation of land it had captured in the 1967 war and allow Palestinian refugees and their descendants to return to Israel. The movement aims to delegitimize Israel through consumer boycotts and isolate the country by convincing businesses and governments to withdraw investments.

The BDS movement claims to oppose antisemitism. Its website states, "The BDS movement stands for freedom, justice and equality . . . and categorically opposes as a matter of principle all forms of racism, including Islamophobia and anti-semitism."[15] Yet, far beyond criticizing the Israeli government for its treatment of Palestinians, advocates of BDS often deny Israel's right to exist. Moreover, many critics of BDS argue that the movement also offers no practical answers to solving the impasse between Israel and the Palestinians. Its major demand is that Israel accept the return of the descendants of Palestinians who left (or were forced out, depending on one's view) during the War of Independence. Yet the strongly prevailing view in Israel is that if millions of Palestinian descendants were allowed to return, Israel would cease to exist as a democratic Jewish state. Most BDS advocates do not mention that the 1948 war displaced both Palestinians and Jews, but with a difference: Israel absorbed hundreds of thousands of Jews thrown out of Arab lands where they had lived for centuries, whereas the Arab countries largely refused to accept homeless Palestinians, leaving them to languish in refugee camps.

Separating BDS from Legitimate Criticism of Israel

In 2002 *New York Times* columnist Thomas Friedman put it simply: "Criticizing Israel is not anti-Semitic . . . but singling out Israel for opprobrium and international sanction out of all proportion to any other party in the Middle East is anti-Semitic, and not saying so is dishonest."[16]

Natan Sharansky, the dissident who fought for the rights of Jews in the Soviet Union, developed a "3D Test" in 2003 to separate legitimate criticism of Israel from antisemitism:

> The first "D" is the test of demonization. When the Jewish state is being demonized; when Israel's actions are blown out of all sensible proportion; when comparisons are made between Israelis and Nazis and between Palestinian refugee camps and Auschwitz—this is anti-Semitism, not legitimate criticism of Israel.
>
> The second "D" is the test of double standards. When criticism of Israel is applied selectively; when Israel is singled out by the United Nations for human rights abuses while the behavior of known and major abusers, such as China, Iran, Cuba, and Syria, is ignored; when Israel's Magen David Adom, alone among the world's ambulance services, is denied admission to the International Red Cross—this is anti-Semitism.

The third "D" is the test of delegitimization; when Israel's fundamental right to exist is denied—alone among all peoples in the world—this too is anti-Semitism.[17]

The BDS movement fails Sharansky's tests by demonizing Israel, applying a double standard for criticizing Israel while ignoring the misdeeds of other countries, and delegitimizing Israel's right to exist as a Jewish state.

Growth of the BDS Movement

Nonetheless, the movement gained traction among left-of-center organizations and university campuses worldwide. Frequently aligning themselves with left-wing social justice groups opposing racism, globalization, and militarization (causes popular with many college students), BDS proponents grew their American base of supporters.

Their lobbying to hinder Israel's economy resulted in some churches, universities, and nonprofit institutions (such as Hampshire College) dropping investments in high-profile companies that do business with Israel, among them Hewlett Packard, Caterpillar, and Airbnb.

Several mainline liberal Protestant denominations have also supported anti-Israel activity. In 2022 the Presbyterian Church (USA) declared Israel an apartheid state. That same year, the New England Conference of the United Methodist Church passed "Identifying and Opposing Apartheid in the Holy Land," a resolution calling on the United States "to condition US funding to Israel upon Israel's willingness to dismantle its apartheid system and implement all the rights due to Palestinians under international law."[18]

To date, the boycotts have not inflicted significant economic damage. While "Israel has been concerned that the BDS movement would succeed in rallying consumers, businesses and governments to shun Israeli products and services, and in the case of governments, deny it trade benefits," a 2015 Knesset report found that despite the movement "chalk[ing] up some successes, . . . the[se] did not have any broad impact."[19] Major world corporations, including Google, Microsoft, Dell, and Phillips, continue to maintain research and development facilities in Israel.

BDS *and College Students*

Support for BDS is particularly high on American university campuses, where since 2012 student government groups at such universities as Brown, Ohio State, and the University of Wisconsin-Madison have passed resolutions calling on their schools to divest from companies that do business with Israel.[20] University officials have largely rejected these calls. Columbia University president Dr. Lee Bollinger represented the majority opinion of college administrators when he said that "at Columbia, questions about possible divestment of endowment funds are not decided by referendum. . . . The University should not change its investment policies on the basis of particular views about a complex policy issue. . . . It is unfair and inaccurate to single out this specific dispute for this purpose when there are so many other comparably deeply entrenched conflicts around the world."[21] Debates over these resolutions have led to inflammatory rhetoric, divisiveness, and manifestations of antisemitism on campuses.

A 2020 AJC survey found that 43 percent of Jewish young people experienced antisemitism on a college campus or knowing someone who did, with much of it expressed as or linked to anti-Zionism.[22] A 2021 ADL-Hillel survey found that 32 percent of Jewish students experienced antisemitism directed at them while another 31 percent witnessed antisemitic activity on campus directed at others. "Fifteen percent reported they felt the need to hide their Jewish identity from others on campus, and 12 percent said they had been blamed for the actions of the Israel government because they are Jewish."[23] Some students ceased wearing kippot or religious jewelry. A Jewish student at New York University, Esther Bildrici, explained, "Somehow it became the cool thing to do, to be anti-Zionist on the college campus. In school or in class, I have a very hard time ever admitting that I've been to Israel and I've studied in Israel."[24]

In classrooms, there have been widely publicized incidents of professors calling Israelis the new Nazis, using maps of the Middle East with Israel missing, teaching that Zionism is racism, and maintaining that Israel should not exist as a Jewish state. For example, at Columbia University, "a number of professors, mainly instructors in Middle East studies, have distinguished themselves in the black art of defaming Israel as a Holocaust emulator."[25] A Jewish student at the University of Michigan reported a professor telling her class that "Jews invented religious persecution."[26] Student protestors with bullhorns drowned out a speech by Jerusalem mayor Nir Barkat at San Francisco State University in 2017, shouting, "Get the [expletive] off our campus!" and "From the River to the sea, Palestine will be free."[27]

Hillel buildings also became targets. University of Massachusetts Hillel was graffitied with the word Palestine, in Arabic, in 2018. Antisemitic and anti-Israel posters were left outside the Hillel House at Tufts University; one read "Destroy Israeli Apartheid Forces and Amerikkkan Pigs Which Fund It. Free Palestine."[28]

Additionally, given university commitments to academic freedom, free speech, and the First Amendment, pro-Palestinian supporters have been able to speak on campus in ways that promulgate such antisemitic tropes as Jews control the media and financial markets and shape political policies. Going further, speaking at the 2022 City University of New York Law School commencement, Nardeen Kiswani, a Palestinian activist who had called for abolishing Israel and claimed that Israel mass-raped Palestinian women, said, "We had peace before Israel was created, so abolishing Israel is the key to peace."[29] A year earlier she told an anti-Israel rally, "I hope that a pop-pop is the last noise that some Zionists hear in their lifetime."[30] An attendee told a reporter, "It's one thing to have a political person who you don't agree with but she calls for the actual murder of Jews. It's really setting a precedent that CUNY is OK with having people in their school who are out to hurt us."[31] American Jewish Committee CEO Jonathan Greenblatt stated, "Freedom of speech does not mean freedom to harass and intimidate. . . . Expressions of antisemitism under the guise of Israel criticism are unacceptable."[32]

Fig. 15. Pro-Israel demonstration in New York, 2014. Ethel Wolvovitz / Alamy Stock Photo.

Fighting Antisemitism on Campus

To counteract these forms of antisemitism on campuses, a number of Jewish advocacy groups, as well as students, have taken action. Hillel, the world's largest Jewish college organization, has instituted several initiatives empowering students to respond to antisemitism on their campuses. In 2021 leaders partnered with the ADL and the SCN to create ReportCampusHate.org, where students can report antisemitic incidents on their campuses and receive immediate legal and emotional support. Hillel also ramped up training for students on countering antisemitism. Additionally, their Campus Climate Initiative (CCI), a college administration, local Hillel, and CCI team partnership "works collaboratively with higher education administrators to ensure a positive campus climate in which Jewish students feel comfortable expressing their identity and values, free of antisemitism, harassment, or marginalization."[33]

In 2020, believing that students who have experienced antisemitism are best equipped to combat it, Jewish students founded the advocacy group Jewish on Campus (JOC), which collects stories about antisemitic activities personally experienced by students and shares them with research institutions to better understand how antisemitism manifests itself and the role universities can play in stopping it on their campuses.

Fighting BDS

To counteract the BDS movement, Jewish communal organizations have focused on educating Jews and non-Jews about Israeli policies and politics; they have also turned to legislation. In 2011 over thirty groups, ranging from the AJC and the ADL to the Jewish Federations of North America and B'nai Brith, issued a joint statement, appearing in newspapers across the country, which read in part, "The BDS movement is antithetical to principles of academic freedom and discourages freedom of speech. The movement silences voices from across the Israeli political spectrum. By pursuing delegitimization campaigns on campus, proponents have provoked deep divisions among students and created an atmosphere of intolerance and hatred."[34] Significantly, in 2017 all fifty state governors and the mayor of the District of Columbia joined an AJC initiative affirming rejection of the BDS movement. As of May 2021, thirty-five states had passed anti-BDS laws, resolutions, or executive orders mostly banning states from doing business with companies that support the BDS movement. They required companies contracting with those states to affirm that they were not participating in a boycott of the Jewish state. Separately, on January 28, 2019, the U.S. Senate passed (by a vote of 74–19) the S.1 bill containing this anti-boycott provision: "The bill allows a state or local government to adopt measures to divest its assets from entities using boycotts, divestments, or sanctions to influence Israel's policies. Such measures shall meet various requirements, including those related to written notice and comment. It also bars lawsuits against investment companies based solely on a company's decision to divest from entities that use boycotts, divestments, or sanctions to influence Israel's policies."[35] On July 24, 2019, the U.S. House of Representatives passed a resolution condemning the boycott of Israel (by a vote of 398–17). In 2020 Secretary of State Mike Pompeo, speaking for the U.S. government, issued a statement declaring "Anti-Zionism is anti-Semitism [and] the United States is therefore committed to countering the Global BDS Campaign as a manifestation of anti-Semitism."[36]

In 2021 Ben and Jerry's announced it would no longer sell its popular ice cream in the West Bank, which they called "occupied Palestinian territory." Founders Bennett Cohen and Jerry Greenfield, both Jewish, insisted they were not anti-Israel. "We are also proud Jews," they said, "We . . . remain today, supporters of the State of Israel, but it's possible to support Israel and oppose some of its policies, just as we've opposed policies of the U.S. government."[37] Cohen and Greenfield, it should be noted, never stopped selling their ice cream in any part of the United States because they disputed U.S. government policy. A wellspring of opposition arose among Jewish and non-Jewish groups. The American Jewish Committee assisted thirty Ben and Jerry's franchisees in the United States in drafting a letter opposing the West Bank ban that read in part: "There is a danger that the pursuit of social justice will . . . result in the adoption of overly simplistic solutions by people who share a single view of the world that misconstrue complex problems in which multiple claims of justice are implicated. . . . The imposition of such narrow prescriptions does not advance social justice, or the pursuit of a values-led business."[38] Hadassah, the Women's Zionist Organization, joined other major Jewish and pro-Israel organizations in urging states with anti-BDS laws to stop investments or business relations with Unilever, Ben and Jerry's parent company. Several states with anti-BDS legislation, including Florida, Texas, Colorado, New York, and Illinois, divested from Unilever.

Israel's Wars, Anti-Israel Attacks

In December 2008, after enduring years of rocket attacks from Hamas-controlled Gaza, Israel invaded Gaza with ground troops in a twenty-two-day war. While the U.S. government reiterated Israel's right to self-defense, the war provoked anti-Israel rallies, antisemitic graffiti, and even a Molotov cocktail thrown at a Chicago synagogue.

Reaction in the United States to a May 2021 Gaza war was even more intense. After Palestinian militants in Gaza fired numerous rockets and mortars into Israel, Israel responded with massive air strikes that destroyed Gaza's infrastructure and resulted in considerable civilian casualties. Televised images from Gaza highlighting these civilian casualties inflamed anti-Israel activity. Terms like "genocide" and "apartheid" were directed at Israel, and the ADL reported evidence of antisemitic assaults linked to events in the Middle East, including Jewish diners being attacked in Los Angeles and a Jewish man wearing a Star of David necklace being punched in New York City.[39] Jewish organizations and government officials reacted swiftly to the attacks. In Washington, both Senate Majority Leader Chuck Schumer and Minority Leader Mitch McConnell issued statements denouncing antisemitism. Speaker of the House Nancy Pelosi stated, "This hatred is horrific and heartbreaking."[40] The ADL found and publicized "a total of 387 incidents . . . reported that month with 297 of the incidents occurring after May 10, the date marking the official start of military action."[41] Police around the country increased patrols in heavily Jewish neighborhoods. Once again, these incidents demonstrated that military campaigns by Israel, regardless of their rationale, trigger antisemitic responses in America and beyond.

The Mapping Project

The connection between anti-Israel and anti-Jewish activities reached a new level in 2022 with the emergence of the Mapping Project: an interactive online map visually linking together hundreds of Massachusetts groups and institutions with ties to Israel—from synagogues and Jewish communal organizations to police departments, businesses, and schools—and accusing them of "supporting the colonization of Palestine."[42] Created anonymously, the Mapping Project was supported by BDS in Boston but later disavowed by the international

BDS organization. Particularly concerning, the map clearly identifies each institution's leaders and provides their addresses, putting them in danger at a time of rising antisemitism. According to the project, "Our goal in pursuing this collective mapping [is] to reveal the local entities and networks . . . so we can dismantle them. Every entity has an address, every network can be disrupted."[43]

The Jewish community, political leaders, and law enforcement were prompt in condemnation. Robert Trestan, the New England Regional Director of the ADL, said, "To be sure, one can legitimately critique the political stances of any organization. But to do so with this kind of bigoted language—while calling for the 'dismantling' of an entire community—is dangerous."[44] Congressman Seth Moulton of Massachusetts observed, "This project is an anti-Semitic enemies list with a map attached."[45] FBI Special Agent in Charge Joseph Bonavolonta explained that the FBI was "very well aware and [we] are tracking the Mapping Project website, and are working to identify additional information regarding this website."[46]

Defining Antisemitism to Help Combat It

One means of combatting antisemitism is securing agreement on what it means. Conflicting definitions of antisemitism over the years were confusing and lacked legal provenance. Rising antisemitism related to Israel led the then thirty-one member countries of the International Holocaust Remembrance Alliance or IHRA (an intergovernmental organization founded in 1998) to adopt this "working definition" of antisemitism in 2016:

> Antisemitism is a certain perception of Jews, which may be expressed as hatred toward Jews. Rhetorical and physical manifestations of antisemitism are directed toward Jewish or non-Jewish individuals and/or their property, toward Jewish community institutions and religious facilities.[47]

To provide contemporary context, the IHRA listed the following as ways of identifying antisemitism:

Calling for, aiding, or justifying the killing or harming of Jews in the name of a radical ideology or an extremist view of religion.

Making mendacious, dehumanizing, demonizing, or stereotypical allegations about Jews as such or the power of Jews as collective—such as, especially but not exclusively, the myth about a world Jewish conspiracy or of Jews controlling the media, economy, government, or other societal institutions.

Accusing Jews as a people of being responsible for real or imagined wrongdoing committed by a single Jewish person or group, or even for acts committed by non-Jews.

Denying the fact, scope, mechanisms (e.g. gas chambers) or intentionality of the genocide of the Jewish people at the hands of National Socialist Germany and its supporters and accomplices during World War II (the Holocaust).

Accusing the Jews as a people, or Israel as a state, of inventing or exaggerating the Holocaust.

Accusing Jewish citizens of being more loyal to Israel, or to the alleged priorities of Jews worldwide, than to the interests of their own nations.

Denying the Jewish people their right to self-determination, e.g., by claiming that the existence of a State of Israel is a racist endeavor.

Applying double standards by requiring of it a behavior not expected or demanded of any other democratic nation.

Using the symbols and images associated with classic antisemitism (e.g., claims of Jews killing Jesus or blood libel) to characterize Israel or Israelis.

Drawing comparisons of contemporary Israeli policy to that of the Nazis.

Holding Jews collectively responsible for actions of the State of Israel.[48]

The IHRA definition and examples are legally nonbinding on government entities but provide a reputable means of identifying antisemitic speech and actions.[49] The United States uses this working definition and has encouraged other governments, international organizations, and individual states to use it as well. In March 2022 Iowa and Kansas become the twenty-third and twenty-fourth states to adopt the IHRA definition.

An example of the double standard listed in the IHRA document was the 2022 report by Amnesty International accusing Israel of being an apartheid country. Their report stated that "Israeli authorities impose a system of domination and oppression against the Palestinian people . . . and deprive Palestinians of their human rights. We conclude this treatment amounts to an institutionalized regime of oppression and domination defined as apartheid under international law."[50] The report also called for the right of return of Palestinian refugees to Israel, which would effectively eliminate Israel's status either as a Jewish state or as a democratic state. It ignored the political and military attacks on Israel fomented by Hamas, Hezbollah, and other Palestinian allies. It also ignored other countries' human rights violations against their own citizens. Using the IHRA definition, Amnesty International's report would itself be seen as antisemitic.

All the while, Americans' impressions of Israel have remained largely positive, with at least 58 percent viewing the nation favorably since 2001. A May 2021 Gallup poll showed that 85 percent of Republicans and 66 percent of Democrats view Israel favorably.[51]

A pivotal election in Israel in 2023 moved the government in Israel further to the right. Proposed reforms to the judiciary, curbing the independence of the Supreme Court, set off mass protests in Israel itself. President Isaac Herzog of Israel and President Joseph Biden of the United States warned the governing coalition of Israeli lawmakers not to make sweeping changes without broader consensus. Yet even under these difficult circumstances, many Israelis and Americans have continued to care deeply about the future of Israel as a Jewish and democratic state, asking what commitment to and support for Israel should look like amid such realities.

12

The Changing Landscape of Hate

Sadly, antisemitic violence has long been part of the American Jewish experience. Various tragic incidents over the years, even in periods when antisemitism seemed to have lulled, reveal the vulnerabilities of Jews and Jewish institutions. At the height of the civil rights struggle in the 1950s and 1960s, antisemites bombed or attempted to bomb Jewish institutions from Miami and Jacksonville, Florida, to Nashville, Tennessee, and Gadsden, Alabama. In Gadsden, on March 25, 1960, members of Congregation Beth Israel had gathered for a festive Friday night service, which included Christian clergy as guests, when a Molotov cocktail was thrown through a stained-glass window. It did not explode. The sixteen-year-old Nazi sympathizer who had thrown the bomb then wounded two congregants who rushed out of the building to confront him. He later told police that he "passionately hated Jews."[1]

On October 8, 1977, a white supremacist, Joseph Paul Franklin, hid in waiting outside Congregation Brith Sholom Knesset Israel near St. Louis. As bar mitzvah guests left the synagogue, he shot into the crowd, killing one and wounding two. Later arrested for other violent acts, including bombing a synagogue in Chattanooga and murdering people in interracial relationships, he was found guilty and executed for his crimes.

Not all attacks on Jews resulted in physical injury or death. On March 9, 1977, seven armed members of the Hanafi Movement (whose founder had broken away from the Nation of Islam) invaded B'nai Brith headquarters in Washington DC, holding more than one hundred hostages captive for three terrifying days before releasing them after negotiations with police and the ambassadors of Iran, Egypt, and Pakistan.

Skokie

That same year, a neo-Nazi group, the National Socialist Party of America (NSPA), revealed plans to hold a march in Skokie, Illinois, just north of Chicago, in full storm trooper regalia with swastikas. Skokie was a deliberate choice since the village was home to a large population of Jews and Holocaust survivors. Religious groups from across the country joined residents in opposing the small Nazi group's right to rally in Skokie. A complicated two-year legal battle ensued. Ultimately, the case landed in the Supreme Court, with the ACLU appointing a Jewish lawyer to support the neo-Nazi NSPA's argument that the proposed march was protected under the First Amendment of the U.S. Constitution.

The court eventually allowed the march in Skokie, but negotiations between the various parties kept the march from taking place there, so the NSPA moved the event to Chicago. On June 24, 1978, about twenty brown-shirted Nazis gathered in front of Chicago's Kluczynski Federal Building, as thousands of shouting counterprotestors threw eggs, rocks, wood, and bottles at them. The rally did not last long—only ten minutes, according to one estimate in the Jewish press; after the NSPA demonstrated its right to rally, members gave a Nazi salute and retreated into the building. Nonetheless, the story dominated national headlines for weeks.

Good Neighbors

The support of non-Jewish neighbors has been important for communities affected by antisemitic events. On the evening of December 2, 1993, a cinder block was thrown through the bedroom window of a five-year-old Jewish boy in Billings, Montana. The boy was unharmed, but the community was already on edge. Hanukkah was approaching, and the boy's family had placed a menorah on the windowsill viewable from the street. Billings, population eighty thousand, including about one hundred Jewish residents, had recently become a hotbed for Ku Klux

Klan and white nationalist activity against American Indians, Blacks, Jews, gays and lesbians, and other groups. Local churches and civic organizations offered their support to the Jewish community. Members of a local church decided to put menorahs in their windows, too, so that would-be antisemitic attackers wouldn't be able to determine which families in town were Jewish. Their idea took off. The local newspaper printed a full-page drawing of a menorah for readers to cut out, and a local store displayed a large sign reading "Not in Our Town! No Hate. No Violence. Peace on Earth."[2] In the end, vandals broke the windows of two churches displaying the images and vandalized a sign at a Catholic high school wishing the Jewish community a Happy Hannukah, all while thousands of homes in the city displayed images of menorahs in their windows as a sign of solidarity with their Jewish neighbors.

Montanans again rose to the occasion in 2016 when a business dispute escalated between a Jewish real estate agent, Tanya Gersh, and the mother of the avowed antisemite and white nationalist Richard Spencer in the resort town of Whitefish, home to a tiny Jewish community. Neo-Nazis soon got involved, publishing articles peddling antisemitic tropes and urging their supporters to act against Gersh. One white supremacist announced plans for an armed march through the town. Alluding to the real estate agent and local Jews, the editor of the Nazi newspaper the *Daily Stormer* wrote, "The Jews are a vicious, evil race of hate-filled psychopaths . . . so then—let's hit 'em up."[3] Death threats and other attempts to intimidate the community followed.

The town was overwhelmingly supportive of the Jewish residents. It was Hanukkah time, and like in Billings years earlier, townspeople displayed paper menorahs in their windows along with a logo of a local activist group called Love Lives Here. Political leaders, including the state's governor, issued a joint statement decrying antisemitism, and community members organized an anti-hate rally. The neo-Nazi march never happened, and instead, on the planned day of the march, local Jews hosted a community matzo ball soup party to show their appreciation for the community's support. Meanwhile, Tanya Gersh sued the *Daily Stormer* editor for invasion of privacy, intentional infliction of emotional distress, and violation of Montana's Anti-Intimidation Act. A court awarded her $14 million in damages.

American Jewry's Lost Innocence

American Jewish visitors to major European cities during the last decades of the twentieth century were often asked, tongue in cheek, how they knew they were approaching a synagogue or Jewish institution. The answer: by the police car out front. Tightened security around Jewish houses of worship in London, Paris, Berlin, and beyond regularly included the placement of highly armed police or soldiers in response to the increasing attacks on Jewish communal buildings in Europe. Americans, comfortable with the openness of Jewish life in their own communities, despite occasional acts of violence, could not imagine their local synagogues and institutions requiring special security. This innocence began to fall apart in 1999. That summer alone, the JTA reported "the torching of three synagogues in Sacramento, the discovery of a 'hit list' of Jewish community leaders in northern California, the shooting spree in Chicago, last week's attack on a Jewish Community Center in Granada Hills, Calif., and a series of other incidents have threatened the Jewish community."[4]

The morning of August 10, 1999, started out normally at the North Valley Jewish Community Center's summer day camp in Granada Hills, California—until 10:45 a.m., when a white supremacist, Buford O. Furrow Jr., entered the building with a high-powered rifle and began shooting, wounding the receptionist, three young campers, and a sixteen-year-old counselor. He went on to murder a Filipino American letter carrier. After his arrest, Furrow told police he "was concerned about the decline of the white race and he wanted to send a message to America by killing Jews."[5] In response to this tragedy, President Bill Clinton declared, "This is another senseless act of gun violence. . . . It calls on all of us not only to give our thoughts and prayers to the victims and their families but to intensify our resolve to make America a safer place."[6] Jewish institutions around the country began increasing security around their buildings.

9/11

On September 11, 2001, two commercial airplanes hijacked by Muslim terrorists struck the twin tower World Trade Center buildings in New York City, while a third plane crashed into the Pentagon and a fourth, on the way to the United States Capitol in Washington, crashed into a Pennsylvania field. Americans, glued to their televisions, watched in aghast horror as the World Trade Center towers collapsed. Nearly three thousand innocent men, women, and children were killed.

Almost immediately, vicious rumors began circulating on antisemitic websites and social media that the Israeli government was behind the World Trade Center attacks and that no Jews had died in the collapse, because all Jewish workers in the buildings had received advance warning not to show up on September 11. In truth, Islamic terrorists were responsible for the horrific attacks, and an estimated 10 to 15 percent of the victims were Jewish. Despite the proven falsehoods, Jewish groups were compelled to refute the baseless charges. According to ADL national director Abraham Foxman, "Anti-Semites in the U.S. have always exploited current events to make the case for blaming America's troubles on Jews and Israel. The September 11 terrorist attacks, however, have created a new dynamic where rhetoric of anti-Semites in this country is being picked up and recycled in some segments of the Muslim and Arab world to advance hateful myths and conspiracy theories about Israel and Jews."[7]

Social Media and the Rise of Hate

When Henry Ford wanted to disseminate hatred against Jews in the 1920s, he used a newspaper. When Father Coughlin spewed out hate in the 1930s, he used radio. By 2017, as ADL CEO Jonathan Greenblatt pointed out, "The racists used to hand out their materials in paper bags on street corners, today they hand out their hate on Facebook."[8]

Beginning with Facebook in the mid-2000s, social media became a major communications vehicle for extremist groups to connect with people who shared similar views and to recruit potential members. As the most widely used social networks, including Facebook, Twitter,

TikTok, Instagram, and YouTube, promised to crack down on hate, a report from the Center to Counter Digital Hate (CCDH) found they actually failed to act upon 89 percent of posts that researchers flagged as antisemitic.[9] On TikTok, over one billion users around the world, including large numbers of impressionable young people, continue to be exposed to antisemitic content, leading to what experts describe as "both normalization of the content and radicalization of the Tik-Tok viewer."[10] Over a span of four months of 2021, another group of researchers found "415 comments [on TikTok] containing one or more of the antisemitic attributes of the IHRA" (see chapter 11).[11] Antisemites using the platform endeavor to avoid detection by the app's algorithm monitoring hate speech "by 'purposefully' misspelling words. [They] replace the word 'Jews' with 'juice' to avoid having accounts deleted."[12]

Perhaps to avoid the threat of being banned from mainstream sites, hate groups began moving to less well-known or hidden sites. On such right-wing sites as Telegram, 8chan, Gab, Parler, and others, formerly less visible hate groups—Holocaust deniers, neo-Nazis, white supremacists, extremists, and others—spread their ideologies, recycled falsehoods, and recruited members. On some sites, users started placing triple parentheses around (((Jewish names))) to easily identify and highlight Jews. Hiding behind an ostensible cloak of anonymity, individuals and groups easily spread misinformation, a trend that continues to this day. Minimal vetting allows the most extreme and outrageous claims to circulate. Organizations such as ADL and the Southern Poverty Law Center (SPLC) monitor these sites to keep aware of threats, but they cannot always outflank radicalized extremists.

At times, the hate spills over from online discussion groups to real life, with devastating consequences. Longtime white supremacist Nazi and Ku Klux Klan supporter Frazier Glenn Cross Jr. adapted his tactics as times changed. On April 13, 2014, he opened fire in the parking lot of the Jewish Community Center in Overland Park, Kansas, killing a sixty-nine-year-old physician and his fourteen-year-old grandson. Cross then killed a woman in the parking lot of the Jewish-sponsored Village Shalom, an assisted-living facility nearby. He was later to learn that the people he murdered were Christians, not Jews. When at his trial, the district attorney charged, "Everything he did that day was with one intent, to kill people," Cross immediately interrupted, saying that his goal was "to kill Jews, not to kill people"—alerting Jewish institutions to the dangers posed by white supremacists.[13]

Charlottesville and the Replacement Theory

On Friday night, August 11, 2017, hundreds of neo-Nazis, Klan members, and armed militias gathered for the Unite the Right rally in Charlottesville, Virginia. The white supremacists ostensibly came to protest the removal of Confederate monuments, but the event quickly turned into a demonstration of hate. Carrying lit tiki torches, reminiscent of Nazi-era parades in Germany, the Charlottesville marchers chanted, "Jews will not replace us" as they paraded through the University of Virginia campus.

The replacement theory is a white supremacist conspiracy theory that alleges nonwhite immigrants are culturally replacing the white, Protestant majority and its accompanying culture. The theory has multiple forms but is generally antisemitic. One version claims that a Jewish elite is trying to bring Muslim and dark-skinned immigrants into the country in large numbers to overwhelm the white population. Largely because of anti-immigrant bias and demographic insecurity, both amplified by social media, the replacement theory has made deep inroads in America. A 2022 Associated Press poll found that around a third of Americans, including half of Republicans, agreed with the statement "There is a group of people in this country who are trying to replace native-born Americans with immigrants who agree with their political views."[14] In response to these developments, news media outlets and Jewish defense organizations began informing the public about the antisemitic canards imbedded in the replacement theory's charges.

On August 12 in Charlottesville, marchers carrying swastika flags and shouting Nazi slogans passed by the only synagogue in the city. "Several times, parades of Nazis passed our building, shouting, 'There's the synagogue!' followed by chants of 'Sieg Heil' and other anti-Semitic language," the synagogue president blogged. Some carried flags with swastikas and other Nazi symbols. The synagogue was not attacked, but elsewhere in the city, one of the white supremacists injured almost forty people and killed counter protestor Heather Heyer by driving his car into a crowd. When he was asked about the event, President Donald Trump responded, "You had some very bad people in that group, but you also had people that were very fine people, on both sides."[15] Many Americans were astounded by the president's remarks. In the opinion of many, by equating the two groups, the president sent a chilling message that neo-Nazis, white nationalists, and antisemites had equal standing with those opposing racism and prejudice. The Charlottsville incident, and the president's remarks about it, are now remembered as a grim milestone in the resurgence of hate in America.

Ramping Up Security

With each new antisemitic event attracting national attention, local Jewish communities ramped up security initiatives. In 2007 the Community Security Service (css) was formed. Working with synagogues and Jewish institutions across the country, css began training community members to identify and react to suspicious behavior. In large cities, Jewish Federations began hiring trained law enforcement specialists to counsel local synagogues, camps, and schools on ways to protect their institutions from attacks. In 2012 the Los Angeles Jewish Federation launched its Community Security Initiative, the area's single point of contact to coordinate intelligence, training, and resources; in recent years, other Jewish communities have added their own security initiatives.

Pittsburgh

In 2017 the Jewish Federation of Greater Pittsburgh hired Bradley Orsini, a retired FBI agent, as the Jewish community security director. Orsini began visiting local Jewish synagogues, schools, and agencies, evaluating their safety status and recommending updates to existing security procedures. He also conducted training sessions for leaders, members, and employees of the Jewish community, including advising them on specific, practical steps to improve safety in the event of a variety of scary, but realistic situations they might face. He counselled people to have cellphones with them even on Shabbat to make instant contact with the police if needed.

His training saved lives on October 27, 2018. That Shabbat morning, a heavily armed gunman carrying a high impact assault rifle and three handguns burst into the Tree of Life building, which housed three separate congregations—Tree of Life, Dor Hadash (New Generation), and New Light, all of which were then holding services—and began shooting. The first to die were two middle-aged brothers in the lobby passing out prayer books. Reportedly shouting "All Jews must die!," the gunman roamed through the building for twenty minutes.[16] Hearing gun shots, four New Light Congregation members hid in a storage closet. One of them, eighty-eight-year-old Melvin Wax, was shot and killed when he opened the closet door.

The shooter then headed upstairs to the Tree of Life Congregation. Rabbi Jeffrey Myers, standing on the bimah, had heard the shooting downstairs. Applying his training, he pulled out his cellphone and called 911 while quickly ushering the four people closest to him out of the sanctuary to safety. He later recounted, "I went up into the choir loft and heard him execute my congregants."[17]

Pittsburgh police arrived within minutes of the first gunshots, as the shooter was trying to escape. A shooting duel commenced as he retreated back into the building. An officer reported, "We are under fire. He's got an automatic weapon. He's firing at us from the synagogue."[18] SWAT officers in battle gear arrived soon after. They escorted surviving congregants out of the building and later exchanged fire with the gunman, who had made his way to the third floor. Ultimately the gunman was wounded and surrendered to the police. He reportedly uttered antisemitic beliefs to the police as he crawled toward them. In all, the gunman, Robert Bowers, killed eleven worshipers and wounded six people (two congregants and four police officers), making this the deadliest attack on Jews in American history.

That evening, more than three thousand people gathered at the intersection of Murray and Forbes Avenues in Squirrel Hill, a neighborhood often seen as the heart of the Jewish community in Pittsburgh, for a solemn vigil. Reverend Vincent Kolb of the Sixth Presbyterian Church across the street told the crowd, "We gather because we are heartbroken but also to show zero tolerance for anti-Semitic speech, anti-Semitic behavior and anti-Semitic violence."[19] Wasi Mohamed, executive director of the Islamic Center of Pittsburgh, also offered words of solace and solidarity with the Jewish community, saying, "Obviously, we're all heartbroken . . . and how could we not be? People were stolen from us."[20] The following day, an overflow crowd at Soldiers and Sailors Memorial Hall and Museum gathered in solemn tribute. Christian, Muslim, and Jewish clergy once again offered prayers while civic leaders mourned the tragedy.

Throughout the country, vigils, religious services, and spontaneous gatherings were held to honor the victims. In Knoxville, Tennessee, Rabbi Yossi Wilhelm told over seven hundred people, including the mayor and interfaith clergy, "Eleven Jews, killed for no reason other than the fact that they were Jewish. An attack against any Jew is an attack against all Jews. An attack against any innocent person is an attack against all of us. An attack against a house of worship in the United States of America is an attack against every American."[21]

As they attempted to make sense of what happened, investigators found that Robert Bowers spent a lot of time on far right-wing websites. His social media posts featured Nazi symbols and false conspiracy theories, including among them the idea that the Holocaust was a hoax. He was fixated on the Hebrew Immigrant Aid Society, founded in 1881, which in the twenty-first century transformed itself to help immigrants of all ethnicities, including Muslims, come to the United States. Two weeks prior to the shooting, Dor Hadash in the Tree of Life building had hosted a HIAS-sponsored National Refugee Shabbat program, raising Bower's ire against Jews. Before entering the syna-

Fig. 16. Demonstration decrying hate in Pittsburgh on October 30, 2018, days after the Tree of Life shootings there. Aaron Jackendoff / SOPA Images / ZUMA Wire / Alamy Live News.

gogue and killing eleven people, Bowers wrote on Gab, "HIAS likes to bring invaders in that kill our people. I can't sit by and watch my people get slaughtered. Screw your optics, I'm going in."[22] (The ADL explains that "the optics debate is a major point of contention among various white supremacist factions: Is it better to promote white supremacist ideology via overtly National Socialist symbolism [swastikas, for example], or with the less overtly racist imagery [including American flags] favored by so-called American Nationalists."[23] For Bowers, the only way to express his hatred of Jews was by violence regardless of the consequences. The ADL adds that "some white supremacists insist that even the best optics won't change anything for their cause."[24])

Within days, the slogan "Stronger than Hate" appeared on signs throughout Pittsburgh. Local sports teams featured those words on their uniforms. Amid controversy over whether he was welcomed in the city (especially due to his Charlottesville remarks), President Donald Trump visited the Tree of Life building to pay respects on behalf

Pittsburgh Post-Gazette

ONE OF AMERICA'S GREAT NEWSPAPERS

$2.00   232 YEARS OF SERVICE   FRIDAY, NOVEMBER 2, 2018   VOL. 92, NO. 93, 11/2/18   **FINAL**

...יתגדל ויתקדש שמה רבה

These are the first words of the Jewish mourners' prayer, 'Magnified and sanctified be Your name,'
to be recited tonight on the first Sabbath since the tragedy at Tree of Life

Alexandra Wimley/Post-Gazette

Mourners gather Thursday at New Light Cemetery in Etna for the burial of Richard Gottfried, who was killed in the Tree of Life synagogue shootings.

Fig. 17. On the third day of funeral services for victims of the Tree of Life shootings, the *Pittsburgh Post Gazette* commemorated the tragic event by displaying, as the newspaper's headline, the first four words in Hebrew of the *Kaddish*, the prayer for the dead. Copyright, *Pittsburgh Post Gazette*, 2022, all rights reserved. Reprinted with permission.

of the country. Meanwhile, the work of protecting Jewish institutions continued. Bradley Orsini said, "Our goal was really to empower all 50,000 folks in the Jewish community of greater Pittsburgh to become first responders. We can't stop every shooting. We know the only thing we can truly do for our community, as citizens, is prepare and train. . . . What we can control is minimized loss of life."[25]

Chabad of Poway

The horror in Pittsburgh dramatically ramped up security concerns for Jewish institutions around the country but did not prevent additional attacks. Exactly six months later, during services on the last day of Passover at the Chabad of Poway Synagogue in California, a nineteen-year-old gunman, John Timothy Earnest, entered carrying an assault rifle and began shooting. A congregant, Lori Gilbert-Kaye, moved quickly to shield Rabbi Yisroel Goldstein before they were both hit. Gilbert-Kaye was killed and the rabbi, shot in the hand, later lost a finger. Two other congregants, including a young child, were also wounded.

Meanwhile the Earnest's weapon unexpectedly jammed; he turned and fled in his automobile. An off-duty armed Border Patrol agent in the synagogue managed to shoot the gunman's car as it sped off; Earnest was arrested shortly thereafter. Later, police investigation revealed that Earnest was inspired by the attack in Pittsburgh and similar attacks on two mosques in Christchurch, New Zealand. He gave the plainest explanation of his motive to the 911 operator he called after the attack: "I'm defending our nation against the Jewish people, who are trying to destroy all white people."[26] Previously he had posted both anti-Muslim and anti-Jewish rants on social media, including an antisemitic tirade on the white supremacist channel 8chan. He was later sentenced to multiple life sentences in prison without the possibility of parole.

Jersey City

Two more violent events of a different genesis occurred later that year. On December 10, 2019, two shooters first killed a police officer in a cemetery and then murdered two Jews and a non-Jewish worker in a nearby kosher market in Jersey City, New Jersey. Weeks later, in nearby Monsey, New York, a man wielding a machete broke into a rabbi's home during a Hanukkah celebration and slashed five Jews, one of whom later died from his injuries.

In both cases the targets were ultra-Orthodox Jews, and the attackers were linked to the Black Hebrew Israelites (which can refer to a number of Black groups which claim to be the true descendants of the ancient Israelites, unlike the views expressed by Black Jews involved with mainstream Judaism). Police later discovered antisemitic writings, drawings of swastikas, and Stars of David among the attackers' writings. Unlike previous violent attacks on Jews by white supremacists, these attackers were Black extremists.

Targeting Orthodox Jews

Providing context for these events, in 2019, the FBI found that 60 percent of reported anti-religious hate crimes were against Jews.[27] Particularly vulnerable were Orthodox Jews, clearly identifiable by their clothing or appearance. In 2021 the ADL found that thirty-four of the fifty-one assaults recorded in New York State that year took place in Brooklyn, mostly against Orthodox Jews whose traditional clothing easily identified them as Orthodox Jews.[28]

On July 1, 2021, Orthodox Rabbi Shlomo Noginski was repeatedly stabbed in front of the Jewish day school in Boston where he taught. Although seriously injured, he survived. The attacker, Khaled Awad, an Egyptian national, was quickly apprehended. According to Assistant District Attorney Margaret Hegarty, Amad had previously said, "All Jews are stingy and evil." Hegarty also told reporters that police had learned "the suspect had strong religious views and opinions against Jews, Christians, and the American culture, which were preconceived notions he arrived with from the Middle East."[29]

Antisemitic Attitudes

By 2020 an AJC poll on the state of antisemitism in America revealed that nearly 90 percent of American Jews felt that antisemitism was a problem. Furthermore, about 25 percent of Jews reported avoiding wearing, carrying, or displaying items that might reveal their religious identity because of antisemitic concerns. Ironically, the same poll surprisingly revealed that nearly half of all Americans were unfamiliar with the term "antisemitism."[30] By 2022 the annual AJC poll found that 82 percent of American Jews thought that antisemitism had increased over the past five years while "38% reported changing their behavior at least once out of fear of antisemitism."[31] The ADL 2022 poll also revealed that "85 percent of American believe at least one anti-Jewish trope, as opposed to 61 percent in 2019," and that "anti-Israel sentiment, including anti-Israel sentiment rooted in antisemitic conspiracy theories, is held by broad swaths of the population."[32]

The ADL's annual tally of hate crimes in America, published in 2022, showed that 2021 witnessed a peak in antisemitic incidents—2,717—the largest number since the organization began tracking such incidents (in 1979). Physical assaults had increased by 167 percent from 33 in 2020, harassment increased by 43 percent, and vandalism rose by 14 percent.[33]

Insurrectionists and Jewish Targets

On January 6, 2021, a group of insurrectionists invaded and rampaged through both houses of Congress in support of President Donald Trump's call to overturn the 2020 presidential election, which would soon put his opponent Joseph Biden in the White House. A motley crew of Trump supporters—white nationalists, neo-Nazis, QAnon adherents and others—paraded through the halls with a variety of flags that communicated their values, including in their mix the white supremacist Confederate flag. Prominent among the insurrectionists were members of the Proud Boys, an extremist group with violent tendencies and the Oath Keepers, armed antigovernment extremists. As commentators later revealed, members of extremist groups flashed secret signs of their white supremacist organizations while inside the Capitol. There were also flags with the logo of Kekistan, an imaginary country invented by the alt-right, with its logo resembling a Nazi military flag. One extremist wore a sweatshirt reading "Camp Auschwitz."[34] Several others wore shirts with the letters "6MWE," an abbreviation for "6 Million Jews Weren't Enough."[35]

Despite their separate ideologies, among many other factors the insurrectionists were fueled by anti-Jewish hate. We know this because they communicated among themselves on social media, including 8chan, a site which permits users to traffic in such traditional antisemitic lies as the claim that Jews (specifically wealthy Jews) aim for global domination of governments, the economy, and world events. Recently, Jewish philanthropist and Holocaust survivor George Soros has become a boogeyman for all kinds of conspiracy myths, such as his sparking protests against police brutality in order to pursue a more sinister agenda or global takeover. The use of his name is a shorthand for alleged Jewish plots to control the United States and manipulate the world.

Code Words and Congress

With the arrival of the COVID pandemic in 2020, antisemites began blaming Jews for creating the virus. Tel Aviv University's Kantor Center reported, "The false theories went like this: Jews and Israelis created and spread the virus so that they could rescue the world with lucrative vaccines [echoing] an ancient form of anti-Semitism that blamed Jews for spreading illnesses."[36] Subsequently, even members of Congress began to connect Jews with the virus and unrelated charges arose. When in May 2021 House Speaker Nancy Pelosi mandated that members of Congress wear masks, Congresswoman Marjorie Taylor Greene of Georgia responded, "You know, we can look back at a time in history where people were told to wear a gold star, and they were definitely treated like second class citizens, so much so that they were put in trains and taken to gas chambers in Nazi Germany and this is exactly the type of abuse that Nancy Pelosi is talking about."[37] House Minority Leader Kevin McCarthy responded, "Let me be clear: the House Republican Conference condemns this language."[38] Jewish organizations and news outlets also publicly rebuked her.

Racist, Islamaphobic, and antisemitic posts from Greene's Facebook page had already begun circulating. Her November 17, 2018, post accused the Rothschilds of using lasers from space to ignite serious forest fires in California. She also liked a Tweet that implicated Israeli intelligence services in the assassination of President John F. Kennedy.

Also concerning was a 2019 statement by Senator Josh Hawley of Missouri: "For years the politics of both Left and Right have been informed by a political consensus that reflects the interests not of the American middle, but of a powerful upper class and their cosmopolitan priorities. This class lives in the United States, but they identify as 'citizens of the world.' They run businesses or oversee universities here, but their primary loyalty is to the global community."[39] Although not antisemitic on its surface, many critics noted the similarity between Hawley's use of the term "cosmopolitan" and Hitler's and Stalin's use of that term referring to Jews. In short, the critics saw Hawley's speech as recycling an older tradition that questions Jews' loyalty to their country because, according to antisemites, they are only loyal to each other and/or are involved in some sort of international cabal. Other terms such as "Deep State," "Hollywood elites," "Rothschild," and "Soros" can hint at Jewish conspiracies to control the world. Other code words or phrases implying Jews include "globalist," "financier," and "New York."

Antisemitism and the Virtual World

The anonymity of social media and use of code words can empower antisemites. Troll attacks and "dog-whistles" magnify their numbers. According to two scholars, "Trolls are people who organize to disrupt. . . . an event held on social media through targeted dissemination of hate speech and disinformation."[40] Similarly, another scholar defines the "dog-whistle politics" or "dog whistling" as "the use of messages embedded in speeches that seem innocent to a general audience but resonates with a specific public attuned to receive them."[41]

However tempting, it is unwise to respond, share, or repost these spurious charges, counsel Brandeis University's Sabine von Mering and her coeditor, Monika Hübscher, in the 2022 publication *Antisemitism on Social Media*: "It actually elevates the visibility of antisemitic posts through engagement with it."[42] Elsewhere, von Mering has explained, "Social media's algorithms reward content that elicits user responses, even if those responses are negative. Even if you denounce an antisemitic post or call out the person who published it, you increase the likelihood that the content will be promoted on the platform."[43] These factors contribute to the difficulty of curbing prejudice in general and antisemitism in particular on social media.

Antisemitic Groups in the United States

Antisemitism flourishes on the extreme ends of both right and left wings of the political spectrum, though almost all experts believe that the problem is graver on the former side than the latter. The Right accuses Jews of being communists; the Left charges they are capitalists. Both the Aryan Nations, a white neo-Nazi group, and the Nation of Islam, a Black nationalist group, have pointed to the fact that both the Federal Reserve and ADL were founded in the same year (1913) as evidence that Jews control the U.S. Federal Reserve System. In reality, the establishment of the two institutions is coincidental. An act of Congress in response to an earlier economic crisis established the Federal Reserve, America's central bank. In contrast, the ADL, a nongovernmental organization, was founded in reaction to the public displays of antisemitism during the Leo Frank case.

By 2020 there were over eight hundred hate groups in the United States, according to the Southern Poverty Law Center. Some are small and locally based; a few have national followers. Some groups, like the Ku Klux Klan, have been around for over a century; others are fairly new, or merge, change names, or disappear, with members forming or joining other groups. There are white nationalist groups that hate all sorts of people who are not white and Protestant, like Jews, African Americans, Muslims, and Catholics; and there are Black nationalist groups that hate whites. A common theme running through many of the groups is a hatred of Jews.

Neo-Nazi groups adopt Nazi regalia, symbols, salutes, and slogans. The New England-based National Social Club (NSC 131) believes that Jews are plotting to exterminate the white race and has taken action against groups it perceives as working against its white nationalist agenda. Other groups include the National Social Movement, National

Alliance, American Nazi Party, Folksfront, and the Nationalist Socialist White People's Party, whose founder Matt Koehl wrote, "Jews are the primary enemy of white people, and their ultimate goal [i]s the orchestrated destruction of the white race in order to achieve global political control."[44]

White supremacist groups such as Patriot Front focus on distributing antisemitic flyers and stickers. Along with other hate groups, they refer to the United States as "ZOG"—the Zionist Occupied Government—the lie that Jews secretly control the U.S government. The Base, another white supremacist group, is preparing for a race war that will create a country only for white people, leaving no room for Jews and other minorities. The Goyim Defense Fund produced tracts accusing Jews of creating the COVID pandemic. In Central Florida, the New Jersey European Heritage Association disseminated leaflets stating, "The Jews control and censor free speech in the media/internet. . . . They always work against their host country thru [sic] usury media control, open borders, porn, feminism, anti-European/anti-white propaganda, gun control, LGBT, transgenderism . . . etc."[45]

Even hate groups with small numbers of followers can have an outsized impact on social media. Their numbers may also belie the fact that they are well organized and some members are armed and unafraid to provoke confrontation. While any violent acts these groups instigate are subject to police response, their written ideologies of hate and misinformation are often protected by the First Amendment, if that speech is judged not to call for imminent bodily harm

Perhaps the strangest extremist group to emerge in recent times, since 2017, is QAnon. Taking its name from an anonymous person or persons known as Q, QAnon claims to expose the "Deep State," a cabal of elitists who, they believe, run the world. Often, the conspiracy theories QAnon claims to expose are bizarre plots, and many of the wild theories seemingly have nothing to do with Jews. Nonetheless, QAnon insurrectionists attacking the U.S. Capitol on January 6, 2021, claimed to be supporting President Trump, who they believed was covertly fighting a cabal of Democrats, Hollywood activists, and liberals, all of whom belong to a Satanic pedophile cult that kidnaps and kills children to use their blood in secret ceremonies—a reworked revival of the ancient blood libel accusing Jews of killing Christian children for their blood. QAnon followers believe in an upcoming event, the Storm, when all members of this imagined Satanic group will be arrested in a violent military takeover of the U.S. government. A 2021 Morning Consult poll found that almost half of all QAnon supporters agreed with the antisemitic claims in *The Protocols of the Elders of Zion* (see chapter 7). News outlets and Jewish organizations continue to counter QAnon's eccentric and paranoid beliefs, even as online followers top one million.

Holocaust Remembrance

All the while, with the passage of time, fewer Americans alive today are aware of the Holocaust than ever before. A 2020 Pew Research Center poll showed that only 45 percent of Americans knew that six million Jews died in the Holocaust.[46] A Conference on Material Claims against Germany poll that same year found that 48 percent of GenZ and millennials could not name a single concentration camp or ghetto, and a majority could not identify the infamous concentration camp Auschwitz-Birkenau.[47] The survey placed part of the blame on Holocaust misinformation on social media. About half of the respondents had witnessed Holocaust denial or distortion online, and almost a third reported seeing Nazi imagery on their social media feeds or in their communities.

Jewish and non-Jewish organizations have responded by focusing on education. Museum of Jewish Heritage president and CEO Jack Kliger explained in the aftermath of the Unite the Right rally and spread of antisemitism on social media: "We must commit to educate in our classrooms and beyond and teach students how to first recognize hate rhetoric and symbols so they can stop it. We must continue to address online hate. . . . And, we must mobilize and address bias, both implicit and explicit, and engage in advocacy."[48]

Fighting Back through Education

"Antisemitism," said Pittsburgh Jewish Federation CEO Jeffrey Finkelstein, "is not a problem promoted by Jews; we are merely the target."[49] As antisemitic events multiplied, American Jews realized that they needed a multitrack response: expanding education to combat antisemitism, ramping up security, and joining forces with like-minded groups to fight hate.

Education about antisemitism has become a key Jewish communal objective, with longstanding "defense" organizations creating initiatives not only to educate Jews but also a wider American audience about hate and bigotry. The United State Holocaust Memorial Museum, dedicated in 1993, aims to teach "millions of people each year about the dangers of unchecked hatred and the need to prevent genocide."[50] The ADL's "A World of Difference Institute ®," launched in 1992, trains school and community groups in bias education, helping students and teachers to recognize the benefits of diversity and to counteract antisemitism. The ADL's Center on Extremism monitors hate group activity, tracks hate incidents, and releases statistical data about anti-Jewish activity in the United States in its annual Audit of Antisemitic Incidents. In 2022 the AJC issued "A Call to Action against Antisemitism in America: American Jewish Committee's Society-Wide Nonpartisan Guide to Address Antisemitism" to proactively unite political, business, and communal leaders to respond to antisemitism. In doing so, the AJC noted, "When societies cannot protect their Jewish populations—by ignoring, minimizing, or redefining antisemitism—they often fail to protect their democracy as well. . . . Because what starts with Jews rarely ends with them."[51]

The American Jewish Congress works with elected officials to develop methods of countering antisemitism. Congress president Jack Rosen explained, "Ignorance, prejudice, and fear drive hatred and violence. We can and should treat those symptoms in our schools and places of worship but we must also gird ourselves as a society against such views and the inevitable violence that accompanies them."[52] The

Fig. 18. The American Jewish Committee's Hands across the Campus program brings together young people of different backgrounds to learn about diversity and the dangers of hate groups. AJC Archives.

congress educates American voters through its nonpartisan Jewish Political Guide explaining candidates' views on Jews in the United States and Israel.[53] Their research has exposed the work of white supremacists and extremist views of certain candidates.

Jewish federations, along with overseeing security needs, have been working with the Jewish defense organizations to provide resources on how to combat antisemitism and anti-Zionism within their communities. For example, the Kansas City Federation created workshops for Jewish students on how to recognize and respond to antisemitism on campus.

Combat Antisemitism Movement (CAM) is an international coalition of over three hundred organizations (including the AJC, American Jewish Congress, B'nai Brith International, and the Jewish Federations of North America) responding to, publicizing, and counteracting antisemitic events. Their Advisory Council includes political, academic, and religious leaders from around the world. CAM's weekly emails inform readers about antisemitic activities worldwide. In 2022 CAM joined with Fighting Online Antisemitism (FOA) to launch a portal called "Report It" to help people report and fight against antisemitic content found on popular social media platforms such as Facebook, Instagram, Twitter, and YouTube.

Protecting the Jewish Community

The FBI's 2021 data on hate crimes showed that the Jewish community was targeted in more than half of all religion-based crimes. While constituting fewer than 2 percent of the American population, Jews accounted for nearly 55 percent of all religious hate crimes that year. "We are a community that faces the most complex and violent threats of any faith based community," says Michael Masters, CEO of the Secure Community Network. "But not exclusively. . . . We are the tip of the spear."[54]

In 2004 the Jewish Federations of North America and the Conference of Presidents of Major American Jewish Organizations founded SCN, "the official homeland security and safety initiative of the organized Jewish community in North America. . . . the central organization dedicated exclusively to the safety and security of the American Jewish community, working across 146 federations, 50 partner organizations, over 300 independent communities as well as with other partners in the public, private, non-profit and academic sectors."[55] As the threats grew, the SCN ramped up its operations, opening a Duty Desk in Chicago to intake threats, reports, and issues; analyze intelligence; and disseminate information. In 2021 SCN created a technology-driven National Jewish Security Operations Command Center serving as a 24/7 staffed central location to coordinate and protect the Jewish community. SCN also provides security training to local Jewish communities, formulates procedures for reacting to threats, and develops relationships with the FBI and Homeland Security in addition to local and state law enforcement (see appendix 2). According to Masters,

"Our effort is firmly rooted on the notion that the backbone of a system is a professionally-led network. Safety and security is a profession that involves knowledge, skill set, and insight. scn views security as layers of an onion: intelligence, information sharing, physical security of a building, locks on windows and doors, situational awareness training and identifying active threats."[56] Working with public safety experts, security professionals, and law enforcement, scn developed a model known as Operation Protective Shield, which engages regional directors and advisors as well as community-based professionals, and deploys best-practice assessments, training, and security policies. scn has also promoted the recruitment and hiring of more experienced law enforcement experts, including retired fbi agents, to oversee training and security for local Jewish institutions.

Security training by scn proved successful on Saturday morning, January 15, 2022, when a lone gunman took four hostages, including the rabbi, at Congregation Beth Israel in Colleyville, Texas. His goal: the release of an imprisoned Islamic terrorist. "He bought into the antisemitic tropes that Jews control the world. Jews control the media. Jews control the banks," Jeffrey Cohen, one of the hostages, later reported. "And because he believed this, he genuinely thought that we could call up President Biden that we could call up President Trump [sic] and have them release her because we're Jews, and we have all this power."[57]

After an eleven-hour standoff, the hostages were able to escape and the hostage-taker was shot dead by police. In the aftermath, Rabbi Charlie Cytron-Walker thanked law enforcement officials, scn, and the adl for the security training his congregation had received. "In the last hour of our hostage crisis," the rabbi explained, "the gunman became increasingly belligerent and threatening. Without the instruction we received, we would not have been prepared to act and flee when the situation presented itself."[58]

In 2021 the scn trained over seventeen thousand people nationwide in situational awareness and/or dealing with active threats and aims to increase those numbers in succeeding years. In the first six months of 2022, SCN had trained over thirty-two thousand people. "We need to prepare every synagogue, school, every camp across the country for these types of attacks," Masters said. "It's unfortunate, but that's the reality we live in."[59]

U.S. Responses

In 2021 the U.S. Congress passed a resolution condemning the rise in antisemitic violence and harassment targeting Jewish Americans; calling on elected officials, faith leaders, and civil society leaders to denounce and combat all manifestations of antisemitism; calling on the President to continue America's leadership role in international efforts to combat antisemitism, support Holocaust education, ensure the security of Jewish institutions, and produce a report that evaluates the threat of antisemitism to the American people; and urging law enforcement agencies to cooperate in the FBI's efforts to collect data on antisemitic hate crimes.

That year, recognizing the global rise in anti-Jewish hate, President Joseph Biden appointed Jewish historian Dr. Deborah Lipstadt to a newly created position as special envoy to monitor and combat antisemitism, with the rank of ambassador. On Passover eve 2023 the president issued a public statement calling antisemitic acts "unconscionable and despicable. They carry in them terrifying echoes of the worst chapters in human history. And they're not only a strike against Jews; they're also a threat to other minority communities and a stain on the soul of our nation. . . . It is our obligation to ensure that hate doesn't grow or become normalized. It is our duty to preserve and protect the sacred ideals enshrined in our Constitution: religious freedom, equality, dignity and respect. That is the promise of America."[60]

The Twenty-First Century Reality

By the twenty-first century, Jews, believing anything was possible in America, had achieved successes unparalleled in Jewish history. American Jews have firmly established themselves in all aspects of life from business to academia. Despite the obstacles faced by earlier generations, Jews find themselves in the boardrooms of America's leading corporations and at the helm of the country's Ivy League universities. Jews are visible in sports, entertainment, literature, and the arts. In political service, as in many other fields, they have often greatly exceeded their percentage of the American population. In 2023 there were eight Jewish members of the United States Senate while the total Jewish population hovered at about 2 percent. In the year 2000, Senator Joseph Lieberman of Connecticut became the Democratic Party nominee for vice president of the United States, and as the first Jew on a major political party's presidential ticket could say, "Anything is possible in America."[61] In 2021, when Kamala Harris became vice president, her Jewish husband, Doug Emhoff, became the first "second gentleman" of the United States. *Editors' Update*: After Hamas's massacre in Israel on October 7 and the Israel-Hamas war that immediately followed, the Anti-Defamation League reported that antisemitic incidents in America "reached the highest number of incidents during any two-month period since ADL began tracking in 1979. . . . Between Oct. 7 and Dec. 7, ADL recorded a total of 2,031 antisemitic incidents, up from 465 incidents during the same period in 2022, representing a 337-percent increase year-over-year."[62] Additionally, the Indiana University Institute for the Study of Contemporary Antisemitism reported: "In just the first three weeks after October 7th, social media websites were inundated with instances of Holocaust inversion, with the memory of the Holocaust weaponized . . . explicitly comparing [Israel] with Nazi Germany and equating its justified acts of self-defense in the Gaza Strip with genocide."[63]

Despite their outward successes, Jews have not become complacent about the antisemitism that continues to threaten them. Overall, they have become more self-confident in standing up for their rights. Going forward, Jews must remember their history and remain vigilant of the threats before them. As Pittsburgh Jewish Federation president and CEO Jeffrey Finkelstein put it, "Our vigilance is not the same as fear. The rise in antisemitism must not make us afraid."[64]

Appendix 1

1. *Hold elected officials accountable for how they react—or fail to react—when Zionism is demonized or Jews are threatened.* Politicians seeking support must understand that these factors matter to many of us. It should be unacceptable for them to get away with practiced soundbites when they appear in front of, say, a synagogue, but then take a different stance elsewhere.

2. *Hold educational institutions accountable.* Some schools and colleges support Jewish and pro-Israel students who feel targeted; others have betrayed their students' trust. This is not about asking institutions to support a particular political stance; rather, it is about ensuring that their environments do not become poisoned by hatred, bigotry, intimidation, or ostracism. Jewish and pro-Israel students have the right to feel safe and free to express their views. If those institutions fail to protect these rights, students, trustees, alumni, parents, and others need to hold them responsible.

3. *Be swivel-headed about antisemitism.* This age-old pathology comes from multiple sources, but too many only call out the threat when it serves their own partisan political preference. So, Jews on the left point their finger at the Far Right, while Jews on the right point their finger at the Far Left, when the truth is they're both correct. We must maintain a 360-degree view.

4. *Show Jewish pride.* This is no time for American Jews to remove the mezuzahs from our doors, or kippahs from our heads, or

the word "Jewish" from the facades of our institutions, or to seek cover or hide in any other way. We can and should openly affirm our identity.

5. *Engage allies.* Antisemitic attacks need to be seen as assaults on the fabric and fiber of America's democratic, pluralistic society. When any minority is threatened, our country as a whole is at risk. We must unite with partners in diverse faith and ethnic groups to counter hate. The Jewish community has been a friend to other groups in America, whether it's been in the fight for civil rights and social justice, or overcoming unjust immigration restrictions, or speaking out for other targeted minorities. True friendships must work both ways.

Excerpted from *A Jewish Call to Action* with permission of the American Jewish Committee

Appendix 2

Founded in 2004 under the auspices of the Jewish Federations of North America and the Conference of Presidents of Major American Jewish Organizations, the Secure Community Network is the official homeland security and safety initiative of the organized Jewish community in North America. Through its operations center and Duty Desk, SCN provides timely, credible threat and incident information to both law enforcement and community partners, serves as the community's formal liaison with federal law enforcement, coordinates closely with state and local law enforcement partners, and develops and implements strategic frameworks that enhance the safety and security of the Jewish people. The following interview was conducted with SCN director Michael Masters.

How Likely Is It That Jews Will Encounter an Active Shooter Attack against One of Our Institutions?

In the two years prior to the pandemic, we saw four deadly attacks on our community: Pittsburgh, Poway, Monsey, and Jersey City. During the pandemic, we saw historic increases in antisemitic rhetoric, incidents, and hate crimes. We then had Colleyville, in addition to incidents that—while not attacks on the Jewish community—occurred within our facilities, from domestic disturbances to violent confrontations due to sports games.

We will not choose the time and place of the next incident. We can choose our preparation. This is what is critical. Every facility must have a security strategy that includes physical security solutions and training. Every community member must be trained.

Is There Anything Individuals Can Do to Possibly Prevent an Active Shooter Attack?

The vast majority of individuals who undertake targeted attacks forecast their intentions: in most cases, they explicitly tell someone of their plans. It is critical that when people see something—or hear something—they say something.

Some common indicators include:

A drastic change in someone's personality or attitude toward others, such as hostility based on claims of injustice or perceived wrongdoing, observable grievances, claims of marginalization, or distancing from friends and colleagues;

Escalations in that person's behavior, such as increasingly erratic, unsafe, or aggressive behaviors, and making statements of retribution;

Sudden and dramatic changes in the person's life experience, such as financial difficulties or pending civil or criminal litigation.

Dramatic changes in appearance, fascination with firearms or violence, etc.

If you do see or hear concerning behavior, report it to law enforcement immediately, as well as your local Jewish security director—if you have one—and SCN's Duty Desk: DutyDesk@SecureCommunityNetwork. org, 844.SCN.DESK (844.726.3375), securecommunitynetwork.org.

Beyond that, work to minimize the likelihood that you, your organization, or facility will become a target. Take security seriously and be consistent as well as comprehensive. While we can never reduce all risk, taking steps to protect against, prevent, and prepare for events— including steps that are readily visible—may minimize an individual selecting you, your facility or organization, or family as a target.

What Steps Can Individuals Take to Prepare in Case of an Attack?

Be situationally aware at all times. Be attentive to exits and entrances, people, the things they are doing, and both where and when they are doing them. If something seems suspicious or out of place, trust your instincts. Relocate to somewhere more safe or secure, if necessary, and contact necessary authorities.

Be prepared to commit to action; do not believe "it cannot or will not happen here." Have a plan.

Most basically, know your surroundings, who is coming in and out of them, and how to get out and get somewhere safe.

Ensure your facility has an assessment, has implemented a plan to address what the assessment identifies, and is undergoing, providing, or supporting training.

Be proactive. Find training for you, your loved ones, and friends. Contact your synagogue, other organization, Federation, or SCN directly.

What Kinds of Training and Support Can SCN Provide Our Jewish Community?

SCN's flagship training courses include "Be Aware: An Introduction to Situational Awareness," which teaches how to identify and report suspicious activity; "Countering Active Threat Training," which teaches how to prepare for the possibility of an active threat, how to apply the Run-Hide-Fight principles if such a threat occurs, and what to do when law enforcement arrives; and "Stop the Bleed®," which teaches lifesaving techniques to control bleeding as recommended by the American College of Surgeons. SCN also develops specialized training courses for urban and rural camps, facility ushers and greeters, and other specific audiences. Contact SCN to learn more.

Notes

Introduction

1. Editors' Note: The author passed away during the production of this volume. The JPS editors added this sentence to update the book prior to its printing.

1. Origins of Hate

1. Rosenblatt, "Is It Still Safe?"
2. "Jew Bashing from a Saint: Christianity-Revealed," accessed August 1, 2023, https://jdstone.org/cr/files/jewbashingfromasaint.html.
3. Schaff and Wace, *Nicene and Post-Nicene Fathers*, 47.
4. Krey, *First Crusade*, 53–54.
5. "Anti-Semitism: Anti-Semitic Legends of Europe," trans, and ed. D. L. Ashliman, Jewish Virtual Library, accessed June 16, 2023, https://jewish virtuallibrary.org/anti-semitic-legends-of-Europe#Stone.
6. "Martin Luther and the Jews," University of Texas, accessed June 16, 2023, https://laits.utexas.edu/bodian/re-MartinLutherAndJews.html.

2. In the Beginning

1. Oppenheim, "Early History of the Jews in New York," 74.
2. Oppenheim, "Early History of the Jews in New York," 5.
3. Oppenheim, "Early History of the Jews in New York," 8.
4. Oppenheim, "Early History of the Jews in New York," 8.
5. Huhner, "Asser Levy," 13.
6. Cyrus Adler and Max J. Kohler, s.v. "Barsimson, Jacob," *Jewish Encyclopedia*, accessed August 14, 2023, https://jewishencyclopedia.com/articles/2553 -barsimson-jacob.
7. Oppenheim, "Early History of the Jews in New York," 20.
8. Oppenheim, "Early History of the Jews in New York," 21.
9. Oppenheim, "Early History of the Jews in New York," 33.
10. Oppenheim, "Early History of the Jews in New York," 1.

11. "Boston Jews Petition for First Cemetery," April 29, 1884, Mass Moments, https://massmoments.org/moment-details/boston-jews-petition-for-first-cemetery.html.

12. Friedman, "Cotton Mather and the Jews," 202.

13. Dinnerstein, *Anti-Semitism in America*, 6.

14. Huhner, "Jews in Connection with the Colleges," 115.

15. Huhner, "Jews in Connection with the Colleges," 103.

16. Fein, *Boston—Where It All Began*, 11.

17. Huhner, "Daniel Gomez," 176.

18. Stern, "Jewish Marriage and Intermarriage," 142.

19. Dinnerstein, *Anti-Semitism in America*, 7.

20. Morgan, "Sheftalls of Savannah," 355.

21. Marcus, "Jews and the American Revolution," 150.

22. "Religious Persecution Fueled Revolution," *Thomasville Times-Enterprise*, January 23, 2020, https://www.timesenterprise.com/opinion/columns/religious-persecution-fueled-revolution/article_115cde09-d605-5cd1-9a09-e5924b789d75.html.

23. Gerber, *Jews of Spain*, 210.

24. Masserman and Baker, *Jews Come to America*, 93.

25. United States Constitution, article 6, accessed August 14, 2023, https://Senate.gov/civics/constitution_ item/constitution.htm.

26. United States Constitution, First Amendment, accessed August 14, 2023, https://www.senate.gov/civics/constitution_item/constitution.htm.

27. "Religious Tests and Oaths in State Constitution," Center for the Study of the American Constitution, accessed August 14, 2023, https://csac.history.wisc.edu/document-collections/religion-and-the-ratification/religious-test-clause/religious-tests-and-oaths-in-state-constitutions-1776-1784/.

28. Lebeson, *Pilgrim People*, 163.

29. Patel, *Sacred Ground*, 14.

30. Text adapted from historian Jonathan Sarna's annotated comments on the Seixas-Washington correspondence at the National Museum of American Jewish History website, accessed August 14, 2023, https://religiousfreedom.nmajh.org/.

31. John Berlau, "When George Washington Met Moses," *National Review*, August 13, 2020, https://www.nationalreview.com/2020/08/george-washington-champion-religious-freedom/#slide-1.

32. Matt Sheley, "Touro Celebrates Tolerance," *Newport Daily News*, August 18, 2013.

33. Sheley, "Touro Celebrates Tolerance."

34. "Paxson Gives Keynote for Washington Letter at Touro," August 17, 2014, https://news.brown.edu/articles/2014/08/touro.

3. Settling In

1. Noah, *Travels*, ix.

2. Noah, *Travels*, 376–77.

3. Noah, *Travels*, 378.

4. Noah, *Travels*, 379.

5. Noah, *Discourse*, 19.

6. David Philipson, "The Jew in America," *American Israelite*, July 8, 1909.

7. "The Noahs," *American Israelite*, March 7, 1873.

8. "Mordecai M. Noah," *United States Telegraph*, November 18, 1828.

9. *United States Gazette*, November 4, 1828.

10. "The Late Re-nomination and Confirmation of Mordecai M. Noah," *New Hampshire Statesman*, June 5, 1830.

11. "Pennsylvania Society for Evangelizing the Jews," *Occident and American Jewish Advocate*, October 1, 1843.

12. "The American Society for Meliorating the Condition of the Jews," *Occident and American Jewish Advocate*, July 1, 1849.

13. Finkelstein, *JPS Guide to American Jewish History*, 72.

14. "An American Dreyfus," *Jewish Voice*, October 13, 1899.

15. Stern and Sternlicht, *Uriah Phillips Levy*, 41.

16. Stern and Sternlicht, *Uriah Phillips Levy*, 63.

17. "Naval General Court Martial," *Baltimore Sun*, April 15, 1842.

18. "Naval General Court Martial."

19. Stern and Sternlicht, *Uriah Phillips Levy*, 57.

20. Eitches, "Maryland's 'Jew Bill,'" 265.

21. Houston, *Israel Vindicated*, 98.

22. Niebuhr, *Beyond Tolerance*, 36.

23. Eitches, "Maryland's 'Jew Bill,'" 273.

24. "Cavetown Meeting," *Torch Light and Public Advertiser*, September 16, 1823.

25. "Maryland Election," *National Advocate for the Country*, October 14, 1823.

26. "The Jews of Damascus," *Leicester Chronicle* (Leicester, England), June 6, 1840.

27. "Jews of Damascus."

28. "Correspondence Relative to the Damascus Persecutions," *Evening Post* (New York), August 31, 1840.

29. "Correspondence Relative to the Damascus Persecutions."
30. "Correspondence Relative to the Damascus Persecutions."
31. "Persecution of the Jews," *National Gazette* (Philadelphia), September 2, 1840.
32. "Foreign News," *Essex County Standard* (Colchester, Essex, England), September 25, 1840.
33. "Treaty with Switzerland," *Richmond Dispatch*, March 22, 1854.
34. Stroock, "Switzerland and the American Jews," 12.
35. Stroock, "Switzerland and the American Jews," 10.
36. Stroock, "Switzerland and the American Jews," 15.
37. "Supplement to the Swiss Question," *Israelite*, October 2, 1857.
38. "Supplement to the Swiss Question."
39. "The Treaty of the United States with the Swiss Confederation," *Israelite*, September 4, 1857.
40. Stroock, "Switzerland and the American Jews," 26.
41. "The Mortara Mass Meeting," *Daily Evening Bulletin* (San Francisco), January 17, 1859.
42. "The Mortara Case," *Daily Exchange* (Baltimore), November 29, 1858.
43. "The Mortara Case," *American Israelite*, April 1, 1909.
44. Gordon, "Board of Delegates of American Israelites," 19.

4. A Country Divided

1. Sarna, *When General Grant Expelled the Jews*, 6.
2. "Expulsion of the Jews from Grant's Department," *Indianapolis Star*, January 5, 1863.
3. Dinnerstein, *Antisemitism in America*, 32.
4. "Letter from the Editor of the Israelite," *Daily Missouri Republican*, January 24, 1863.
5. Markens, "Lincoln and the Jews," 228.
6. "Gen. Grant's Order against the Israelites," *Louisville Daily Journal* (Kentucky), January 3, 1863.
7. Rockaway and Gutfeld, "Demonic Images," 370.
8. "On Persecution," *Occident and American Jewish Advocate*, February–March 1863, http://theoccident.com/civilwar/on_persecution.html.
9. Sarna and Mendelsohn, *Jews and the Civil War*, 42.
10. Lewis Regenstein, "Jews and Anti-Semitism in the American Civil War: America's Worst Anti-Jewish Action," *Jewish Magazine*, accessed August 14, 2023, https://jewishmag.com/110mag/civilwar/civilwar.htm.

11. "Expulsion of the Jews from Grant's Department," *Indianapolis Star*, January 5, 1863.

12. Markens, "Lincoln and the Jews," 229.

13. Markens, "Lincoln and the Jews," 229.

14. Markens, "Lincoln and the Jews," 229–30.

15. Markens, "Lincoln and the Jews," 230.

16. "Abraham Lincoln (1809–1865)," Jewish Virtual Library, accessed August 14, 2023, https://jewishvirtuallibrary.org/abraham-lincoln.

17. Schmier, "Notes and Documents," 15.

18. Schmier, "Notes and Documents," 22.

19. Donald Altschiller, s.v. "Jews," *Encyclopedia of the American Civil War*, 1070–71.

20. Aaron O'Neill, "Number of Soldiers Who Were Enlisted during the American Civil War from 1861 to 1865, by Army," Statista, June 21, 2022, https://statista.com/statistics/1009782/total-army-size-american-civil-war-1861-1865/.

21. Barash, "American Jewish Chaplaincy," 9.

22. Markens, "Lincoln and the Jews," 226.

23. Rywell, "Judah Benjamin," 35.

24. Rywell, "Judah Benjamin," 29.

25. "Senator Wilson's Notorious Speech," *Israelite*, July 19, 1872.

26. Dinnerstein, *Anti-Semitism in America*, 33.

27. Benet, *John Brown's Body*, 69–70.

28. Morais, "Jewish Ostracism in America," 270.

29. Michael Meyer, "The German-Jewish Legacy in America," the 2010 Paul Lecture, https://jsp.sitehost.iu.edu/docs/Legacy%20Indiana.pdf.

30. Michael A. Meyer, "Thank You, Moritz Loth: A 125-Year UAHC Retrospective," *Reform Judaism* vol. 27, no. 1 (Fall 1998): 30–34, 36–39.

31. "The News This Morning," *New York Tribune*, June 1, 1876.

32. "A Sensation at Saratoga," *New York Times*, June 19, 1877.

33. "Sensation at Saratoga."

34. "Sensation at Saratoga."

35. "Trouble Continues," *Daily Inter Ocean* (Chicago), June 21, 1877.

36. "Judge Hilton's Position," *New York Times*, June 20, 1877.

37. "Selecting Their Guests," *New York Times*, June 21, 1877.

38. Livney, "Let Us Now Praise Self-Made Men," 81.

39. "Reviving a Prejudice," *New York Daily Herald*, July 22, 1879.

40. "Jews Barred from Hotel," *Chicago Tribune*, May 18, 1907.

41. "Civil Rights in New Jersey, 1945–2020: Discrimination in Social Life," New Jersey State Library, accessed August 14, 2023, https://libguides.njstatelib.org/discrimination/public.

42. Halperin, "Jewish Problem in U.S. Medical Education," 140.

5. The Great Wave

1. Volkman, *A Legacy of Hate*, 31.

2. Goodkind, *Prominent Jews of America*, 119.

3. Livingston, *Must Men Hate?* 3.

4. "Jewish Objection to Christianizing Efforts," *Literary Digest*, May 14, 1910.

5. "To Seek Warrants for Hoe Employees," *New York Times*, August 3, 1902.

6. "Our New York Letter," *Independent-Record* (Helena, Montana), August 12, 1902.

7. "Jews Offer Reward," *New York Tribune*, August 1, 1902.

8. Dinnerstein, *Uneasy at Home*, 171.

9. Sarna, *American Judaism*, 433.

10. Dimont, *Jews in America*, 165.

11. Leo Trachtenberg, "Philanthropy That Worked," Winter 1998, https://www.city-journal.org/html/philanthropy-worked-12156.html.

12. Ernest K. Coulter, "Allen Colonies and the Children's Court," *North American Review*, November 1904.

13. "New Home for Jews," *New York Tribune*, May 13, 1907.

14. "Tell of Good Work in Saving Bad Boys," *New York Times*, May 15, 1911.

15. John J. Douquette, "Anti-Semitism: A Darker Chapter in History of Our Adirondack Region," *Adirondack Daily Enterprise*, February 2, 1987.

16. American Library Association, "Melvil Dewey Medal," accessed August 14, 2023, https://www.ala.org/awardsgrants/ala-medal-excellence.

17. "From Readers," *New York Times*, January 6, 1906.

18. Theodore A. Bingham, "Foreign Criminals in New York," *North American Review*, September 1908.

19. Ribak, "Jew Usually Left Those Crimes to Esau," 2.

20. "Jewish Disclaimer of Gambler Profanation," *Literary Digest*, August 24, 1912.

21. "Dr. Chase Preaches on Rosenthal Case," *Brooklyn Times Union*, November 18, 1912.

6. A Lynching and a Lawyer

1. Finkelstein, *Captain of Innocence*, 18.

2. While Dreyfus was imprisoned on Devil's Island, France was torn apart with the surfacing of evidence that he was innocent. Brought back to France for a new military trial in 1899, Dreyfus was again found guilty but "with extenuating circumstances." To avoid further embarrassment, the government pardoned him and released him from prison. He returned to the army.

3. Connolly, *Truth about the Frank Case*, 42.

4. Lawson, *American State Trials*, 264.

5. Connolly, *Truth about the Frank Case*, 18.

6. Golden, *Lynching of Leo Frank*, 227.

7. "As Appeared in *B'nai Brith News*, October 1913," Anti-Defamation League, accessed August 14, 2023, https://www.adl.org/excerpt-anti-defamation-league-founding-charter.

8. "While Leo Frank Is Loafing at the State Farm, the Rich Jews Continue to Defame the People and the Courts of Georgia," *Jeffersonian*, July 15, 1915.

9. "Why Do They Keep Up the Big Money Campaign against the People and the Courts of Georgia?" *Jeffersonian*, August 12, 1915.

10. "John M. Slaton Talks in Alaska. Attacks Senators Smith and Hardwick. Is Coming Back to Run for the Senate," *Jeffersonian*, August 19, 1915.

11. "Opinions," *Crisis*, October 1915.

12. "Georgia Disgraced," *Akron Beacon Journal*, August 17, 1915.

13. "The Shame of Georgia," *Brooklyn Times Union*, August 17, 1915.

14. "Marshall Indicts Tom Watson as Frank's Slayer," *Buffalo Courier*, August 19, 1915.

15. "After 69 Years of Silence, Lynching Victim Is Cleared," *New York Times*, March 8, 1982.

16. "Brandeis on Zionism," World Zionist Organization, accessed August 14, 2023, https://www.wzo.org.il/index.php?dir=site&page=articles&op=item&cs=3276.

17. "Anti-Semitic Letter from Ex-President Taft Up for Auction," History News Network, April 24, 2016, https://historynewsnetwork.org/article/162644.

18. Todd, *Justice on Trial*, 85.

19. Todd, *Justice on Trial*, 143.

20. Todd, *Justice on Trial*, 92.

21. "Why the Difference," *New York Age*, February 2, 1916.

22. Katz, "Henry Higginson vs. Louis Dembitz Brandeis," 80.

23. "Brandeis and the Senate," *Washington Times*, February 6, 1916.

24. American Jewish Congress pamphlet, *The American Jewish Congress: What It Is and What It Does*, 1936, 9.

25. "Jewish Welfare Board, Purpose Scope Achievement," pamphlet issued in 1918 by the Jewish Welfare Board in New York, 1.
26. "Says Mass of Jews Oppose Bolshevik," *Atlanta Constitution*, February 23, 1919.

7. The Bigoted 1920s

1. Nilus, *Jewish Peril*, 48.
2. Henry Ford, "The International Jew: The World's Foremost Problem," *Dearborn Independent*, May 22, 1920.
3. Henry Ford, "The Jewish Aspect of the 'Movie' Problem," *Dearborn Independent*, February 12, 1921.
4. "Jewish Jazz Becomes Our National Music," *Dearborn Independent*, August 6, 1921.
5. Ford, *International Jew*, 128.
6. Finkelstein, *Forged in Freedom*, 72.
7. Baldwin, *Henry Ford and the Jews*, 120.
8. Baldwin, *Henry Ford and the Jews*, 120.
9. "America's Jewish Enigma—Louis Marshall," *Dearborn Independent*, November 26, 1921.
10. "'Jewish Rights' to Put Studies Out of Schools," *Dearborn Independent*, March 19, 1921.
11. *The "Protocols," Bolshevism, and Jews*, American Jewish Committee pamphlet, 1921, 14.
12. "How T. Roosevelt Estimated Ford," *San Francisco Examiner*, March 10, 1921.
13. "Ford's Misguided Tirade Against Jews in America," *Vicksburg Herald* (MS), December 29, 1920.
14. "The Jews Fight Back," *Appeal* (Saint Paul MN), April 2, 1921.
15. "Henry Ford—Pogromist," *Butte Daily Bulletin* (MT), December 23, 1920.
16. "Jew Baiting in Michigan," *Leavenworth Times* (KS), December 4, 1920.
17. "Two Libel Suits against Ford May Be Ended," *Detroit Free Press*, July 6, 1927.
18. "Statement by Henry Ford," 386–87.
19. Wallace, *American Axis*, 123.
20. "Imperial Wizard Explains Workings of Ku Klux Klan," *Passaic Daily Herald* (NJ), October 24, 1923.
21. "Should There Be a Jewish Fight on the Klan?" *Washington Jewish Chronicle*, December 8, 1922.
22. "Letter from Charles D. Levy to President Calvin Coolidge Requesting Protection for Jews from the Ku Klux Klan," June 24, 1924, https://docsteach

.org/documents/document/letter-from-charles-d-levy-to-president-calvin -coolidge-requesting-protection-for-jews-from-the-ku-klux-klan.

23. "Jews, Attention!," *Denver Jewish News*, August 23, 1922.

24. "Many Jews Go to College," *Nation*, June 14, 1922.

25. "Jews Facing a Closing College Door," *Literary Digest*, July 8, 1922.

26. "May Jews Go to College."

27. Halperin, "Jewish Problem in U.S. Medical Education," 141.

28. Dinnerstein, *Anti-Semitism in America*, 86.

29. Stephen Steinberg, "How Jewish Quotas Began," *Commentary*, September 1971, https://www.commentary.org/articles/stephen-steinberg/how-jewish -quotas-began/.

30. "Jew Baiting at the U.S. Naval Academy," *American Israelite*, June 22, 1922.

31. "Naval Academy Incident Closed," *Riverside Daily Press* (CA), June 15, 1922.

32. Wortman, *Admiral Hyman Rickover*, 112.

33. American Jewish Committee, *To Bigotry No Sanction*, 20.

34. Cohen, "Jews, Jobs, and Discrimination," 3.

35. Elias Lieberman, "The Difficult Art of Being a Jew," *Outlook*, January 10, 1923.

36. "Jews, Attention!," *Denver Jewish News*, August 23, 1922.

37. "Jews, Attention!," *Denver Jewish News*, August 23, 1922.

38. Higham, "Social Discrimination against Jews in America," 371.

39. "Jewish Patronage Not Solicited," *Wisconsin Jewish Chronicle*, May 25, 1923.

40. "Our New 'Nordic' Immigration Policy," *Literary Digest*, May 10, 1924.

41. "Shall America Bar the Jew?" *Wisconsin Jewish Chronicle*, January 11, 1924.

42. "The Massena Blood Libel," My Jewish Learning, accessed August 14, 2023, https://www.myjewishlearning.com/article/the-massena-blood-libel.

43. "Governor Smith Orders Probe of 'Massena Incident,'" *Boston Globe*, October 4, 1928.

44. "Inquiry Promised by Smith in Massena Jewish Trouble," *Cincinnati Enquirer*, October 4, 1928.

45. "Mayor Apologizes for Accusing Jews of Ritual Murder," *Wisconsin Jewish Chronicle*, October 12, 1928.

46. "Smith Orders Investigation into 'Messina Incident,'" *Plain Speaker* (Hazleton PA), October 4, 1928.

47. "Better Understanding between Christians and Jews in America," *Lebanon Daily News* (PA), October 8, 1928.

8. The Rising Storm

1. "Ludendorf and Hitler Declare War on Jews," *Wisconsin Jewish Chronicle*, November 9, 1923.
2. "Rabbi Stephen S. Wise, WJC Past President," World Jewish Congress, accessed August 14, 2023, https://www.worldjewishcongress.org/en/bio/rabbi-stephen-s-wise.
3. "No German Steel for Triboro Bridge, Laguardia Orders," *Jewish Telegraphic Agency*, November 15, 1935, https://www.jta.org/archive/no-german-steel-for-triboro-bridge-laguardia-orders.
4. "Nazis End Attacks on Jews in Reich, Our Embassy Finds," *New York Times*, March 27, 1933.
5. "Western Penn. Jewry Protest to Washington," *Indiana (pa) Gazette*, March 28, 1933.
6. "McNutt Protests Attacks on Jews," *Indianapolis Star*, March 28, 1933.
7. Thomas L. Blanton (TX), "Extension of Remarks in the Congressional Record," *Congressional Record* 77 (1933): 885.
8. "Bulletin no. 3. The Silver Shirts: Their History, Founder and Activities," August 24, 1933, https://ajcarchives.org/ajc_data/Files/thr-ss1.pdf.
9. "Bulletin no. 3. The Silver Shirts."
10. "The Jewish Hymn: Onward Christian Soldiers," United States Holocaust Memorial Museum, accessed August 14, 2023, https://perspectives.ushmm.org/item/the-jewish-hymn-onward-christian-soldiers.
11. "Report True Wants 15 Big Jews Bumped Off," Jewish Telegraphic Agency, August 21, 1936, https://www.jta.org/archive/report-true-wants-15-big-jews-bumped-off.
12. "Inter-Group Relations," 213.
13. Irwin, *Inside the "Christian Front"*, 3.
14. Handlin, "Twenty Year Retrospect," 309.
15. "Jews, New Deal Denounced; Few Heads Cracked," *Knoxville News-Sentinel*, February 21, 1939.
16. "Bund Head Assailant Is Given 10 Days," *Evening Sun* (Baltimore), February 21, 1939.
17. Marc Shapiro, "When Jewish Children Were the Ones Being Separated," *Baltimore Jewish Times*, July 19, 2018.
18. "US Immigration Laws and the Refugee Crisis," Holocaust Encyclopedia, United States Holocaust Memorial Museum, https://encyclopedia.ushmm.org/content/en/article/wagner-rogers-bill.

19. Herbert Manasse, "Jewish Refugees on German Ship Seek Divine Aid in Finding Home," https://www.newspapers.com/image/382741690/?terms =jewish%20refugees%20ship&match=1.

20. "Breckinridge Long's Memorandum," June 26, 1940, https://www.facing history.org/rescuers/breckinridge-long-memorandum.

21. Welch, "American Public Opinion," 622.

22. Charles Lindbergh, "Des Moines Speech," delivered in Des Moines, Iowa on September 11, 1941, http://charleslindbergh.com/americanfirst/speech.asp.

23. Lindbergh, "Des Moines Speech."

24. Lindbergh, "Des Moines Speech."

25. Dorothy Thompson, "Mr. Lindbergh and the Facts," *Boston Globe*, September 17, 1941.

26. "Two Groups Hit Speech by Lindbergh," *Pittsburgh Post-Gazette*, September 19, 1941.

27. "Peace Group Hits Flier for Attack on U.S. Jews," *Oakland Tribune* (CA), September 21, 1941.

28. "As the Press of America Views the Lindbergh Speech," *Daily Times* (Davenport IA), September 16, 1941.

29. "As the Press of America Views the Lindbergh Speech."

30. "As the Press of America Views the Lindbergh Speech."

31. "Says Talk 'Like Berlin,'" *Capital Times* (Madison WI), September 12, 1941.

32. Welch, "American Public Opinion," 624.

33. Francis L. Hurwitz, "Humor That's Dangerous," *Jewish Sentinel*, 1944, https://idaillinois.org/digital/collection/p16614coll14/id/49154.

34. "The Riegner Telegram," Holocaust Encyclopedia, United States Holocaust Memorial Museum, https://encyclopedia.ushmm.org/content/en/article /the-riegner-telegram.

35. "Riegner Telegram."

36. "Franklin Roosevelt Administration Report on Meeting of Jewish Leaders with Roosevelt (December 8, 1942)," https://www.jewishvirtuallibrary.org /report-on-meeting-of-jewish-leaders-with-roosevelt-december-1942.

37. "Franklin Roosevelt Administration Report on Meeting of Jewish Leaders with Roosevelt (December 8, 1942)."

38. Rafael Medoff, "The Bergson Group vs. the Holocaust—and Jewish Leaders vs. Bergson" (Part II), June 13, 2007, https://www.jewishpress.com/indepth /front-page/the-bergson-group-vs-the-holocaust-and-jewish-leaders-vs -bergson-part-ii/2007/06/13/.

39. Medoff, *Jews Should Keep Quiet*, 187–88.
40. Medoff, *Jews Should Keep Quiet*, 190.
41. Matt Lebovic, "As the Holocaust Raged, US Newspapers Buried Reports on Hitler's Final Solution," July 29, 2022, https://www.timesofisrael.com/as-the-holocaust-raged-us-newspapers-buried-reports-on-hitlers-final-solution/.
42. Medoff, "Bergson Group vs. the Holocaust."
43. "Roosevelt Sets Up War Refugee Board," *New York Times*, January 23, 1944.
44. Finkelstein, *Shelter and the Fence*, 45–46.
45. "Saltonstall Chases Writer out of State House," *Charlotte Observer*, October 19, 1943.
46. "Saltonstall Chases Writer out of State House."
47. "Saltonstall Challenged," *Baltimore Sun*, October 19, 1943.
48. "Young Hoodlums Blamed by Mayor for Racial Trouble," *Boston Globe*, October 30, 1943.
49. "Hearings before a Subcommittee on the Post Office and Post Roads House of Representatives," 33.
50. "New York Mayor to Get Report on Investigation of Anti-Semitism," *Wisconsin Jewish Chronicle*, January 7, 1944.
51. "Must Be No Room for Class or Race Persecution in U.S.," *York Daily Record* (PA), February 14, 1944.
52. "Anti-Semitism in U.S. Plays Hitler's Game, National Rally Told," *Wisconsin Jewish Chronicle*, February 18, 1944.
53. Dinnerstein, "Anti-Semitism Exposed and Attacked," 142.

9. Into the Mainstream

1. "Amicus Brief Jewish Coalition Shelley v. Kraemer": "Interest of the Amici," Supreme Court of the United States. *Shelley v. Kraemer*, 334 U.S. 1 (1947), 2, https://www.scribd.com/document/533525391/Amicus-Brief-Jewish-Coalition-Shelley-v-Kraemer.
2. "Civil Rights Unit Reports on Housing Bias against Jews," *Wisconsin Jewish Chronicle*, September 18, 1959.
3. "Civil Rights Unit Reports on Housing Bias against Jews."
4. Milton Friedman, "Washington Week," *Wisconsin Jewish Chronicle*, November 14, 1952.
5. Harry S. Truman, "Statement by the President upon Signing the Displaced Persons Act," June 25, 1948, https://www.trumanlibrary.gov/library/public-papers/142/statement-president-upon-signing-displaced-persons-act.

6. Drew Pearson, "General MacArthur Can Handle Russians," *Star Press* (Muncie IN), July 20, 1948.

7. "Shocking Words," *American Jewish World*, May 6, 1949.

8. Quoted in Leonard Dinnerstein, "American Immigration Policy, 1945–1950," Yad Vashem, accessed August 14, 2023, https://www yadvashem.org/articles /academic/american-immigration-policy.html.

9. Gerald L. K. Smith, *Jew-Communist Internationalism*, leaflet of the Christian Nationalist Party, 1951, 20.

10. Milton Friedman, "Franco's 'Be Kind to Jews' Campaign," *Wisconsin Jewish Chronicle*, March 3, 1950.

11. *Appendix to the Congressional Record*, v. 89 part 10, March 26, 1943, Washington DC: United States Government Printing Office, A1471.

12. "Rankin Continues Attacks on Jews, Evades Publicity," *American Jewish World*, April 18, 1947.

13. "Rankin Continues Attacks on Jews, Evades Publicity."

14. David Turner, "America after the Holocaust," *Jerusalem Post*, March 27, 2013; Rankin, quoted in Harold Brackman, "The Attack on Jewish Hollywood," *Modern Judaism*, February 2000.

15. Turner, "America after the Holocaust,"

16. Larry Tye, "McCarthy Was Anti-Communist. Was He Also Anti-Semitic?" *Boston Globe*, July 7, 2020.

17. "Groups Denounce Communists in Rosenberg Case," *American Jewish World*, May 23, 1952.

10. Civil Rights and Legal Rights

1. Kevin Schultz, "Favoritism Cannot Be Tolerated," *American Quarterly*, September 2007.

2. Pfeffer, *Church, State and Freedom*, 348.

3. "Religious Program Brings School Suit," *New York Times*, July 28, 1948.

4. United States Supreme Court, "Engel v. Vitale" (1962), no. 468, https:// caselaw.findlaw.com/us-supreme-court/370/421.html.

5. "Catholic Lay Organ Renews Defense on School Prayer Ban," *Wisconsin Jewish Chronicle*, September 28, 1962.

6. "Catholic Lay Organ Renews Defense on School Prayer Ban."

7. "Carson v. Makin," *Oyez*, accessed August 14, 2023, https://www.oyez.org /cases/2021/20-1088.

8. Sotomayor quoted in Amy Howe, "Court Strikes Down Maine's Ban on Using Public Funds at Religious Schools," June 21, 2022, https://www.scotusblog

.com/2022/06/court-strikes-down-maines-ban-on-using-public-funds-at
-religious-schools/.

9. Ron Kampeas, "Supreme Court Decision on Coach's Prayer Throws Doubt on a 30-Year-Old-Victory for a Jewish Family," June 27, 2022, https://www .jta.org/2022/06/27/politics/supreme-court-decision-on-coachs-prayer -throws-doubt-on-a-30-year-old-victory-for-a-jewish-family.

10. Kaitlin Smith, "It Takes a Village: The Success of *Brown v. Board*," June 3, 2019, https://facingtoday.facinghistory.org/it-takes-a-village-the-success -of-brown-v.-board.

11. "West Virginia State Board of Education v. Barnette (1943)," National Consti-tution Center, accessed August 14, 2023, https://constitutioncenter.org/the -constitution/supreme-court-case-library/west-virginia-board-of-education -v-barnette.

12. Finkelstein, *Schools of Hope*, 28.

13. "Amici Curiae Brief," Sweatt v. Painter, 1950, found on Google Books, https://google.com/books/edition/Records_and_Briefs_of_the_United _States/u4xyRvBdrhuc?hl=en&gbpv=1&dq=Inequality+is+an+inevitable +concomitant+of+segregation+of+racial+groups+in+public+educational +facilities+and+as+such+violated+the+equal+protection+of+the+laws +provision+of+the+Fourteenth+Amendment&pg=ra3-pr1&printsec= frontcover.

14. *McLaurin v. Oklahoma State Regents*, 339 U.S. 637 (1950), https://supreme .justia.com/cases/federal/us/339/637/.

15. Justin Jacobs, "Jews Play Important, Supporting Role in 'Freedom Rid-ers,'" May 13, 2011, https://jewishchronicle.timesofisrael.com/jews-play -important-supporting-role-in-freedom-riders/.

16. "Dr. Blake among 283 Held in Racial Rally in Maryland," *New York Times*, July 5, 1963.

17. Quoted in "The Temple Bombing," The Temple, accessed August 15, 2023, https://www.the-temple.org/bombing.

18. "G.O.P. Probers Learn of Anti-Semitic Parodies," *St. Louis Jewish Light*, March 30, 1966.

19. "Goals of the Rights March," *New York Times*, August 29, 1963.

20. "The Problem of Silence: Rabbi Joachim Prinz Speech at the March on Washington," American Jewish Archives, accessed August 14, 2023, https:// www.americanjewisharchives.org/snapshots/the-problem-of-silence-rabbi -joachim-prinz-speech-at-the-march-on-washington/.

21. Rabbi Ari Sunshine, "I Felt My Legs Were Praying," January 4, 2018, https://www.shearith.org/blog/i-felt-my-legs-were-praying.

22. Greene, *Temple Bombing*, 180.

23. "Conversation with Martin Luther King," Gendler Grapevine Project, March 25, 1968, https://www.gendlergrapevine.org.

24. "Conversation with Martin Luther King."

25. James Baldwin, "Negroes Are Anti-Semitic Because They're Anti-White," *New York Times*, April 9, 1967, https://archive.nytimes.com/www.nytimes.com/books/98/03/29/specials/baldwin-antisem.html?_r=2.

26. Podair, *Strike That Changed New York*, 124.

27. "Code Switch, Pt 2: Black Parents Take Control, Teachers Strike Back," NPR, February 12, 2020, https://www.npr.org/transcripts/803382499.

28. Celestine Bohlen, "Teacher Accused of Past Anti-Semitism Quits Dinkins Camp," *New York Times*, October 12, 1989.

29. Marjorie Ingall, "Goodbye to Julius Lester, the Ultimate Contrarian," *Tablet*, January 22, 2018.

30. Quoted in Cooks, *Exhibiting Blackness*, 69.

31. Quoted in Greenberg, "How Affirmative Action Fractured the Black-Jewish Alliance," 85.

32. Eunice G. Pollack, "Black Antisemitism in America: Past and Present," Institute for National Security Studies, June 1, 2022, https://inss.org.il/publication/black-antisemitism/.

33. Bruce Buursma, "Muslim Leader Drawing Fire," *Fort Worth Star-Telegram*, April 15, 1984.

34. E. R. Shipp, "Tape Contradicts Disavowal of 'Gutter Religion' Attack," *New York Times*, June 29, 1984.

35. "Louis Farrakhan," Southern Poverty Law Center, accessed August 14, 2023, https://www.splcenter.org/fighting-hate/extremist-files/individual/louis-farrakhan.

36. Quoted in Kenneth S. Stern, "Dr. Jeffries and the Anti-Semitic Branch of the Afrocentrism Movement," American Jewish Committee *Issues in National Affairs* 1, no. 2 (1991), https://www.bjpa.org/content/upload/bjpa/issu/issues%202.pdf.

37. *The Anti-Semitism of Black Demagogues and Extremists*, Anti-Defamation League pamphlet, 1992, 23.

38. "Hate Grows in Brooklyn," *Jewish Daily Forward*, August 21, 1991.

39. Craig Horowitz, "The New Anti-Semitism," *New York*, January 11, 1993.

40. Jeff Dunetz, "How Anti-Semitism Replaced Historic Black-Jewish Alliance," *Jewish Star*, February 9, 2020, https://www.thejewishstar.com/stories/how-anti-semitism-came-to-replace-the-historic-black-jewish-alliance,18745.

41. Jeff Jacoby, "The Flames of Hatred in the Age of Farrakhan," *Boston Globe*, December 14, 1995.

42. "On Protest Tape," *Daily News* (New York), December 13, 1995; Minoo Southgate, "Racist Rhetoric Fueled Harlem Inferno," *Daily News*, December 18, 1995.

43. "Antisemitic Attitudes in the U.S.A. Guide to ADL's Latest Poll," Anti-Defamation League, January 27, 2020, https://www.adl.org/survey-of-american-attitudes-toward-jews.

44. Ben Sales, "The Stats of US Anti-Semitism: A New Survey Has Some Clear and Dismal Data," August 9, 2022, https://www.timesofisrael.com/the-stats-of-us-anti-semitism-a-new-survey-has-some-clear-and-dismal-data/.

45. "Then and Now: Black-Jewish Relations in the Civil Rights Movement," University of Pennsylvania, Penn Today, accessed August 14, 2023, https://penntoday.upenn.edu/news/black-jewish-relations-civil-rights-movement.

46. Marc H. Morial and Harriet P. Schleifer, "Black, Jewish Leaders: We Are Standing Together to Fight Bigotry in America," September 9, 2020, https://www.usatoday.com/story/opinion/2020/09/09/black-jewish-leaders-how-we-fight-racism-bigotry-together-column/5743874002/.

11. Zionism = Judaism?

1. See Troy, *Zionist Ideas*.

2. "Mrs. Meir Warns of Danger of Nasser's Anti-Israel Hate Campaign; Protest Made to Moscow on Propaganda Drive," *Wisconsin Jewish Chronicle*, November 14, 1958.

3. Marrus, *Lessons of the Holocaust*, 72.

4. "Elimination of All Forms of Racial Discrimination: Zionism as Racism," Resolution Adopted by the UN General Assembly, https://un.org/unispal/document/auto-insert-181963/.

5. "Americans Disagree with U.N. on Zionism as Racism," *Longview Daily News* (WA), December 15, 1975.

6. Donald Kirk, "Zionism Is Racism, UN Votes; 'Terrible Evil Loose,' U.S. Says," *Chicago Tribune*, November 11, 1975.

7. Liskofsky, "UN Resolution on Zionism," 110.

8. Vernon E. Jordan Jr., "Zionism, Racism-and Anti-Semitism Too," *Record* (Hackensack NJ), November 18, 1975.

9. Richard Brunher, "Local Bigoted Talk Is Well Below Professional Levels," *Morning Call* (Allentown PA), April 7, 2002.

10. "Americans' Sympathy for Israel Rising," *San Bernardino County Sun* (CA), December 23, 1973.

11. Elihai Braun, "UN World Conference against Racism, Racial Discrimination, Xenophobia and Related Intolerance-Durban, South Africa," Jewish Virtual Library, accessed August 14, 2023, https://www.jewishvirtuallibrary .org/durban-i-un-conference-against-racism-2001.

12. Braun, "UN World Conference."

13. Richard Goldstone, "Israel and the Apartheid Slander," *New York Times*, November 1, 2011.

14. "Allegation: Israel Is an Apartheid State," Anti-Defamation League, May 3, 2022, https://www.adl.org/resources/glossary-term/allegation-israel -apartheid-state.

15. "Isn't a Boycott of Israel Anti-Semitic?" BDS, accessed August 14, 2023, https://bdsmovement.net/faqs#collapse16241.

16. Alan Dershowitz, "Ben & Jerry's Defense Is Hard to Swallow," *Daily News* (NY), August 1, 2021.

17. Natan Sharansky, "3D Test of Anti-Semitism: Demonization, Double Standards, Delegitimization," *Jewish Political Studies Review* 16, nos. 3–4 (Fall 2004): 5–8.

18. Yonat Shimron, "American Jewish Groups Denounce Presbyterian Church for Calling Israel 'Apartheid,'" July 11, 2022, https://religionnews.com/2022 /07/11/american-jewish-groups-denounce-presbyterian-church-for-calling -israel-apartheid/.

19. "Knesset Report: BDS Movement Has No Impact on Economy," *Haaretz*, January 9, 2015, https://www.haaretz.com/2015-01-09/ty-article/.premium /knesset-report-bds-movement-has-no-impact-on-economy/0000017f-db7d -d3ff-a7ff-fbfd76de0000?lts=1660841408639.

20. "Campus Divestment Resolution in the USA (2005–2022)," Jewish Virtual Library, accessed August 14, 2023, https://www.jewishvirtuallibrary.org /campus-divestment-resolutions.

21. "President Bollinger Comments on College Student Vote on Israel," Columbia University of the City of New York, September 29, 2020, https://president .columbia.edu/news/president-bollinger-comments-college-student-vote -israel.

22. "2020 AJC Surveys on the State of Antisemitism in America: Jewish Sample and General US Public Sample Comparisons," accessed August 15, 2023, https://www.jewishdatabank.org/databank/search-results/study/1112.

23. "One-Third of Jewish Students Experienced Antisemitism on College Campuses in Last School Year, New Survey Finds," October 25, 2021, https://www.adl.org/news/press-releases/one-third-of-jewish-students -experienced-antisemitism-on-college-campuses-in.

24. Josefin Dolsten, "What It's Like to Support Israel at NYU," April 24, 2018, https://www timesofisrael.com/what-its-like-to-support-israel-at-nyu/.

25. "Martin Kramer Says Columbia University Professors Claim Israelis Are the New Nazis," https://historynewsnetwork.org/article/156750.

26. Talia Katz, "Anti-Semitism, Run Amok on Campus," *Daily News* (New York), October 13, 2018.

27. Rosanna Xia, "Anti-Semitism Alleged at San Francisco State," *Los Angeles Times*, June 20, 2017.

28. Jeremy Fox, "Anti Israel Poster Found at Tufts Hillel," February 13, 2109, https://www.bostonglobe.com/metro/2019/02/13/anti-israel-posters -found-tufts-jewish-center/KbgClPbahgwyUol4iu9xxp/story.html.

29. Jacob Henry, "Anti-Israel Commencement Speaker Sparks Fresh Antisem- itism Debate at CUNY," May 21, 2022, https://www.timesofisrael.com/anti -israel-commencement-speaker-sparks-fresh-antisemitism-debate-at-cuny/.

30. Eitan Fischberger, "The Groups Intimidating New York Jews," *New York Daily News*, May 19, 2022, https://www.nydailynews.com/opinion/ny -oped-groups-intimidating-new-york-jews-20220519-dqlyi5xp3rgrpkrtd gzxpwzlru-story.html.

31. Henry, "Anti-Israel Commencement Speaker."

32. "ADL Report: Inflammatory Anti-Israel Activity and BDS Calls Are Vilifying Many Jewish Students on Campus," December 7, 2021, https://www.adl.org /resources/press-release/adl-report-inflammatory-anti-israel-activity-and -bds-calls-are-vilifying.

33. Hillel International, "Campus Climate Initiative," August 14, 2023, https:// www.hillel.org/cci.

34. "Statement of Jewish Organizations on Boycott, Divestment and Sanctions (BDS) Campaigns against Israel," February 2011, https://www.stopbds.com /?page_id=1318.

35. "Strengthening America's Security in the Middle East Act of 2019," Congress. gov, accessed August 14, 2023, https://congress.gov/bill/116th-congress /senate-bill/1/all-info.

36. "BDS Israel Boycott Group Is Anti-Semitic, Says US," BBC, November 19, 2020, https://bbc.www.com/news/world-middle-east-54999010.

37. John O'Connor, "Ill. Regulators Threaten Ben & Jerry's over Israel," *Rutland Daily Herald* (VT), July 30, 2021.

38. "American Jewish Committee Applauds Ben & Jerry's U.S. Franchisees Letter of Concerns," August 4, 2021, https://www.ajc.org/news/american -jewish-committee-applauds-ben-jerrys-us-franchisees-letter-of-concerns.

39. "Following Start of Mideast Violence, Antisemitic Incidents More Than Double in May 2021 vs May 2020," Anti-Defamation League, June 7, 2021, https://www.adl.org/resources/blog/following-start-mideast-violence -antisemitic-incidents-more-double-may-2021-vs-may.

40. Luis Andres Henad, "Americans Must Come Together," *Tyler Morning Telegraph* (Tyler TX), May 29, 2021.

41. "ADL Audit Finds Antisemitic Incidents in United States Reached All-Time High in 2021," April 25, 2022, Anti-Defamation League, https://www.adl .org/news/press-releases/adl-audit-finds-antisemitic-incidents-in-united -states-reached-all-time-high-in.

42. Anti-Defamation League, "What Is the Mapping Project?" accessed August 14, 2023, https://www.adl.org/boston-mapping-project.

43. "The Mapping Project," accessed August 14, 2023, https://mapliberation.org.

44. Ross Crisantiello, "Mass. Jewish Leaders, Politicians, Condemn New Pro-Palestine Site 'The Mapping Project,'" June 14, 2022, https://www.boston .com/news/local-news/2022/06/14/jewish-leaders-politicians-condemn -pro-palestine-mapping-project/.

45. Linda Matchan, "The Mapping Project: How Worried Should Jews Be?" *Jewish Journal*, June 23, 2022.

46. Ross Crisantiello, "Mass. Jewish Leaders, Politicians, Condemn New Pro-Palestine Site 'The Mapping Project,'" June 14, 2022, https://www.boston .com/news/local-news/2022/06/14/jewish-leaders-politicians-condemn -pro-palestine-mapping-project/.

47. U.S. Department of State, "Defining Antisemitism," accessed August 14, 2023, https://www.state.gov/defining-antisemitism/.

48. U.S. Department of State, "Defining Antisemitism."

49. Some individuals and groups committed to combatting antisemitism have also raised concerns about the IHRA definition and proposed alternative approaches.

50. Amnesty International, "Crime of Apartheid: The Government of Israel's Systematic Oppression against Palestinians," accessed August 14, 2023, https://www.amnestyusa.org/campaigns/end-apartheid/.

51. "Key Trends in U.S. Views on Israel and the Palestinians," May 28, 2021, https://news.gallup.com/poll/350393/key-trends-views-israel-palestinians .aspx.

12. The Changing Landscape of Hate

1. "Jews in Gadsden Reassured; Youth Who Bombed Synagogue Is Arrested," *Jewish Telegraphic Agency*, March 28, 1960.
2. Roger Rosenblatt, "Their Finest Minute," *New York Times*, July 3, 1994. https://www.nytimes.com/1994/07/03/magazine/their-finest-minute.html.
3. Quoted in Andrew Romano, "How the Town of Whitefish Defeated Its Neo-Nazi Trolls," *Yahoo! News*, January 19, 2017.
4. Lauren Stein, "In Era of the 'Lone Wolf' Extremist, Anti-Semitic Terror Hard to [*sic*]," *Jewish Telegraphic Agency*, August 17, 1999, https://www.jta .org/1999/08/17/lifestyle/behind-the-headlines-in-era-of-the-lone-wolf -extremist-anti-semitic-terror-hard-to.
5. James Sterngold, "Shootings in Los Angeles: The Overview; Man with a Past of Racial Hate Surrenders in Day Camp Attack," *New York Times*, August 12, 1999.
6. "Jewish Community Center Shootings," c-Span, August 10, 1999, https:// www.c-span.org/video/?151557–1/jewish-community-center-shootings.
7. "ADL Says U.S. Based Anti-Semites Are Feeding Sept. 11 Rumor Mill," *US Newswire*, November 9, 2001.
8. "Anti-Defamation League Steps Up Efforts to Combat Anti-Semitism Online," NPR, September 21, 2016, https://www.npr.org/sections/alltech considered/2016/09/21/494914690/anti-defamation-league-steps-up-efforts -to-combat-anti-semitism-online.
9. Deepa Shivaran, "Antisemitic Posts Are Rarely Removed by Social Media Companies," NPR, August 2, 2021, https://www.npr.org/2021/08/02/10238 19435/antisemitic-posts-are-rarely-removed-by-social-media-companies -a-study-finds.
10. Sabine von Mering and Monika Hubscher, "There Is a Lot of Antisemitic Hate Speech on Social Media—and Algorithms Are Partly to Blame," *Conversation*, July 26, 2022, https://theconversation.com/there-is-a-lot-of-antisemitic -hate-speech-on-social-media-and-algorithms-are-partly-to-blame-185668.
11. Weimann and Masri, "New Antisemitism on Tik Tok," 173.
12. Gabriel Weimann and Natalie Masri, "Tik Tok's Spiral of Antisemitism," *Media*, November 18, 2021, https://www.mdpi.com/2673–5172/2/4/41.

13. John Eligon, "White Supremacist Convicted of Killing 3 at Kansas Jewish Centers," *New York Times*, September 1, 2015, https://www.nytimes.com/2015/09/01/us/white-supremacist-convicted-of-killing-3-at-kansas-jewish-centers.html.

14. Samuel Breslow, "What Is the Great Replacement Theory and What Does It Say about Jews," *Forward*, May 16, 2022, https://forward.com/news/502579/great-replacement-theory-jews-blacks-tucker-carlson-antisemitism.

15. Amy Wong, "Trump Faces New Foreign Back Lash," *Philadelphia Inquirer*, August 17, 2017.

16. Chrystal Hayes, Kevin Johnson, Candy Woodall, "Who Is Robert Bowers? Accused Pittsburgh Synagogue Shooter Left Anti-Semitic Trail," *USA Today*, October 27, 2018, https://www.usatoday.com/story/news/nation/2018/10/27/pittsburgh-shooting-robert-bowers-identified-suspect-synagogue/1789239002/.

17. Ben Sales, "How the Pittsburgh Synagogue Shooting Unfolded," *Jewish Telegraphic Agency*, October 29, 2018, https://www.jta.org/2018/10/29/united-states/pittsburgh-synagogue-shooting-unfolded.

18. Sales, "How the Pittsburgh Synagogue Shooting Unfolded."

19. Marylynne Pitz and Peter Smith, "Thousands Gather for Vigil Honoring Victims in Squirrel Hill Shooting," *Pittsburgh Post-Gazette*, October 27, 2018.

20. Marylynne Pitz and Peter Smith, "Thousands Gather for Vigil Honoring Shooting Victims," *Pittsburgh Post-Gazette*, October 28, 2018.

21. Amy McRary, "Vigil Remembers Victims of Pittsburgh Shooting," *Knoxville News-Sentinel*, October 31, 2018.

22. Masha Gessen, "Why the Tree of Life Shooter Was Fixated on the Hebrew Immigrant Aid Society," *New Yorker*, October 27, 2018, https://www.newyorker.com/news/our-columnists/why-the-tree-of-life-shooter-was-fixated-on-the-hebrew-immigrant-aid-society.

23. "Tree of Life Shooting Revives 'Optics' Debate among White Supremacists," Anti-Defamation League, November 6, 2018, https://www.adl.org/blog/tree-of-life-shooting-revives-optics-debate-among-white-supremacists.

24. "Tree of Life Shooting Revives 'Optics' Debate."

25. Lucretia Wimbley and Andrew Goldstein, "Fearing the Worst, Houses of Worship Tighten Security," *Pittsburgh Post-Gazette*, October 25, 2019.

26. "Man Gets Life in Prison for '19 Synagogue Attack," *Boston Globe*, October 2, 2021.

27. "2019 Hate Crime Statistics," Federal Bureau of Investigation, accessed August 14, 2023, https://ucr.fbi.gov/hate-crime/2019/topic-pages/incidents-and-offenses.
28. "ADL: New York Leads the Nation in Antisemitic Incidents; Assaults Surge to All-Time High," April 26, 2022, Anti-Defamation League New York New Jersey, https://nynj.adl.org/news/2021-audit-ny/.
29. John Ellement and Andrew Bricker, "Man Who Allegedly Stabbed Rabbi in Brighton Faces Hate Crime, Civil Rights Charges," *Boston Globe*, July 8, 2021.
30. American Jewish Committee, *State of Antisemitism in America 2020*, 12.
31. "5 Key Takeaways from AJC State of Antisemitism in America Report 2022," *ajc Global Voice*, February 13, 2023, https://www.ajc.org/news/5-key-takeaways-from-ajcs-state-of-antisemitism-in-america-report-2022.
32. "Antisemitic Attitudes in America: Topline Findings," Anti-Defamation League, January 12, 2023, https://www.adl.org/resources/report/antisemitic-attitudes-america-topline-findings.
33. "ADL Audit Finds Antisemitic Incidents in United States Reached All-Time High in 2021," Anti-Defamation League, April 25, 2022, https://adl.org/news/press-releases/adl-audit-finds-antisemitic-incidents-in-united-states-reached-all-time-high-in?print=1s.
34. "The Jan. 6 Rioter Who Wore a 'Camp Auschwitz' Sweatshirt Gets 75 Days in Jail," National Public Radio, September 16, 2022, https://www.cnn.com/2021/01/09/us/capitol-hill-insurrection-extremist-flags-soh/index.html.
35. "Proud Boys' Bigotry Is on Full Display," Anti-Defamation League, December 24, 2020, https://www.adl.org/resources/blog/proud-boys-bigotry-full-display.
36. Laurie Kellman, "Report: Pandemic Amped Up Anti-Semitism, Forced It Online," Associated Press, April 7, 2021, https://apnews.com/article/race-and-ethnicity-conspiracy-theories-israel-coronavirus-pandemic-financial-markets-32bc8c63d8759ded9c1f2cb8ca7301e0.
37. Ryan Nobles, "Marjorie Taylor Green Compares House Mask Mandate to the Holocaust," CNN, May 22, 2021, https://www.cnn.com/2021/05/21/politics/marjorie-taylor-greene-mask-mandates-holocaust/index.html.
38. Quoted in Barbara Sprunt, "Kevin McCarthy Leads House GOP in Blasting Marjorie Taylor Greene's Holocaust Remarks," National Public Radio, May 25, 2021, npr.org/2021/05/25/1000129271/marjorie-taylor-greenes-holocaust-remarks-blasted-by-republicans-leaders.

39. Ben Sales, "Senator's Speech of 'Cosmopolitan Elites': Anti-Semitic Dog Whistle or Poli-Sci Speak?" *Jewish Telegraphic Agency*, July 19, 2019, https://www.jta.org/2019/07/19/united-states/a-missouri-senator-gave-a-speech-opposing-a-powerful-upper-class-and-their-cosmopolitan-priorities-um.

40. Hubscher and Walter, "Attacks on Democracy," 74.

41. Langer, "Deep State, Child Sacrifices and the 'Pandemic,'" 21.

42. Hubscher and von Mering, *Antisemitism on Social Media*, 10.

43. Sabine von Mering, "How Social Media Fuels Antisemitism," Brandeis University, May 13, 2022, https://www.brandeis.edu/jewish-experience/social-justice/2022/may/antisemitism-social-media.html?feature.

44. Quoted in Cassie Miller, "Social Media and System Collapse," 98.

45. Quoted in Alessandro Marazzi Sassoon, "Hateful Ideology on Display in Brevard," *Florida Today*, February 28, 2021.

46. "What Americans Know about the Holocaust," Pew Research Center, January 22, 2020, https://www.pewresearch.org/religion/2020/01/22/what-americans-know-about-the-holocaust/.

47. "First-Ever 50 State Survey on Holocaust Knowledge of American Millennials and Gen-Z Reveals Shocking Results," Conference on Jewish Material Claims Against Germany, September 20, 2020, https://www.claimscon.org/millennial-study.

48. Jack Kliger, "Holocaust Denial Is a Plague: Social Media Is Finally Trying to Inoculate Itself," Museum of Jewish Heritage, October 24, 2020, https://mjhnyc.org/press/holocaust-denial-is-a-plague-social-media-is-finally-trying-to-inoculate-itself/.

49. "Federation Response to Antisemitism," Jewish Federation of Greater Pittsburgh, January 14, 2022, https://jewishpgh.org/federation-response-to-antisemitism.

50. United States Holocaust Memorial Museum, "About the Museum," accessed August 14, 2023, https://www.ushmm.org/information/about-the-museum.

51. "A Call to Action against Antisemitism in America," American Jewish Committee, accessed August 14, 2023, https://www.ajc.org/call-to-action/report.

52. Jack Rosen, "The Many Faces of Antisemitic Terror," American Jewish Congress, January 20, 2022, https://ajcongress.org/op-ed/jack-rosen-the-many-faces-of-antisemitic-terror/.

53. American Jewish Congress, Jewish Political Guide, accessed August 15, 2023, https://ajcongress.org/jewishpoliticalguide/.

54. Author interview with Michael Masters, August 31, 2022, via Zoom.

55. "About SCN," Secure Community Network, accessed August 14, 2023, https://securecommunitynetwork.org.

56. Author interview with Michael Masters.

57. "'I Did Not Think We Would Get Out'; Congregation Beth Israel Hostage Shares Terrifying Experience," CBS News, January 17, 2022, https://www.cbsnews.com/dfw/news/colleyville-texas-congregation-beth-israel-hostage-terrifying-experience/.

58. Bill Hutchinson, "Texas Rabbi 'Grateful to Be Alive' as Synagogue Hostage-Taking suspect ID'd," ABC News, January 16, 2022, https://abcnews.go.com/US/texas-rabbi-grateful-alive-deadly-synagogue-hostage-standoff/story?id=82294717.

59. Faygie Holt, "We Can Never Let Guard Down Says Jewish Security Official, Urging Congregant Training Drills," Jewish News Syndicate, January 17, 2022, https://www.jns.org/we-can-never-let-guard-down-says-jewish-security-official-urging-congregant-training-drills/.

60. President Joe Biden, "To Fight Antisemitism, We Must Remember, Speak Out and Act," April 5, 2023, https://www.whitehouse.gov/briefing-room/statements-releases/2023/04/05/icymi-president-joe-biden-op-ed-to-fight-antisemitism-we-must-remember-speak-out-and-act/.

61. "Senate Seat Secured as Lieberman Waits," *Hartford Courant*, November 8, 2000.

62. "ADL Reports Unprecedented Rise in Antisemitic Incidents Post-Oct. 7," December 11, 2023, https://www.adl.org/resources/press-release/adl-reports-unprecedented-rise-antisemitic-incidents-post-oct-7.

63. Editors' Note: The author passed away during the production of this volume. The JPS editors added this paragraph to update the book prior to its printing. "New ISCA Report Raises Alarm over Sharp Post-October 7th Rise in Holocaust Denial, Distortion, and Inversion on Social Media," Combat Antisemitism Movement, December 12, 2023, https://combatantisemitism.org/studies-reports/new-isca-report-raises-alarm-over-sharp-post-october-7th-rise-in-holocaust-denial-distortion-and-inversion-on-social-media/.

64. Jeffrey Finkelstein, "Feeling Safe while Finding Togetherness," *Pittsburgh Jewish Chronicle*, January 23, 2022, https://jewishchronicle.timesofisrael.com/feeling-safe-while-finding-togetherness/.

Bibliography

American Jewish Committee. *To Bigotry No Sanction: A Documental Analysis of Anti-Semitic Propaganda, Prepared by the American Jewish Committee.* New York: American Jewish Committee, 1944.

——. *The State of Antisemitism in America 2020.* New York: American Jewish Committee, 2020.

Ashton, Diane. *Rebecca Gratz: Women and Judaism in Antebellum America.* Detroit: Wayne State University Press, 1998.

Baldwin, Neil. *Henry Ford and the Jews.* New York: Public Affairs, 2001.

Barash, Louis. "The American Jewish Chaplaincy." *American Jewish Historical Quarterly* 52, no. 1 (September 1962): 8–24.

Benet, Stephen Vincent. *John Brown's Body.* Garden City NY: Doubleday and Duran, 1928.

Britt, Tevis. "Jews Not Admitted: Anti-Semitism, Civil Rights, and Public Accommodation Laws." *Journal of American History* 107, no. 4 (March 2021): 847–70.

Cohen, J. X. *Jews, Jobs, and Discrimination.* New York: American Jewish Congress, 1937.

Cohen, Naomi. *Encounter with Emancipation: The German Jews in the United States, 1830–1914.* Lincoln: University of Nebraska Press, 1994.

Connolly, Christopher Powell. *The Truth about the Frank Case.* New York: Vail-Ballou, 1915.

Cooks, Bridget R. *Exhibiting Blackness.* Amherst: University of Massachusetts Press, 2011.

Dimont, Max. *The Jews in America.* New York: Simon and Schuster, 1978.

Diner, Hasia. *The Jews of the United States.* Berkeley: University of California Press, 2004.

Dinnerstein, Leonard. "Anti-Semitism Exposed and Attacked, 1945–1950." *American Jewish History* 71, no. 1 (September 1981): 134–49.

———. *Anti-Semitism in America*. New York: Oxford University Press, 1994.

———. *Uneasy at Home: Antisemitism and the American Jewish Experience*. New York: Columbia University Press, 1987.

Dye, Ira. *Uriah Levy: Reformer of the Antebellum Navy*. Gainesville: University Press of Florida, 2006.

Ehlrich, Walter. *Zion in the Valley: The Jewish Community of St. Louis*. Vol. 1, *1807–1907*. Columbia: University of Missouri, 1997.

———. *Zion in the Valley: The Jewish Community of St. Louis*. Vol. 1, *The Twentieth Century*. Columbia: University of Missouri, 2002.

Eiseman, Alberta. *Rebels and Reformers*. New York: Zenith Books, 1976.

Eitches, Edward. "Maryland's 'Jew Bill.'" *American Jewish Historical Quarterly* 60, no. 3 (1971): 258–79.

Evans, Eli. *Judah P. Benjamin: The Jewish Confederate*. New York: Free Press, 1988.

Fein, Isaac M. *Boston—Where It All Began*. Boston: Boston Jewish Bicentennial Committee, 1976.

Finkelstein, Norman H. *Captain of Innocence: France and the Dreyfus Affair*. New York: Putnam, 1991.

———. *Forged in Freedom: Shaping the Jewish American Experience*. Philadelphia: The Jewish Publication Society, 2002.

———. *Heeding the Call: Jewish Voices in America's Civil Rights Struggle*. Philadelphia: The Jewish Publication Society, 1997.

———. *JPS Guide to American Jewish History*. Philadelphia: The Jewish Publication Society, 2007.

———. *Schools of Hope: How Julius Rosenwald Helped Change African American Education*. Honesdale PA: Highlights, 2014.

———. *The Shelter and the Fence*. Chicago: Chicago Review Press, 2021.

Ford, Henry. "Aspects of Jewish Power in the United States." In *International Jew*, vol. 4, 1–246.

———. *The International Jew*. Vol 4. Dearborn MI: Dearborn Publishing, 1922.

———. "The International Jew: The World's Foremost Problem." In *The International Jew*, vol. 1, 1–235. Dearborn MI: Dearborn Publishing, 1920.

Frankel, Jonathan. *The Damascus Affair: "Ritual Murder," Politics, and the Jews in 1840*. Cambridge UK: Cambridge University Press, 1997.

Friedman, Lee M. "Cotton Mather and the Jews." *Publications of the American Jewish Historical Society* 26 (1918): 201–10.

Friedman, Saul S. *The Incident at Massena: The Blood Libel in America*. New York: Stein and Day, 1978.

Gerber, Jane S. *The Jews of Spain: A History of the Sephardic Experience*. New York: Free Press, 1992.

Golden, Harry. *The Lynching of Leo Frank*. New York: Cassell, 1966.

Goldstein, Eric and Deborah Weiner. *On Middle Ground: A History of the Jews of Baltimore*. Baltimore: John Hopkins University Press, 2018.

Gonda, Jeffrey D. *Unjust Deeds: The Restrictive Covenant Cases and the Making of the Civil Rights Movement*. Chapel Hill: University of North Carolina Press, 2015.

Goodkind, S. B. *Prominent Jews of America*. Toledo OH: Hebrew Publishing, 1918.

Gordon, Bezalel. "Board of Delegates of American Israelites." In *Encyclopaedia Judaica*, vol. 4, edited by Michael Berenbaum and Fred Skolnik, 19–20. New York: Macmillan, 2007.

Greenberg, Cheryl Lynn. "How Affirmative Action Fractured the Black-Jewish Alliance." *Journal of Blacks in Higher Education* 52 (Summer 2006): 85–88.

Greenberg, Mark I. "Ambivalent Relations: Acceptance and Anti-Semitism in Confederate Thomasville." *American Jewish Archives* 45, no. 1 (1993): 13–29.

Greene, Melissa Fay. *The Temple Bombing*. New York: Da Capo Press, 2006.

Halperin, Edward C. "The Jewish Problem in U.S. Medical Education 1920–1955." *Journal of the History of Medicine and Allied Sciences* 56, no. 2 (April 2001): 140–67.

Handlin, Oscar. "A Twenty Year Retrospect of American Jewish Historiography." *American Jewish Historical Quarterly* 65, no. 4 (1976): 295–309.

"Hearings before a Subcommittee on the Post Office and Post Roads. House of Representatives November 15 and 16, 1943." Washington DC: United States Government Printing Office, 1943.

Heidler, David Stephen, Jeanne T. Heidler, and David J. Coles, eds. *Encyclopedia of the American Civil War: A Political, Social, and Military History*. New York: W. W. Norton, 2000.

Higham, John. "Social Discrimination against Jews in America 1830–1930." In *The Jewish Experience in America*, vol. 5, edited by Abraham Karp, 349–81. New York: Ktav, 1969.

Houston, George. *Israel Vindicated: Being a Refutation of the Calumnies Propagated Respecting the Jewish Nation*. New York: Abraham Collins, 1823.

Hubscher, Monica, and Sabine von Mering, eds. *Antisemitism on Social Media*. London: Routledge, 2022.

Huhner, Leon. "Asser Levy: A Noted Jewish Burgher of New Amsterdam." *Publications of the Jewish American Historical Society* 8 (1900): 9–23.

——. "Daniel Gomez, a Pioneer Merchant of Early New York." *Publications of the American Jewish Historical Society* 41 (1951): 107–25.

——. "Jews in Connection with the Colleges of the Thirteen Original States Prior to 1800." *American Jewish Historical Quarterly* 19 (1910): 101–24.

Hutchinson, Dennis J. "Brown v. Board of Education." In *The Oxford Guide to United States Supreme Court Decisions*, 2nd ed., edited by Kermit L. Hall and James W. Ely Jr. (online). Oxford University Press, 2009.

"Inter-Group Relations." *American Jewish Year Book* 41 (1939–40): 209–23.

Irwin, Theodore. *Inside the "Christian Front."* Washington DC: American Council on Public Affairs, 1940.

Jackson, Kenneth T. *Crabgrass Frontier: The Suburbanization of the United States.* Oxford: Oxford University Press, 1987.

Karabel, Jerome. *The Chosen: The Hidden History of Admission and Exclusion at Harvard, Yale, and Princeton.* Boston: Houghton Mifflin Harcourt, 2005.

Katz, Irving. "Henry Higginson vs. Louis Dembitz Brandeis." *New England Quarterly* 41, no. 1 (March 1968): 67–81.

Kertzer, David. *The Kidnapping of Edgar Mortara.* New York: Vintage, 1997.

Krey, August C. *The First Crusade: The Accounts of Eyewitnesses and Participants.* Princeton NJ: Princeton University Press, 1921.

Langer, Armin. *Deep State, Child Sacrifices, and the "Plandemic": The Historical Background of Antisemitic Tropes within the QAnon Movement.* New York: Routledge, 2022.

Lawson, John D. *American State Trials.* St. Louis: F. H. Thomas Law, 1918.

Lebeson, Anita Libman. *Pilgrim People.* New York: Harper and Brothers, 1950.

Leffler, Phyllis. "Insiders or Outsiders: Charlottesville's Jews, White Supremacy, and Antisemitism." *Southern Jewish History* 21 (2018): 61–120

Liskofsky, Sidney. "UN Resolution on Zionism." *American Jewish Year Book* 77 (1977): 97–126.

Livingston, Sigmund. *Must Men Hate?* New York: Harper and Brothers, 1944.

Livney, Lee. "Let Us Now Praise Self-Made Men: A Reexamination of the Hilton Seligman Affair." *New York History* 75, no. 1 (1994): 66–98.

Marcus, Jacob Rader. *Early American Jewry.* Vol. 1, *The Jews of New York, New England and Canada 1649–1794.* Philadelphia: JPS, 1951.

——. *Early American Jewry.* Vol. 1,: *The Jews of Pennsylvania & the South, 1655–1790.* Philadelphia: JPS, 1953.

———. "Jews and the American Revolution: A Bicentennial Jewish Documentary." *American Jewish Archives* 27 (November 1975): 103–257.

Markens, Isaac. "Lincoln and the Jews." In *The Jewish Experience in America*, vol. 3, edited by Abraham Karp, 220–76. New York: Ktav, 1969.

Marrus, Michael R. *Lessons of the Holocaust.* Toronto: University of Toronto Press, 2016.

Masserman, Paul, and Max Baker. *The Jews Come to America.* New York: Bloch, 1932.

Medoff, Rafael. *America and the Holocaust: A Documentary History.* Philadelphia: The Jewish Publication Society, 2022.

———. *The Jews Should Keep Quiet: Franklin D. Roosevelt, Rabbi Stephen S. Wise, and the Holocaust.* Philadelphia: The Jewish Publication Society, 2019.

Menendez, Albert J and Edd Doerr, eds. *Great Quotations on Religious Freedom.* New York: Prometheus, 2002.

Miller, Cassie. *Social Media and System Collapse: How Extremists Built an International Neo-Nazi Network*, New York: Routledge, 2022.

Morais, Nina. "Jewish Ostracism in America." *North American Review* 123, no. 298 (September 1881): 265–75.

Morgan, David T. "The Sheftalls of Savannah." *American Jewish Historical Quarterly* 62, no. 4 (June 1973): 348–61.

Niebuhr, Gustav. *Beyond Tolerance: Searching for Interfaith Understanding in America.* New York: Viking, 2008.

Nilus, Sergei. *The Jewish Peril: Protocols of the Learned Elders of Zion.* London: Britons, 1920.

Noah, Mordecai M. *Discourse on the Restoration of the Jews.* New York: Harper & Brothers, 1845.

———. *Travels in England, France, Spain and the Barbary States in the Years 1813–14 and 15.* New York: Kirk and Meicein, 1819.

O'Donnell, Edward T. "Hibernians versus Hebrews? A New Look at the 1902 Jacob Joseph Funeral Riot." *Journal of the Gilded Age and Progressive Era* 6, no. 2 (2007): 209–25.

Oney, Steve. *And the Dead Should Rise: The Murder of Mary Phagan and the Lynching of Leo Frank.* New York: Pantheon, 2003.

Oppenheim, Samuel. "The Early History of the Jews of New York." *Publications of the American Jewish Historical Society* 18 (1909): 1–91.

Patel, Eboo. *Sacred Ground: Pluralism, Prejudice, and the Promise of America.* Boston: Beacon Press, 2013.

Pfeffer, Leo. *Church, State and Freedom.* Rev. ed. Eugene OR: Wipf and Stock, 2018.

Podair, Jerald. *The Strike That Changed New York: Blacks, Whites, and the Ocean Hill-Brownsville Crisis.* New Haven: Yale University Press, 2004.

Porwancher, Andrew. *The Jewish World of Alexander Hamilton.* Princeton NJ: Princeton University Press, 2021.

Ribak, Gil. "'The Jew Usually Left Those Crimes to Esau': The Jewish Responses to Accusations about Jewish Criminality in New York, 1908–1913." *ajs Review* 38, no. 1 (April 2014): 1–28.

Rockaway, Robert, and Arnon Gutfeld. "Demonic Images of the Jew in the Nineteenth Century, United States." *American Jewish History* 89, no. 4 (December 2001): 355–81.

Rosenblatt, Gary. "Is It Still Safe to Be a Jew in America?" *Atlantic,* March 15, 2020, https://www.theatlantic.com/ideas/archive/2020/03/anti-semitism-new-normal-america/608017/.

Rywell, Martin. *Judah Benjamin: Unsung Rebel Prince.* Asheville NC: Stephens Press, 1948.

Sarna, Jonathan. *American Judaism.* New Haven: Yale University Press, 2004.

———. *Jacksonian Jew: The Jewish World of Mordecai Noah.* New York: Holmes & Meieer, 1980.

———. *When General Grant Expelled the Jews.* New York: Schocken, 2012.

Sarna, Jonathan D. and Benjamin Shapell. *Lincoln and the Jews: A History.* New York: Thomas Dunne Books, 2015.

Sarna, Jonathan, and David Mendelsohn. *Jews and the Civil War: A Reader.* New York: New York University Press, 2010.

Schaff, Philip, and Henry Wace, eds. *Nicene and Post-Nicene Fathers of the Christian Church.* Vol. 3. Oxford: Christian Literature, 1892.

Schmier, Louis. "Notes and Documents on the 1862 Expulsion of Jews from Thomasville, Georgia." *American Jewish Archives* 32, no. 1 (April 1980): 9–22.

Shapiro, Edward S. *Crown Heights: Blacks, Jews, and the 1991 Brooklyn Riot.* Waltham MA: Brandeis University Press, 2006.

Sharansky, Natan. "3D Test of Anti-Semitism: Demonization, Double Standards, Delegitimization." *Jewish Political Studies Review* 16, nos. 3–4 (Fall 2004): 5–8.

Singerman, Robert. "The American Career of the *Protocols of the Elders of Zion.*" *American Jewish History* 71, no. 1 (1981): 48–78.

Smith, Ellen. "Strangers and Sojourners: The Jews of Colonial Boston." In *The Jews of Boston,* edited by Jonathan D. Sarna, Ellen Smith, and Scott-Martin Kosofsky, 21–43. Lebanon NH: Northeastern University Press, 1995.

"Statement By Henry Ford." *American Jewish Year Book* 29 (1927): 383–89.

Stern, Malcolm H. "Jewish Marriage and Intermarriage in the Federal Period (1776–1840)." *American Jewish Archives* 19, no. 2 (November 1967): 142–43.

Stern, Malcolm H., and Sanford Sternlicht, eds. *Uriah Phillips Levy: The Blue Star Commodore.* Norfolk VA: Norfolk Jewish Community Council, 1961.

Stroock, Sol M. "Switzerland and the American Jews." *Publications of the American Jewish Historical Society* 11 (1903): 7–52.

Sussman, Lance. *Isaac Leeser and the Making of American Judaism.* Detroit: Wayne State University Press, 1995.

Todd, Aiden L. *Justice on Trial.* New York: McGraw Hill, 1964.

Troy, Gil. *The Zionist Ideas: Visions for the Jewish Homeland—Then, Now, Tomorrow.* Philadelphia: JPS, 2018.

Urofsky, Melvin I. *Louis D. Brandeis: A Life.* New York: Pantheon, 2009.

Volkman, Ernest. *A Legacy of Hate: Anti-Semitism in America.* New York: Franklin Watts, 1982.

Weimann, Gabriel, and Natalie Masri. "New Antisemitism on Tik Tock." In *Antisemitism on Social Media,* edited by Monika Hubscher and Natalie Masri, 167–80. New York: Routledge, 2022.

Weiss, Nancy. "Long-Distance Runners of the Civil Rights Movement: The Contribution of Jews to the NAACP and the National Urban League in the Early Twentieth Century." In *Struggles in the Promised Land: Toward a History of Black-Jewish Relations in the United States,* edited by Jack Salzman and Cornel West, 123–52. New York: Oxford University Press, 1997.

Welch, Swan. "American Public Opinion toward Jews During the Nazi Era." *Social Science Quarterly* 95, no. 3. (September 2014): 615–35.

Wallace, Max. *The American Axis.* New York: St. Martin's Press, 2003.

Wortman, Marc. *Admiral Hyman Rickover: Engineer of Power.* New Haven: Yale University Press, 2022.

Index

Page numbers in italics indicate illustrations.

American Jewish Congress (AJC), 97–98, 115, 121–23, 137, 145–46, 151, 155, 158–59, 161, 162, 163, 229–30
American Jewish Historical Society, 67
American Jewish Joint Distribution Committee (JDC), 98–99, 134–35, 142
American Jewish Publication Society, 40
American Jewish Year Book, 98
American Jews: and antisemitism, 131, 143–45, 222–23, 229–31, 233; and the Black community, 177–80; and the Board of Delegates of American Israelites, 53–54, 60–61; and Charles Lindbergh, 137; and the Damascus Affair, 48–49; and the end of World War II, 149; and expulsions, 58–62; and George Washington's Letter, 26–31; and Grant's Order no. 11, 55–61; and Henry Ford, 104; and immigration, 73–76, 79–80; and Isaac Leeser, 39–40; and Jewish contributions to American life, 67–69; and Jewish leadership, 46, 130, 158; and the kidnapping of Edgardo Mortara, 52–53; and the Ku Klux Klan (KKK), 110; and legal of activism, 79–80; lost innocence of, 212–13; other advocates against, 127–29; and prayer in public schools, 69, 161–65; and public protests, 121–26; and the "Red Scare," 99–100; and the Revolutionary War, 24; in the twenty-first century, 234; and unwelcoming places, 115–17; and the U.S. Con-

stitution, 24–25, 31, 39; and the U.S.-Switzerland Treaty, 49–51; and World War I, 98
American Library Association, 83
American Revolution, 21–22
American Society for Evangelizing the Jews, 39
American Society for Meliorating the Condition of the Jews, 39
American university campuses, 200–201
amicus curiae. *See* friends of the court briefs
Amnesty International, 197, 208
Anderson, Marian, 167
Anderson, Robert, 114
Annapolis MD, 113–14
Anne (Queen), 21
anti-BDS legislation, 203–4
anti-Christian hatred, 103
Anti-Defamation League (ADL): and accusations of apartheid, 197; and annual tally of hate crimes, 223; and anti-Israel activity, 205; and antisemitic groups in the United States, 226; and antisemitism in the Black community, 184; and antisemitism on campus, 202; and discrimination in graduate school, 168; and discrimination in housing, 150; and equality in education, 161, 163; establishment of, 91; and expanding education to combat antisemitism, 229; and Hillel survey, 200; and laws against libel, 104; and monitoring right-wing websites, 214; and radio programs on civil rights, 153; and rejection

anti-Zionism, 190, 192–94, 200–201, 230

apartheid state accusation, 196–97, 199, 208

Appeal, 105

Arab-Israeli conflict, 188, 190–91, 192–94, 198

Ararat, 37–39

army chaplains, 146

Arnold, Reuben, 89–90

Aronson, Arnold, 173

Article 6, United States Constitution, 25

Aryan Nations, 226

assimilation, 12, 73–74

Associated Press, 59, 137, 215

Atlanta GA, 88–93, 171, 185

Atlanta Journal, 90

Atlantic City NJ, 71–72

A. T. Stewart department store, 70

attacks on Jews: and assaults on American Jews, 143–45; and B'nai B'rith headquarters hostages, 209–10; and the Chabad of Poway Synagogue, 221; and the Christian Front, 130–31; and the Crusades, 5–6; and the Damascus Affair, 46–49; and desecration of Jewish cemeteries, 145; and Granada Hills, California day camp, 212–13; and Hamas's October 7 massacre in Israel, xv, 234; and Henry Ford, 104–5; and the Inquisition, 9–10; and Jersey City NJ, 221–22; on Jewish communal buildings in Europe, 212; in Kishinev, Bessarabia, 79; and Kristallnacht, 129–30; and march in Skokie, Illinois, 210; and mass extermination of Jews,

13–14, 139–40; and Monsey NY, 221; and Overland Park KS, 214; and the R. Hoe and Company incident, 76–79; in Seville, Spain, 9; and the Silver Shirts, 127; and support of non-Jewish neighbors, 210–11; and the targeting of Orthodox Jews, 221–22; and Tree of Life building, 217–21; and the Ukrainian Cossacks, 12. *See also* expulsions; pogroms

Audit of Antisemitic Incidents, 229

Auschwitz death camp, 143

Austria-Hungary, 73

Awad, Khaled, 222

Babylonian conquest, 187

badge laws, 3, 9

Bakke, Allan, 179–80

Baldwin, James, 177

Ballad of Mary Phagan (Carson), 90

Baltimore MD, 51, 171

banking, 115

baptism, 9, 20

Barbary Coast, 34–36

Barghouti, Omar, 197

Barkat, Nir, 201

Barnum, P. T., 105

Barretto, Francisco, 16

Barsimson, Jacob, 18

The Base, 227

Battle of Bunker Hill, 23

BDS (Boycott, Divestment and Sanctions) movement, 197–201, 203–4, 205–6

Becker, Charles, 85

Belgium, 135

Ben and Jerry's, 204